History on Film/Film on History

History: Concepts, Theories and Practice

Series editor: Alun Munslow, University of Staffordshire

The New History
Alun Munslow

History on Film / Film on History
Robert A. Rosenstone

Imperialism
Barbara Bush

History on Film/
Film on History

ROBERT A. ROSENSTONE

PEARSON
Longman

Harlow, England • London • New York • Boston • San Francisco • Toronto
Sydney • Tokyo • Singapore • Hong Kong • Seoul • Taipei • New Delhi
Cape Town • Madrid • Mexico City • Amsterdam • Munich • Paris • Milan

Pearson Education Limited
Edinburgh Gate
Harlow CM20 2JE
United Kingdom
Tel: +44 (0)1279 623623
Fax: +44 (0)1279 413059
Website: www.pearsoned.co.uk

First edition published in Great Britain in 2006

ISBN-13: 978-0-582-50584-1
ISBN-10: 0-582-50584-4

British Library Cataloguing in Publication Data
A CIP catalogue record for this book can be obtained from the British Library

Library of Congress Cataloging-in-Publication Data

Rosenstone, Robert A.
    History on Film / Film on History / Robert A. Rosenstone.– 1st ed.
        p. cm. – (History: concepts, theories and practice)
    Includes bibliographical references and index.
    ISBN-13: 978-5825058443 (pbk.)
    ISBN-10: 0-582-50584-4 (pbk.)
    1. Motion pictures and history. 2. Historical films—History and criticism.   I. Title.
    II. Series.

    PN1995.2.R667 2006
    791.46'658–dc22

                                                            2005044980

10 9 8 7 6 5 4 3 2 1
10 09 08 07 06

Set by 35 in 11/13pt Bulmer MT
Printed in Malaysia

The Publisher's policy is to use paper manufactured from sustainable forests.

For Alun Munslow

an inspiration and a friend

Contents

Preface to the series

*H*istory: Concepts, Theories and Practice is a series that offers a coherent and detailed examination of the nature and effects of recent theoretical, methodological and historiographical developments within key fields of contemporary historical practice. Each volume is open to the idea of history as a historicist cultural discourse constituted by historians as much as it is reconstructed from the sources available about the past. The series examines the discipline of history as it is conceived today in an intellectual climate that has increasingly questioned the status of historical knowledge.

As is well known, questioning of the status of history, indeed of its very existence as an academic subject, has been seen in several recent scholarly developments that have directly influenced our study of the past. These include the emergence of new conceptualisations of 'pastness', the emergence of fresh forms of social theorising, the rise of concerns with narrative, representation and the linguistic turn, and a self-conscious engagement with the issues of relativism, objectivity and truth. All these are reflected in the appearance of new historical themes and frameworks of historical activity.

In acknowledging that history is not necessarily nor automatically authorised by one foundational epistemology or methodology and that history cannot stand outside its own genre or form, all volumes in the series reflect a multiplicity of metanarrative positions. Nevertheless, each volume (regardless of its own perspective and position on the nature of history) explains the most up-to-date interpretational and historiographic developments that fall within its own historical field. However, this review of the 'latest interpretation and methodology' does not diminish the broad awareness of the 'challenge to history as a discipline' reflected in the tensions between referentiality, representation, structure and agency.

Each volume offers a detailed understanding of the content of the past, explaining by example the kinds of evidence found within their own field as well as a broad knowledge of the explanatory and hermeneutic demands historians make upon their sources, the current debates on the uses to which evidence is put, and how evidence is connected by historians within their field to their overall vision of What is history?

Alun Munslow

Acknowledgements

M y deep gratitude to the following institutions and people for the support and encouragement that helped bring this book into being: the California Institute of Technology for providing an open-minded atmosphere where one is encouraged to think outside the box. The Division of Humanities and Social Sciences and its recent chairpersons, John Ledyard and Jean Ensminger, for time off, as well as financial aid for travel and research. My secretary, Sheryl Cobb, for handling all the details which I so often forget. The Getty Research Institute for allowing me to have wonderful scholar year with nothing to do but read, think, and write. The European University Institute; Oxford University; Manchester University; the University of Barcelona; the University of La Laguna on Tenerife in the Canary Islands; Salvador de Bahia Federal University, Brazil; and the University of Tolima, in Ibague, Colombia, for allowing me to teach courses or give a lecture series that let me try out the ideas that comprise this book. The American Centers in Osaka and Tokyo; Australia National Film and Sound Archive; the British Academy; the University of Buenos Aires; Capetown University; the Centres d'etudes critique of the University of Paris; the Center for Interdisciplinary Research, Bielefeld University; the Film Museum of Amsterdam; Fluminense Federal University, Niteroi, Brazil; Ghent University; Hebrew University Jerusalem; the University of Leuven; the Medieval and Renaissance Center of UCLA; Kyushu University, Fukuoka; National University of Colombia, Bogota; Ohio University; the University of Madrid, Complutense; the University of Michigan; St. Anthony's College, Oxford; Scripps College; York University, Toronto for hosting conferences on history and film or for providing a forum at which I could lecture and an audience was able to ask hard questions about my work. Jose Maria Caparros Lera, Rafael de Espana,

Sergio Alegre, Magi Crusells and all the others associated with the Center for Cinematic Research who helped to make my time at the University of Barcelona such a joy; along with Roman Gubern, whose vast knowledge of cinema became part of my education. All the other wonderful hosts I have had throughout the world: Juan Jose Cruz in Tenerife; Bo Straat and Angela Schenck in Florence; Hilda Machado in Rio de Janeiro; Jorge Novoa and Rosa Julina in Salvador de Bahia; Luis Rozo, Arlovich Correa and Jorge Prudencio Lozano, in Ibague, Colombia; Julio Cesar Goyes in Bogota; Leonardo Neuman in Buenos Aires; Leen Engelen, Willem Hesling, and Bruno de Wever in Belgium; Sandra and Bart Kisters in Amsterdam; Kyoko Chinami and Fujio Kayama in Japan; Moshe Sluhovsky in Jerusalem; and Vivian Bickford-Smith and Richard Mendelsohn in Capetown. Filmmakers Warren Beatty, Mel Bucklin, Charles Burnett and Howard Dratch for teaching me things about the medium that I didn't even know I was learning. Alun Munslow, an editorial colleague, source of inspiration, and wonderful friend whose encouragement brought this book to fruition. And not last, but first, Nahid Massoud, without whose love and support, none of the rest would matter.

Pacific Palisades, California
30 March 2005

Publisher's acknowledgements

The publishers are grateful to the following for permission to reproduce copyright material:

Blackwell Publishing Ltd for text derived from Robert A. Rosenstone (2002) 'Film, television and historical thought' in Sara Maza and Lloyd Kramer (eds) *The Blackwell Companion to Western Historical Thought*. Oxford: Blackwell; text derived from '*October* as History', *Rethinking History: The Journal of Theory and Practice*, 5 (1), Summer, 2001; the University of California Press for text derived from Robert A. Rosenstone (2003) 'The Reel Joan of Arc: Reflections on the theory and practice of the historical film', *The Public Historian*, 25 (3), Summer, © 2003 by The Regents of the University of California and the National Council on Public History; a small part of Chapter 2 was derived from Robert A. Rosenstone's review essay of Natalie Zemon Davis, *Slaves on Screen: Film and historical vision*, in *History and Theory*, 41, December 2002, 134–44, © 2002 Wesleyan University; *Cineaste* for text derived from Robert A. Rosenstone (2001) 'Inventing historical truth on the silver screen', *Cineaste*, 29 (2), Spring; Texas A&M University Press for text derived from Robert A. Rosenstone (2006) 'In praise of the biopic: the truth of fictional lives on screen' in Richard Francaviglia and Jerry Rodnitzky (eds) *History and Film: Portraying the past in cinema*. Arlington, TX: Texas A&M University Press; University Press of Kansas for text derived from Robert A. Rosenstone (2000) 'Oliver Stone as historian', in Richard Toplin (ed.) *Oliver Stone's USA*, Lawrence: University Press of Kansas.

In some instances we may have been unable to trace the owners of copyright material, and we would appreciate any information that would enable us to do so.

Chapter 1

History on film

This shouldn't be a book. You need more than words on a page to understand how film presents the world of the past. You need moving images
on a screen and music and sound effects as well. Words aren't fully up to the
task of comprehending the film experience. But to agree to contribute to a
series of books devoted to historical thought and practice in the early twenty-
first century is to confine oneself to the limitations of words on the page. And
to read the book is to agree to share that limitation. But let us never forget, you
and I, that somewhere outside the confining walls of these words lies a world
of colour, movement, sound, light, and life, a world on the screen that points
towards, refers to, represents – let us not worry the precise language right here,
at the outset, we shall get to that in time – to a realm of the past, a vanished
world in which people made wars and love, built things and tore them down,
suffered trauma and felt joy, identified themselves as male or female (or both or
something in between), engaged in personal or class struggle, hoped and
dreamed, led revolutions or followed leaders, lynched other men, prayed to
God, watched their children grow, buried their loved ones – did, in short, all
the things you and I will do or see done or hear about during our own lifetimes.

It is not a real world, of course but then again, neither is that other historical world, the one conjured up for us in the textbooks we endured in grammar
and high school and university. The world that came to us in lectures and lists
of dates, in paragraphs memorized from founding documents, in papers we
ourselves (at least those of us who went to graduate school) had to write on the
origins of parliament, or the terror during the French Revolution, or the ideas
of some Greek philosopher, or the exploits of this emperor or that king, or the
discoveries of one intrepid voyager or another, or the growth of consciousness
of some peasant woman in a Balkan village during early modern times. We take

this to be history, but let us never forget that these are only words on the page, words that got there because of certain rules for finding evidence and producing more words of our own and accepting the notion that they tell us about what is important in the vanished land of the past.

This opening section, then, clearly involves my thesis, one I will argue in the pages ahead – that the familiar, solid world of history on the page and the equally familiar but more ephemeral world history on the screen are similar in at least two ways: they refer to actual events, moments, and movements from the past, and at the same time they partake of the unreal and the fictional, since both are made out of sets of conventions we have developed for talking about where we human beings have come from (and also where we are and where we think we are going, though this is something most people concerned with the past don't always admit). My aim here is not only to get you to see the parallels, but also to show how that vanished world can be, and has been, represented in film to convince you that the world of history on the screen is one worth attending to, one that can render an important past, do a kind of history that is complex enough so that we must learn how to read it. The burden of this book will be just that – to begin to learn how to read and understand this (relatively) new, visual word of the past. (I am, of course, writing this introduction after the chapters have been completed, so for me the learning has already taken place.)

To accept film, especially the dramatic feature film, as being able to convey a kind of serious history (with a capital H), runs against just about everything we have learned since our earliest days in school. History is not just words on the page, but on pages which are for the most part contained in thick tomes whose weight and bulk help to underscore the solidity of the lessons they teach. And film, why that's just entertainment, a diversion from the serious business of life, one of the places we go in an attempt to escape the sorts of social and political problems which fill the pages of our newspapers and those same history books. Sure, films set stories in the past, but these are romances, simple-minded tales of good guys, bad guys, and beautiful heroines. They have nothing to do with the serious world of events and developments described in books. Motion pictures are all about making a reputation for the director and the stars and money for the production companies. For them, history is just another tool to sell tickets.

The 'we' I have been using here is meant in at least two different ways: as the 'we' of the history profession, those of us trained to research and report on our findings about the past, and the simpler 'we' of you and I, author and reader, who are rather more alike than different in our approaches to understanding the world. In the pages that follow I want to explain my ideas to you about why and how the dramatic history film can relate to and even do something we might label 'history' (in truth, we need another word for how film handles the past, but alas we seem stuck with this one, and so throughout this book I will use the term 'history film' for works which consciously try to recreate the past) – at least if by that term we mean something that seriously attempts to make meaning out of the traces left to us from that vanished world. At the same time I wish to share with you part of the personal experiences that have become part of my arguments. This will not be (I trust) autobiographical musings simply to indulge my ego, but rather to help give some insight into the process of how a historian's ideas can develop and change. How I could go from my training as a *Dragnet* historian ('Just the facts, m'am') to a person who has been labelled a 'post-modern' historian, one of those folk who, in the eyes of some critics, are involved in the apparently gleeful task of what one staunch traditionalist has called in the title of his book, *The Killing of History* (Windschuttle 1996).

We who are called 'post-modernist historians' certainly don't see ourselves as involved in a pursuit aimed at such dire consequences. Rather, we are (some of us) engaged in at attempt to bring the practice of history kicking and screaming into the twenty-first century. We want our deep interest in and caring for the past to be expressed in forms congenial to both a contemporary sensibility and to intellectual systems consonant with our own era. Almost 40 years ago, the brilliant theorist, Hayden White, famously told us that the much vaunted 'art' of history consisted in books that were written in the style of the nineteenth-century British novel. Where, he lamented, were the works which matched the moods of twentieth-century life and sensibility, where were the examples of, say, 'surrealist, expressionist, or existentialist historiography' (White 1978: 43–43). Four decades later, a small but growing band of histori-ans have begun to answer White's implicit call for different forms of historical narrative. Some of us – Richard Price, Greg Dening, James Goodman, Simon Schama, and yours truly, to name but a few – have published books that incor-porate contemporary literary moves such as the self-reflexive, the mosaic, the pastiche, the multiple voices of the carnivalesque (Rosenstone 2001a). Many of these innovators have published books or printed essays in *Rethinking History: The Journal of Theory and Practice*, the only publication in the pro-fession which encourages experimental forms of history writing.

The desire to express our relationship to the past by using contemporary forms of expression, as well as the desire to appeal to a contemporary sensibil-ity, sooner or later has to point us in the direction of the visual media. First the motion picture, and then later its electronic offspring, television, became sometime during in the twentieth century the chief medium for carrying the stories our culture tells itself – be these set in the present or the past, be they factual, fictional, or a combination of the two. Blockbuster history films, mini-series, documentaries, docu-dramas – all these genres are increasingly important in our relationship to the past and to our understanding of history. To leave them out of the equation when we think of the meaning of the past is to condemn ourselves to ignore the way a huge segment of the population has come to understand the events and people that comprise history.

One indication of the importance of the visual media are the huge public controversies that regularly erupt over history films. In the United States, Oliver Stone's *JFK* was bitterly attacked by the press and politicians even before it got to the screen, while a 2003 mini-series on Ronald Reagan aroused so much pre-airing opposition that it was moved from a network to a cable channel. In France, Marcel Ophul's three-and-a-half-hour documentary about French collaboration with the Nazis, *The Sorrow and the Pity*, was kept off the government channel which funded it, and when the *The Battle for Algiers*, banned for two decades, finally opened in the 1980s, right-wing hoodlums trashed some movie theatres where it was playing. In Germany, *The Nasty Girl* was denounced for showing that a town's leaders were complicit with the Nazi régime; in Japan, major distributors refused to carry *The Emperor's Native Army Marches On* after a public controversy arose over its depiction of cannibalism among starving soldiers on Pacific Islands during World War II; and in Canada a huge debate among ex-military personnel and the general public followed the airing of a Canadian Broadcasting System documentary, *The Valour and the Horror*, over the behaviour of that country's military personnel in the Second World War (Bercuson and Wise 1994).

The importance of the media also shows in the way certain works are praised for their positive contributions. When screened in Germany, the American mini-series, *Holocaust* first caused an uproar, as if the nation's history was being stolen by foreigners. Yet soon enough, the work was being credited with opening a debate over the meaning and legacy of the Third Reich, leading to new scholarship on the period, and spurring the creation of films by directors of the New German Cinema, who explored and presented a variety of perspectives on the Nazi régime. In Argentina, the dramatic feature, *The Official Story*, publicized the case of *los desparacidos*, those who had been 'disappeared' by the military régime, and provided support to the Mothers of the Plaza de Mayo, a movement of women seeking their vanished sons and daughters. In the United States, the controversy surrounding *JFK* led to the opening of a Congressional inquiry into the Warren Committee's Report on the assassination of the President.

These examples (and one could produce more of them) of controversies or contributions point to something more widespread and more deeply-seated in our psyches – that history films, even when we know they are fanciful or ideological renditions of history, have an effect on the way we see the past. In most cases, a subtle effect, but an effect none the less. You can hear it in the voice of an African American undergraduate who, after seeing *Glory*, the story of the 54th Massachusetts Regiment, a much decorated Black unit in the Civil War, says to me with some emotion, 'I never realized we help to free ourselves'. Or from the Armenian student who, after being exposed to *Ararat*, Atom Egoyan's complex and convoluted rendition of the Turkish massacre of Armenians during World War I and its lingering effect on subsequent generations, seems to stand a little taller as he says, 'At last our story has been told'. Or even from the remaining band of Schindler's people, who joyfully endorsed Steven Spielberg's depiction of their lives during the Nazi period, at the moment when some critics were savaging the film for being sentimental and atypical of the Holocaust experience (on the grounds that few Jews had a Schindler to save them).

What I am getting at is this: something more is going on with the history film than those of us trained as historians and keepers of the flame are likely to admit. The kind of history we teach in our classrooms sets the norms for almost everyone else – film critics, reviewers for newspapers and magazines, politicians, pundits, TV talking heads, students of cinema studies, high-school teachers, students, and the general public (at least as sampled in 'Letters-to-the-editor' columns). We see history (with a capital) as a particular kind of practice, one that insists on a certain kind of historical truth and tends to exclude others. We may pay lip service to the oral tradition, to good historical museums or especially noteworthy exhibitions, even to the occasional film (usually a documentary). But we have little doubt that the truth of the past resides in an empirically-based discourse, one that developed over the last two centuries, was drummed into us in graduate school, and is constantly reinforced by the norms of the profession.

My aim in what follows is not at all to dispute the great strengths of traditional written history. Nor do I mean to ignore the gains of the history profession over the centuries and, more particularly, the creativity of the last fifty years, when revolutions in research methodologies have made for a broad and complex view of humanity, undreamed of by earlier generations of historians. One result of such endeavours is that now we can hear the voices of those who were for so long silent – women, subalterns, slaves, workers, farmers, country folk, commoners, sexual minorities. Now we also have a chance not just to hear these folk, but to see them as well. To say we can do so is to breach a long-time practice which has come to seem carved in stone – the notion that a truthful past can only be told in words on the page. It's a risky business, for to change the medium of history is to change the message as well. Plato suggested this more than two millenia ago in saying that when the mode of the music changes, the walls of the city shake. The mode in this case, the past told in moving images, doesn't do away with the old forms of history – it adds to the language in which the past can speak. How to begin thinking about this, how to understand that language, how to see where history on film sits in relation to written history, how to understand what film adds to our understanding of the past – the posing of such questions, the problems of dealing with them, and some (very tentative) answers are what will fill the pages of the chapters to come.

Questions about the truths of history, or about in what sense history can at all be called 'true', and what that word means with regard to historical discourse, have been on my mind since the early 1990s. Such questions were raised in part by an involvement with projects in the visual media, in part by an encounter with the world of historical theory. They were certainly not with me in graduate school. We students in the 1960s were taught how to find those facts and then use them to create narratives about the past, narratives whose underlying truths we did not question. Never did we learn anything about what might creep into those stories because we were writing a literary form that had its own demands. Never did we learn that the kind of history we were doing was only one way of approaching the truth of the past. We knew that what we had been taught to write was the real history. Certainly we would have been shocked if anyone had said that truths about the past could be expressed on screen, in film or television.

My first involvement with film came when directors decided to make films on the topics of my first two scholarly books – *Crusade of the Left: The Lincoln Battalion in the Spanish Civil War* (1969) and *Romantic Revolutionary: A Biography of John Reed* (1975) – and asked me to participate in the process. For the modest ($250,000, largely funded by the National Endowment for the Humanities) feature-length documentary on the Lincoln Battalion, *The Good Fight* (1983), I both served as an adviser and wrote the narration. For the big budget ($45 million, probably the most expensive movie made up till then), Academy Award winning drama, *Reds* (1982), I was unofficial historical consultant for seven years of pre-production and then on the payroll during the year of filming. The experiences working on those productions taught me a good deal about the difference between constructing a world in the visual media and on the page, yet my interest in the visual media as a way of conveying history predated these involvements. Something must have attuned me to the increasing role of the media in our culture, the fact that the world past and present more and more comes to us in the form of images, for I created a history on film course in 1975, some time before my connection with either project.

My aim in teaching the course, as in my subsequent research, has been to try to understand where films are situated with regard to other kinds of historical discourse. To answer the question: just what, if anything, do history films convey about the past, and how do they convey it? Not that I would have phrased the issues that way when I began. My first essay on the topic resulted from an invitation by a historical journal to take a look at *Reds* from the dual perspective of both insider and outsider (Rosenstone 1982). The essay turned out to be both an appreciation and a critique, one based on the reactions of a (rather) traditional historian who focused on details and themes yet ignored what later became so obvious to me – that words and images work to express and explain the world in somewhat different ways. That a film will never be able to do precisely what a book can do, and vice versa. That history presented in these two different media would ultimately have to be judged by different criteria.

Such ideas developed over the course of a decade. During that period I wrote a number of essays in response to calls from conference organizers and journal editors. The late 1980s and early 1990s were a time when discussions about history and film began to surface in the profession. Most historians tended to approach the history film in the same simple-minded, *ad hoc* way as I did in my first essay – often trying to assess why a particular film did such violence to a topic without considering the nature of the medium or its possibilities. My own work turned slowly towards more theoretical concerns – in part because of my simultaneous involvement with another historical narrative, a work on the topic of American sojourners in nineteenth-century Japan. After I had narrowed my focus to three emblematic figures – a missionary, a scientist, and a writer – composition proved to be difficult, for the straightforward style used in my first two books was not letting me get close enough to my subjects to render their days, the powerful and jarring experiences and encounters, the sights, sounds, smells, and feelings that had so affected their attitudes and lives (Rosenstone 1988). In my search for a new, more expressive way of writing the past, I for the first time encountered the post structuralist critique of historical practice one finds in the work of such critics as Hayden White and Frank Ankersmit. Their writings provided an intellectual underpinning for my studies of film, for they allowed me to see the limitations of traditional history and thus suggested the possibilities of representing the past in new and different ways – one of those being with the visual media.

It took more than a decade of thinking and writing about history film to work my way towards the simple insight that underlies the chapters of this book: film makers can be and already are historians (some of them), but of necessity *the rules of engagement of their works with the stuff of the past are and must be different from those that govern written history.* The breakthrough for me came with *Walker* (1987), directed by Alex Cox, a little known film based on the life of William Walker, an American freebooter who in 1855 led a troop of 58 armed men into Nicaragua to support one side in an ongoing Civil War. A year later, Walker became president of the country, which he ruled for ten months, until the combined armies of Honduras and Guatemala defeated his men and led to his final gesture – torching Granada, then reputed to be the most beautiful city in the Americas. The film, *Walker*, told this story as a kind of absurdist, black comedy, full of overt anachronisms (computers, Mercedes automobiles and *Time* magazine all put in a brief appearance) and outrageous humour. And yet when I went back and read everything written on the topic since the 1850s in English, Spanish, and French (seven books and numerous chapters, essays and articles), it turned out that the film not only gave a stunningly believable portrait of the democrat as imperialist, but also provided a provocative interpretation of the man and his exploits that could stand among all the others. *Walker* clearly situated itself within and commented upon the ongoing discourse surrounding Walker (and American imperialism), and in its aesthetic, its notes of dark absurdity, added something to that tradition (Rosenstone 1995b).

Accepting the notion that film makers can be historians meant sloughing off lessons that were learned in graduate school and reinforced by the gatekeepers of the profession. Not that those rules are all that clear or fixed, but certain practices are. Film, particularly the dramatic film, makes special demands on the traditional historian in that it goes beyond (as theorists argue all historians do) *constituting* its facts, that is, creating facts by picking out certain traces of the past (people, events, moments) and highlighting them as important and worthy of inclusion in a narrative, and instead indulges in *inventing* facts, that is, making up traces of the past which are then highlighted as important and worthy of inclusion. Without dwelling at length on what I will explore in the chapters to come, let me only suggest here that ultimately I think there are two ways of looking at the inventions of characters, dialogue, and incidents that are an inevitable part of the dramatic history film and not unknown in the documentary. You may see the contribution of such works in terms not of the specific details they present but, rather, in the overall sense of the past they convey, the rich images and visual metaphors they provide to us for thinking historically. You may also see the history film as part of a separate realm of representation and discourse, one not meant to provide literal truths about the past (as if our written history can provide literal truths) but metaphoric truths which work, to a large degree, as a kind of commentary on, and challenge to, traditional historical discourse.

The notion of seeing the history film in relation to the larger discourse is central to the argument of the chapters that follow. Indeed, it is, I think, the unique contribution of this book. This approach is also why, though all of my examples come from motion pictures, the arguments made here are equally applicable to history made for television. Whether the screen is large or small, the central questions approached in this book are the same: How do you tell the past? How do you render that vanished world of events and people in the present? How can we (try to) understand the human generations who came before us? Such questions ensure that what you have here is different from a work on the history film by a scholar in cinema or cultural studies, or by a historical theorist. It accounts for the fact that while the argument utilizes both film theory and historical theory, it does so in a manner different from academics in those fields. In what follows you will find some detailed analyses of individual sequences, but only insofar as they work to illuminate a historical vision. Similarly, while certain ideas of historical theory underlie my argument, they remain in the background while I focus on not just how the stories of the past are told, but also on their contents.

In terms of both structure and contents, this book approaches its topics in a rather *ad hoc* way. So little has been written on the history film, that one has the burden (and liberty) of devising an approach to the topic. Since this is a field still in the making, my chapters are meant to be suggestive and provocative rather than definitive. After Chapter 2, an introduction to and brief overview of the development of the field and its issues, each subsequent chapter focuses on a particular topic and undertakes a detailed analysis of one or more films. Chapter 3 deals with the most common standard or mainstream historical drama (focus on *Glory*), and Chapter 4 with its opposite, the innovative or opposition drama (*October*). Chapter 5 is devoted to the documentary (focus on films about the Spanish Civil War, including *The Spanish Civil War*, *The Good Fight*, *Mourir à Madrid*, and *El Perro Negro*), and Chapter 6 to that most popular form, the biopic, or as I prefer to call it, the biofilm (three films about John Reed, *Reds*, *Red Bells*, and *Reed – Insurgent Mexico*). Chapter 7 raises the issue of in what sense is the filmmaker a historian (Oliver Stone, especially his Vietnam films), and Chapter 8 exemplifies how a group of works devoted to a single topic can engage the larger discourse (eight films on the holocaust). Chapter 9 sums up my arguments and attempts to make a case for film as a new form of historical thinking.

Like historical narrative itself, my way of dealing with this topic also tends towards the *ad hoc*. What I have learned over the years is that to find the historical meaning of a film (or a book), you must work at a certain distance from it. Getting in too close, falling in love with the endless details of an individual image or sequence, and you are likely to lose a sense of the larger historical picture or argument. Getting too far away, backing off into theoretical considerations, and the details that constitute the stuff of the past go out of focus. My method is to work at a kind of middle distance, occasionally moving in for a close-up or a detailed analysis, occasionally stepping back into the realm of theory, but always returning to a position from which one can see and understand that the work would not exist except for the traces of particular historical characters and events about which much is already known. This approach may seem a lack of method to those more theoretically trained, but in truth it is like history, itself, for ultimately no single agreed-upon method has ever been devised for rendering the past.

Chapter 2

To see the past

To see the past. To watch history unfold before our eyes. To have a machine that lets us view the deeds of our forebears and the major events that shaped our world. Such a desire no doubt precedes the invention by Louis and Auguste Lumière of that most elegant and revolutionary piece of equipment, the cinematograph. Just four years after the brothers held their first public screening of short, actuality films in the basement of a Paris café, George Melies was in 1900 staging recent historical scenes such as *The Dreyfus Affair* for the camera. Within a decade, films set in the past – long lost works we know today mostly by their titles, *The Assassination of the Duc of Guise* (1908) from France, *The Last Days of Pompeii* (1908) and *The Capture of Rome* (1905) from Italy, and *Uncle Tom's Cabin* (1903) from the United States – were being distributed around the world. In countries as diverse in culture and history as Japan, Russia, England and Denmark, some of the earliest dramatic films (often based upon stage plays) involved the depiction of historical events and characters. Long before cinema reached its twentieth birthday in the mid-teens of the twentieth century, the 'historical' was a regular part of screen fare.

Early on in the history of the new medium, a few people saw part of its promise as just this ability to make us see the past. A French drama critic in 1908 described the aspirations of film as not only the ability to reproduce the contemporary world, but also 'to animate the past, to reconstruct the great events of history through the performance of the actor and the evocation of atmosphere and milieu' (Tredell 2002: 15). D.W. Griffith, director of one of the first major and certainly the most controversial of history films, *Birth of a Nation*, was a virtual missionary on the topic. In 1915 he claimed that the greatest contribution of the motion picture had been 'the treating of historical subjects', and he liked to quote 'educators' who had told him (or so he said) that a film 'can impress upon a people as much of the truth of history in an evening, as many months of study will accomplish' (Silva 1971: 98, 59).

More than a century after the birth of cinema, historians, critics, reviewers, and the general public still wonder if (indeed, most doubt that) this promise of film as history has been fulfilled. For those who care about the topic, the important questions raised by the telling of the past in the visual media have yet to be answered – or even really asked. Do such depictions really count as history? Do they add to or detract from our knowledge of the past? Can any depiction of the past on the screen be taken seriously? Does any film count as 'historical thinking' or contribute to something we might call 'historical understanding'? Can any such visual work be properly labelled with that capitalized term, History?

Attempts to answer such questions will occupy the rest of this book. At the outset, it is important to realize that this sort of question would not have been asked for most of the 100+ years that movies have existed. Yet now, early in the twenty-first century, answering them has become an issue of some importance. Each day it becomes clearer to even the most academic of historians that the visual media are the chief conveyor of public history in our culture. That for every person who reads a book on a historical topic about which a film has been made, especially a popular film such as *Schindler's List* (1993), many millions of people are likely to encounter that same past on the screen. Rather than dismissing such works – as many professional historians and journalists continue to do – as mere 'fiction' or 'entertainment', or lamenting their obvious 'inaccuracies', it seems more judicious to admit that we live in a world shaped, even in its historical consciousness, by the visual media, and to investigate exactly how films work to create a historical world. This means focusing on what we might call their rules of engagement with the traces of the past, and investigating the codes, conventions, and practices by which they bring history to the screen.

At the outset, some background is in order. So are a few analytical distinctions. The early dramatic 'historicals' were not meant as serious investigations into the meaning of past events. They were brief, often no more than theatrical tableaux, national moments of a sort that the audience was bound to recognize – Lincoln at Gettysburg, Dreyfuss on Devil's Island, Marat lying dead in the bath tub. But even as such works grew in length during the second decade of cinema, they failed to become serious about the kinds of questions that usually concern historians. Rather than attempting to understand or explain events or movements or people, they tended to be romances, 'costume dramas' which used (and misused) the past as a mere setting for tales of adventure and love.

Not only has this kind of 'historical' been a part of virtually every national cinema, it has become a tradition, or genre, that continues up to this day in such works as *Titanic* and *Gladiator*.

Popular as they are, such costume dramas are not the only kind of film set in the past. Since the late teens there has grown up another tradition of historical, one that does not hesitate to pose serious questions of, and make serious interpretations about, the meaning of the past. Without contesting questions of precedence or insisting on a precise lineage, let me suggest that among the first of these, certainly in the United States, was Griffith's *Birth of a Nation* (1915). Today one must be cautious in lauding this film because it is so overtly racist, so overflowing with vicious stereotypes of African Americans as barbaric, uneducated, and uncultured. Yet its depiction of the American Civil War, its view of the South as suffering under the depredations of ex-slaves and carpetbaggers during reconstruction, its exaltation of the Ku Klux Klan as heroes in a racial conflict, and its (literally) dreadful stereotypes of African Americans were (alas) direct reflections of the major interpretations of the era in which it was produced – not just the beliefs of the citizen in the street but the wisdom of the most powerful school of American historians of that era. When the film was released, Woodrow Wilson, whose historical works are cited as one of its sources, was residing in the White House, and on 18 February 1915, the director screened *Birth of the Nation* in the presidential mansion. A Southerner by birth, Wilson was deeply moved by the film and his response to it – quoted second-hand but accepted by historians as more or less authentic – both suggests something about the prevailing historical wisdom and proved to be prophetic for the future role of the historical film: 'It's like writing history with lightning. And my only regret is that it is all so terribly true' (Schickel 1984: 270).

A decade after this morally and politically regressive masterpiece, Russian film maker Sergei Eisenstein began to use film to provide the fledgling Soviet Union with its own history and foundation myths – the two notions being in Russia, as in all countries, closely intertwined. In an effort to create a new and revolutionary theory and practice of film for a new and revolutionary régime, Eisenstein created a kind of montage that helped him to construct epic works which promoted the twin-edged theme of the masses entering history and history entering the masses. His films of the 1920s feature no heroes or even individual characters, save for the few who (much the same as in a written narrative history) rise out of the crowd for a moment to articulate an idea or symbolize an event. The first of these, and his acknowledged masterpiece, *Battleship Potemkin* (1925), leaned a long way towards myth as it took a minor incident from the revolution of 1905, a mutiny on a Black Sea battleship, and turned it into a stunning metaphor meant to show how the proletariat can overturn oppression and make a revolution. Three years later, his film to honour the tenth anniversary of the Bolshevik Revolution, *October* (1928) – for all its invented interludes such as the storming of the Winter Palace – stayed close to the details of the so-called Ten Days That Shook the World, even as it downplayed the contribution of both Lenin and his party. Though labelled propaganda by many, and full of tropes that were (and are) unusual in a historical work – humour, repetition, visual metaphor, mini-essays, the poetry of movement – *October* manages to provide an overall interpretation of its subject that is not so different from those argued by major historians of the revolution (as I will show in some detail in Chapter 3).

The Bolshevik Revolution also provided the topic for what is probably the first of the important history documentaries, Esfir Shub's compilation film, *The Fall of the Romanov Dynasty* (1927). Desiring to depict the birth of the new régime in which she lived, Shub painstakingly exhumed and catalogued the extensive home movies of Czar Nicholas, then intercut sequences of royal boating parties, croquet matches, and religious rituals with actuality (newsreel) footage of farm labour, factories, politicians, cavalry on parade, soldiers marching, artillery firing, and revolutionary street demonstrations. Underscoring these images were strong inter-titles – a close shot of a munitions assembly line followed by: 'The hands of workers preparing the death of their brothers' – a comment that can be interpreted as either propagandistic or historical, but is really both at the same time (Roberts 1999: 50–72).

Griffith, Eisenstein, and Shub may be considered the originators (or, to avoid arguments over precedence, at least very early practitioners) of the three types of arguably serious history films that have been produced ever since: the mainstream drama (and its longer sibling the television mini-series or docudrama), the opposition or innovative history, and the compilation documentary. The American created what we might call the 'standard' work of history on film, the 'realistic' (melo) drama that depicts the plight of heroes, heroines and villains caught up in the sweep of huge historical events, men and women whose stories show both the impact of such events on individual lives and, through the figure we know as synecdoche, serve to exemplify larger historical themes – in this case, supposedly how Northern carpetbaggers manipulated ignorant ex-slaves to oppress and exploit the conquered South, which was happily saved from destruction by the bravery of the Ku Klux Klan. Shub is equally 'realistic' as she edits together footage of actual historical moments to create a sense of the past 'as it really was', or at least as some of its moments looked through the lens of a camera from a particular point of view. Eisenstein, by contrast, makes no attempt at anything we might wish to call 'realism'. His aesthetic and style make it impossible to see the screen as some sort of direct window onto a past reality. Through a refusal to focus on individuals, radical editing techniques (four times as many cuts as in the standard film of the time), and overt visual metaphors (a screen full of raised sickles represents the peasantry; raised rifles stand in for the army; turning wheels mean a motorcycle brigade; a statue being torn down indicates the fall of the Czar; the same statue reassembling itself suggests the provisional government has taken over the role of Czar), a work like *October* clearly reveals that it is constructing rather than reflecting a particular vision of the past.

With their varying approaches to history on the screen, each of these types of film makes somewhat different assumptions about historical reality, about what is important for us to know of the past. These, along with the kind of world each form creates on the screen, will be elaborated upon and analyzed in later chapters. Here it should be enough to point out that the *historical assumptions* of such works do not change with later alterations or improvements in the technology of the medium itself. Adding spoken dialogue in the late nineteen twenties, improving upon sound effects, moving from black and white to colour film, enlarging and widening the screen, introducing surround sound, digitalizing the image or shrinking it to fit the size of a television monitor in a living room – none of these changes does anything to alter the kind of historical thinking we encounter in the visual media. The real differences lie between the three kinds of history films. All insist, as they must, on the primacy of the image, but each utilizes images in a different way to create historical meaning.

The dramatic feature film, directed by the descendants of Griffith, has been and continues to be, in terms of audience and influence, the most important form of history in the visual media. Everywhere in the world, movies mean dramatic feature films, with the documentary consigned to a marginal status and the innovative film hardly recognized at all, except among small circles of devotees. This pattern certainly holds true for the 'historical'. Works such as *Gandhi* (1982), *The Night of the Shooting Stars* (1983), *Born on the Fourth of July* (1989), *Schindler's List* (1993), *Underground* (1998) and *Frida* (2002) reach a wide audience and sometimes become the focus of public debate about history, a debate that often swirls around the issue of whether or not the film got the facts right. As I shall later argue, the accuracy of fact is hardly the first or even most important question to ask about the kind of historical thinking that takes place on the screen.

Whether the mainstream drama focuses on documented people or creates fictional characters and sets them amidst some important event or movement (most films contain both actual and invented characters), the historical thinking involved is much the same: individuals (one, two, or a small group) are at the centre of the historical process. Through their eyes and lives, adventures and loves, we see strikes, invasions, revolutions, dictatorships, ethnic conflict, scientific experiments, legal battles, political movements, holocausts. But we do more than see: we feel as well. Using image, music, and sound effect along with the spoken (and shouted, whispered, hummed, and cooed) word, the dramatic film aims directly at the emotions. It does not simply provide an image of the past, it wants you to feel strongly about that image – specifically, about the characters involved in the historical situations that it depicts. Portraying the world in the present tense, the dramatic feature plunges you into the midst of history, attempting to destroy the distance between you and the past and to obliterate – at least while you are watching – your ability to think about what you are seeing. Film does more than want to teach the lesson that history hurts; it wants you, the viewer, to experience the hurt (and pleasures) of the past.

The major way we experience – or imagine we experience – the past on the screen is obviously through our eye. We see bodies, faces, landscapes, buildings, animals, tools, implements, weapons, clothing, furniture, all the material objects that belong to a culture at a given historical period, objects that are used and misused, ignored and cherished, objects that sometimes can help to define livelihoods, identities, and destinies. Such objects, which the camera demands in order to make a scene look 'real', and which written history can easily, and usually does, ignore, are part of the texture and the factuality of the world on film. What in written history Roland Barthes once called 'reality effects', and dismissed as mere notations, achieve on the screen a certain, important 'thingness' (Ankersmit 1994: 139–41b). Because they tell us much about the people, processes, and times, 'reality effects' in film become facts under description, important elements in the creation of historical meaning.

The ability to elicit strong, immediate emotion, the emphasis on the visual and aural, and the resulting embodied quality of the film experience in which we seem to live through events we witness on the screen – all these are no doubt the practices that most clearly distinguish the history film from history on the page, especially that produced by academics. By focusing on the experience of individuals or small groups, film situates itself closer to biography, micro-history, or popular narrative history than to the academic variety, and while each of these three genres has occasionally been criticized as not sufficiently 'historical' by some of the professoriat, each has also won enough supporters to qualify as an accepted form for rendering out relationship to, and increasing our understanding of, the past.

Other aspects of the dramatic film seem much closer to the common practice of historians. Like the academic, the film maker tells a story with a beginning, a middle, and an end, one that includes a strong moral flavour. Like the academic, the film maker's story is almost always embedded in a progressive view of the past, and this is true even with the such unlikely subjects as slavery, the Holocaust, or the mass atrocities of the Khmer Rouge. Like the academic, the film maker can maintain such a viewpoint only through the very act of telling the past: whatever humanity has lost – runs the implicit message – is now redeemed by the creation of this work, by the witnessing of the historical wrongs that this film allows us to share (Rosenstone 1995a: 54–61).

The documentary film, considered as a mode of historical understanding, shares a great deal with the dramatic feature: it tells a linear and moral story, often deals (especially in recent years) with large topics through the experience of a small group of participants, spends a good deal of time on the thingness of objects, and aims to stir the emotions not only through the selection, framing, and juxtaposition of still and moving images, but also by employing a sound-track overflowing with language, sound effects, and music of the era being depicted. Unlike the dramatic film, the majority of its images are not staged for the camera (though occasionally some are), but are gathered from museums and from photo and film archives – a major exception being the 'talking heads', contemporary interviews with participants in the historical events or experts, often professors of history, whose words are used to give shape to and create the broader meaning of the past.

The implicit claim of the documentary is that it gives us direct access to history. That its historical images, through their indexical relationship to actual people, landscapes, and objects, can provide a virtually unmediated experience of the past – certainly more direct than the created past of the feature film, which must stage scenes to film them. But this is no more than a kind of mystification. Except in its contemporary interviews, the document-ary, unlike the dramatic feature, speaks with some regularity not in the present tense but in a specifically visual tense we might dub 'nostalgia', a tense whose emotional appeal can pull in a huge audience, such as that which followed Ken Burns' series, *The Civil War*, which originally appeared on the Public Broadcast System, or that for his subsequent series on baseball and jazz. These works overflow with old photos, actuality footage, and clips from old feature films – all of which, by their original aesthetic, their deterioration over the years, and their reminder of what once was or wasn't there, come bathed in a warm feeling about how times have changed, how much we have gained, how much we have lost. The people in those photos and film clips did not find – as we do – each other's hair or clothing styles quaint, or the furniture they sit on, the buildings they front, the tools and weapons they hold, old fashioned or outmoded. Such images can never bring a direct experience of history, for the intervening years always intrude too much upon the viewer's consciousness.

The opposition or innovative historical film constitutes a baggy category, one that contains a wide variety of theories, ideologies, and aesthetic approaches with both potential and real impact upon historical thought. These are largely works of opposition to what we may designate as 'Hollywood', works consciously created to contest the seamless stories of heroes and victims that make up the mainstream feature and the standard documentary. They are, at the same time, part of a search for a new vocabulary in which to render the past on the screen, an effort to make history (depending upon the film) more complex, interrogative, and self-conscious, a matter of tough, even unanswerable questions rather than of slick stories. The best of these films propose new strategies for dealing with the traces of the past, strategies that point towards new forms of historical thought, forms that need not be limited to the screen, but might, with necessary alterations due to the medium, be carried back to the printed page.

So diverse and hidden (since few are popular) are these kinds of films, that here I can do no more than point to a few and suggest how they attempt to rethink history on the screen. Eisenstein has had a few heirs, film makers (mostly from the Third World) who create dramatic features which place the collective or the masses rather than the individual at the centre of the historical process. Brazil's Carlos Diegues does this and then something even more radical in *Quilombo* (1984), a history of Palmyra, a long-lived seventeenth-century runaway slave society, which is portrayed in song and dance (samba) by actors costumed as if partaking in Carnival. A similar attack on a 'realistic' portrayal of historical events has been pursued by other film makers – Ousmane Sembene in *Ceddo* (1977), a highly stylized story of religious and tribal upheaval in Senegal; Luis Valdes in *Zoot Suit* (1980), which uses song and dance and a mythical central character, El Pachuco, the spirit of the Barrio, to portray Anglo-Mexican tensions and conflict in World War II Los Angeles; Alex Cox, in his anachronism-laden (Mercedes automobiles, helicopters, and computer terminals in the 1850s) black comedy, *Walker* (1987). Other critiques of the 'period look' of film have come in documentaries – Claude Lanzmann's *Shoah* (1985), a work on the Holocaust that contains no images from the 1940s, or Hans Jurgen Syberberg's *Hitler, a Film from Germany* (1977), which uses puppets, sets, historical objects, actors, and back-projection to create the Third Reich on what is clearly shown to be a sound stage.

Such staples of film as the dramatic story and the heightening of emotion have also been called into question. In a series of consciously de-dramatized works – among them *The Age of Iron* (1964), *The Rise of Louis XIV* (1966), and *The Age of the Medici* (1972) – Roberto Rossellini, probably the most prolific director of historical films in the history of the medium, uses non-actors to haltingly deliver lines which are far closer in form to lectures than dialogue, and lets the 'reality effect' of sumptuous costumes and settings carry the argument for his highly materialist interpretation of the past. History as a single story with a clear (moral) conclusion can also be contested. In *Far From Poland* (1984), a work that mixes documentary and drama, director Jill Godmilow presents a history of the Solidarity Movement through competing voices and images that refuse to coalesce into a single story or meaning. Using a similar mixture of genres, Trinh T. Min-ha, in *Surname Viet Given Name Nam* (1989) dispenses with linear story in favour of incident, pastiche, rumination; the very form of the film is historically unsettling, a kind of theme and variation that is signalled in the opening sequence, a dance in which a group of women combine and re-combine in patterns that repeat and vary in endless combinations.

Works by Godmilow, Trinh, and Syberberg (along with a number of other films I have examined elsewhere, see Rosenstone 1995a: 198–225) belong to a small body of films about the past which, more than almost anything done on the printed page, would properly fit into a category labeled post-modern history – at least as defined by theorists of the postmodern. These are histories which do some or all of the following: foreground their own construction; tell the past self-reflexively and from a multiplicity of viewpoints; forsake normal story development, or problematize the stories they recount; utilize humour, parody, and absurdist as modes of presenting the past; refuse to insist on a coherent or single meaning of events; indulge in fragmentary or poetic knowledge; and never forget that the present moment is the site of all past representation. By using such offbeat tropes and techniques, these works issue a sharp challenge to both the practices of the mainstream drama and documentary and the traditional claims of empirical history – a challenge parallel to that issued by post-structuralist theorists, only here the challenge is embodied (or envisioned) in works which combine both a new theory and a practice of history.

Film-makers create films, not theories about film, let alone theories about history, which means it is to their finished productions rather than their stated intentions that we usually must go to understand the historical thinking we find on the screen. To this general rule, there are some exceptions. Eisenstein, a major theorist, does occasionally invoke the Marxist dialectic in reference to history, but only in passing; clearly more interested in notions of montage or what he called 'intellectual' cinema, the Russian never does any sustained explication of the relationship between his historical works and the past events they evoke or describe. Roberto Rossellini, whose more than a dozen films about the past may be the most sustained historical œuvre of any director, provided contradictory ideas about his portrayal of history without ever bothering to resolve them. On the one hand, he invokes notions of the didactic film, one which can objectively describe the past and create a direct, unmediated vison; on the other, he insists that his works are based upon a moral vision, without admitting that such a moral vision inevitably creates a point of view which cannot be objective. More recent directors concerned with history have overtly admitted its subjective components. Rainer Werner Fassbinder, director in the 1970s of several films dealing with the Third Reich and its legacy, did not hesitate to explain, 'We make a particular film about a particular time from our point of view'. Oliver Stone, who in half-a-dozen films has charted aspects of American society from the Vietnam war into the 1980s, initially claimed to be creating history, but then retreated under attacks from the press, particularly about *JFK* (1991) and *Nixon* (1998), to an extreme subjectivist position, asking: 'What is history? Some people say it's a bunch of gossip made up by soldiers who passed it around a campfire'. (Stone 2000: 47)

For any sustained thinking about history and film, one must turn to the work of a handful of professional historians, since all but a few academics have considered the topic outside the pale of their interests or duties. Most historians would probably like to turn Oliver Stone's words against historical films – and see them as a bunch of (mostly untrue) stories that directors put upon the screen. Such a distaste for film has been possible because for most of the twentieth-century historians saw their own work as a thoroughly empirical undertaking, a human science that properly made certain kinds of truth claims about the past, claims that could hardly be matched by the costume dramas, swashbucklers, and romances that were regularly turned out by studios around the world. So rarely did historians comment upon the topic that Peter Novick's book, *That Noble Dream* (1988: 194), a lengthy survey of American historical practice in the twentieth century, contains but a single reference to motion pictures. In a 1935 letter that is highly revealing about professional attitudes, Louis Gottschalk of the University of Chicago wrote to the president of Metro-Goldwyn-Mayer: 'If the cinema art is going to draw its subjects so generously from history, it owes to its patrons and its own higher ideals to achieve greater accuracy. No picture of a historical nature ought to be offered to the public until a reputable historian has had a chance to criticize and revise it'.

Factors other than the quality of films kept historians from considering motion pictures a serious way of recounting the past. The visual media fell on the wrong side of the once enormous wall that separated high culture from low (or mass) culture, which meant that films could not be taken seriously until that wall collapsed – as it began to do in the 1960s. More importantly, for at least the first half of the century academics were secure in the belief that their kind of knowledge of past politics, and economic, social and cultural life, was 'true' knowledge, and they were certain that the culture at large accepted the truths about the past that professional historians could provide. But after mid-century, as the claims of traditional history and its Euro-centred meta-narratives increasingly began to be called into question from a variety of disciplines and quarters – by feminists, ethnic minorities, post-colonial theorists, anthropologists, narratologists, philosophers of history, deconstructionists, and post-modernists – a climate developed that allowed academics to take popular culture more seriously and to begin looking more closely at the relationship between film and historical knowledge.

Not until the late 1960s did the number of historians interested in film reach a large enough mass to begin to create the meetings, essays, journals, and books that indicate a topic is on the scholarly map. A first conference, 'Film and the Historian', was hosted by University College, London, in April 1968, to be followed in the early and mid-1970s by similar gatherings at the universities in Utrecht and Gottingen, at Bielefeld's Centre for Inter-disciplinary Research, and at the Imperial War Museum in London. Attended mostly by scholars from the continent (France, Germany, Denmark, the Netherlands and Belgium) and the UK, with a couple of visitors from the United States, these gatherings focused largely on the production, reception, and value of the actuality (documentary) rather than the fictional film. Out of such conferences grew the International Association for Audiovisual Media and History, which since 1981 has published the *International Journal of Film, Radio, and Television* (Fledelius 2004).

The three books that emerged from these early meetings dealt for the most part with two questions: first, how actuality film could be used as a document for purposes of historical research and second, how it could be used as a teaching tool in the classroom. First to be published was *The Historian and Film* (1976), a collection of essays by (mostly) British historians which focused upon questions of newsreel, movies in the classroom, and how to evaluate films as historical evidence. Three years later, *History and the Audio-Visual Media*, divided its essays into three categories: Didactic Problems, Film and TV Materials as Source Material for Historians, and Content Analysis and Mass Communication. This was followed in 1981 by a volume entitled *Feature Films as History*, the first book to deal with dramatic works, and more particularly with the question of how clusters of films made in certain periods could serve as windows onto an exploration of particular ideologies or climates of opinion – antisemitism in Europe, the Popular Front of the 1930s, or national consciousness in Germany and France in the 1920s (Smith 1976; Short 1981).

A single essay in the volume tentatively edged in a radical new direction. In analyzing Sergei Eisenstein's classic work, *Battleship Potemkin*, D.J. Wenden of Oxford considers the question of how a film, even though its content is largely fictionalized, might yet illuminate an historical event. After comparing the film's account of the ship's mutiny with written histories on the same topic, Wenden suggests that rather than creating a literal reality, Eisenstein makes 'brilliant use of the ship's revolt as a symbol for the whole revolutionary effort of the Russian people in 1905' (Wenden 1981: 40). This is the first instance (at least the first in print known to me) in which a historian makes a move towards suggesting that film might have its own specific way of telling the past, that the very nature of the medium and its practices of necessity create a particular kind of history (here dubbed symbolic history) that is different from what we normally expect to find upon the page.

Two historians in France during the 1970s also took steps towards a notion of film as what we might wish to call historical discourse. Marc Ferro, whose path-breaking essays were eventually collected in *Cinema et histoire* (1977), focuses most of his effort on the notion that film (but not necessarily historical film) is a cultural artifact, one which not only reveals much about the time period in which it is made but that at its best provides what he calls a 'counter analysis' of society. Only in the last essay in the volume does he confront the more problematic (and interesting) issue: 'Does a filmic writing of history exist?' Ferro's initial response is 'No'. Film makers, he argues, blindly incorporate either a national or a leftist ideology into their renditions of the past, and their films thus end up being no more than transcriptions 'of a vision of history which has been conceived by others'. But – and here a radical new notion begins to emerge – Ferro then admits that there are exceptions to this rule. A few directors (he names Andrei Tarkovsky, of Russia; Ousmane Sembene, Senegal; Hans Jurgen Syberberg, Germany; Luchino Visconti, Italy, and a group of Polish film makers) possess such strong historical visions that they are able to transcend the ideological forces and traditions of their countries. Such film makers create independent interpretations of history and thereby make 'an original contribution to the understanding of past phenomena and their relation to the present' (Ferro 1988: 158–64).

Pierre Sorlin, who devotes all of *The Film in History* (1980) to the issue of how the dramatic feature 'restages the past', does not venture as far as Ferro. A certain ambivalence towards film as history runs through the volume, and the internal confusion of his chapter on Sergei Eisenstein's *October* mirrors the difficulties historians inevitably have in dealing with works about the past in a medium that can seem so elusive. Initially Sorlin dismisses *October* as no more than 'propaganda', but a long analysis leads him to contradict himself and by the end of his chapter term it a view of the Russian Revolution that is independent of Bolshevik ideology – a judgement which at least tends toward Ferro's 'filmic writing of history'. The more general problem Sorlin raises about historical films is that they are ultimately 'all fictional'. Even those based on historical evidence 'reconstruct in a purely imaginary way the greater part of what they show'. Nonetheless, he does demonstrate how, with regard to certain topics (the French Revolution, the Italian *Risorgimento,* the American Civil War), groups of historical films do relate to the larger realm of discourse generated by professionals in the field. In an argument too often ignored by historians (and journalists) today, Sorlin suggests that precisely like written histories, films must be judged not against our current knowledge or interpretations of a topic but with regard to historical understanding at the time they were made. This means that when, say, we are condemning the vicious racism of D.W. Griffith's classic, *Birth of a Nation,* we must keep in mind that the film was neither a bizarre personal nor a purely commercial interpretation of the Civil War and Reconstruction, but in fact a decent reflection of the best academic history of its own time, the early twentieth century (Sorlin 1980: 21, 159, 186).

In the quarter century since publication of *The Film in History,* an increasing number of historians have been willing to confront the challenge of the visual media. The first major move into the topic in the United States was a Forum entirely devoted to film in the December 1988 issue of that most conservative and traditional of journals, *The American Historical Review.* Here, my own opening essay, 'History in images/History in words: reflections on the possibility of really putting history onto film', which argued in favour of beginning to take film seriously as a way of thinking about the past, was answered by four historians, three of whom agreed to a greater or lesser extent (although not without some criticisms). A highlight of the forum came in the essay by Hayden White, who took the opportunity to coin an important and useful term, 'historiophoty', which he defined as 'the representation of history and our thought about it in visual images and filmic discourse' (White 1988: 1193). Exploring that topic is precisely the burden of this book you are reading.

Since that initial forum, historians in America, Australia, and Europe have increasingly been drawn to the topic of the visual media. For the most part, this has been in the form of reviews of individual films, which – as a sign of changing times – are now carried by virtually every historical journal; as well as in essays, many of which have appeared as part of edited volumes. The usual tasks of such pieces is to set documentary and dramatic films in their historical context, or try to explain in an *ad hoc* sort of way how much of a particular film is 'true' and how much of it is mistaken or invented, or to deal with the reception or impact of a work. And while occasionally one of these essays by historians, or the comparable works undertaken by scholars in film studies or communications, brush against the question of how and where film sits with regard to traditional historical discourse, attempts to deal directly and fully with the concept of historiophoty are non-existent. The closest attempt to write any sort of sustained, theoretically-informed work that faces the questions raised by Wenden, Ferro, Sorlin, and the AHR Forum is *Slaves on Screen* by Natalie Davis. Because she is a highly regarded scholar of early modern France, and someone who has served as a consultant on a film made on the same topic as her earlier book, *The Return of Martin Guerre*, Davis' work is worth an extended look, in part because of its conscious attempt to broaden the discourse on film and move it in new directions.

Slaves on the Screen is not, it must be said at the outset, a broad or exhaustive examination of its topic. Growing out of a series of lectures delivered at the University of Toronto, the book consists of five short chapters that examine five films dealing with slavery, placing each work in both historical and historiographical contexts. Without using the word, Davis here ventures into the realm of 'historiophoty'. Her aim is to investigate 'what kind of historical inquiry' these films undertake and, in a sense, to elaborate on her idea of film as a kind of 'thought experiment' which were first voiced in conjunction with her work as historical consultant on *The Return of Martin Guerre* (Davis 2000: 121, xi).

The first question that has to be asked by anyone writing historiophoty is that posed by Ferro: can there be a filmic writing of history? Davis puts it in different language: 'What is film's potential for telling about the past in a meaningful and accurate way?' If the whole book is an attempt to provide an answer, the theoretical underpinnings of the argument are present in the first chapter, 'Film as Historical Narrative'. Not that her answer is crystal clear. Davis approaches the issue of 'whether we can arrive at a historical account faithful to the evidence if we leave the boundaries of professional prose for the sight, sound, and dramatic action of film' by invoking the change in ideas of how to tell the past from Homer to Herodotus to Thucydides; then going on to mention Aristotle's distinctions between poetry and history, between 'what happened (and) . . . what might happen', between the 'general truths' of the poet and the 'specific events' of the historian. These classical distinctions, she points out, 'were often blurred in practice' – the speeches recounted by the supposedly rigorous Thucydides were largely invented, and he, too, often resorted to the 'possible' rather than the actual in order to round out his historical accounts (Davis 2000: 4, 3).

The ancients are important to Davis as an oblique way of legitimating film. Implicit is the notion that because history has, over time, been practised

according to different rules, it is now legitimate to devote one's energy to a
study of the practise of history in this (relatively) new medium. Or, to be
specific, one kind of practise. For purposes of this work, Davis has chosen to
analyze only dramatic features because she finds them 'a more difficult case
than documentary films'. More difficult because although critics often like to
create a sharp contrast between 'fiction films' as products of the 'imagination'
and non-fictional documentaries as carriers of 'truth', it is precisely this
dichotomy she wishes to question. Ostensibly more indexical and thus truer
in its relationship to reality, the documentary also involves a 'play of invention', while the dramatic feature, despite fictive elements, 'can make cogent
observations on historical events, relations, and processes' (Davis 2000: 5).

Such dramatic works communicate to us in a medium which has had but a
century to develop its genres, a brief moment compared to 2,500 years in
which Westerners have explored and discarded many different forms for written history. Davis distinguishes between two kinds of history films – those
based on documentable events; and those with imagined plots, in which
verifiable events are intrinsic to the action. She sees the normal feature film as
recounting the past in one of two modes: the historical biography or the micro-
history (which she herself has written). The former may address such questions as 'how and why political decisions are made in different historical
régimes, and their consequences'. The latter, like good social history, can let
us in on the dynamics of family life, or let us share the experience of 'people at
work', medieval peasants sowing and harvesting, Chinese dyers staining cloth
in great vats, women in twentieth-century factories bent over machines. This
said, we still must beware of succumbing too much to their 'reality', for ultimately films do not quite show, but, rather, '*speculate* on . . . how the past was
experienced and acted out, how large forces and events were lived through
locally and in detail' (Davis 2000: 7).

The note of caution in this statement marks the rest of the opening chapter
– indeed, the rest of the book. On the one hand, Davis exults in what she calls
the 'multiple techniques' with which film can narrate the past and make it
coherent and exciting, the very visual and aural language that makes this such
a powerful medium: image, acting, colour, editing, sound, location, design,
costume. On the other, she insists on the importance of traditional require-
ments for telling the past as 'developed over the centuries'. These include
following the obvious ideals (often violated in practice, as she knows) that are
taught to students of history in graduate school: seeking evidence widely,
keeping an open mind, telling readers the sources of the evidence, revealing
one's own assumptions, not letting normative judgements get in the way of
understanding, never falsifying evidence, and labelling our speculations.

Since the dramatic film, by its very nature, cannot fulfill most of these practices (something Davis can never quite get herself to admit directly), it seems to be relegated to a subsidiary role in telling the past. Bearing in mind 'the differences between film and professional prose', she says we can take film seriously 'as a source of valuable and even innovative historical vision'. We can even 'ask questions of historical films that are parallel to those we ask of historical books'. But we cannot wholly trust the answers, for ultimately film makers are not quite historians, but 'artists for whom history matters' (Davis 2000: 11, 15).

With such ideas in mind, Davis approaches five films made between 1960 and 1998, treating them chronologically and, in a general way, setting them against the historiographical context of post-war studies on slavery by such scholars as M.I. Finley, David Brion Davis, and Eugene Genovese. Each film is also loosely connected to a particular social mood. The classic spectacle, *Spartacus* (1960), based on the Howard Fast novel and directed by a young Stanley Kubrick, gets linked both to the Cold War and to scholarly concerns over the 'slave personality'. Two foreign films of the 1970s reflect the outbreak of revolution and independence movements in the Third World – *Burn!* (1969), directed by Italy's Gillo Pontecorvo (best-known for the anti-colonialist masterpiece, *The Battle for Algiers*), the story of a failed revolution on a fictional sugar-producing island; and *The Last Supper* (1976), by Cuba's Tomas Gutierrez Alea, based on a prize-winning (from the American Historical Association) book by historian Morena Fraginal, *The Sugar Mill*, which describes a 1790 revolt on a plantation. Two American productions from the 1990s belong to what Davis calls our growing concern with the horrors of victimization – Stephen Spielberg's *Amistad* (1997), the story of the takeover of a slave ship by African slaves, and the subsequent trials of its leaders in Massachusetts, and *Beloved* (1998), the Jonathan Demme production (from the Toni Morrison novel) that explores the psychic scars left on ex-slaves after gaining their freedom, were produced, in Davis' words, 'under the shadow of the Holocaust' (Davis 2000: 70).

The strategy for analyzing each work consists of three parts. First the genesis – who got the idea for the film, what were its sources, how did various producers-writers-directors bring it to the screen and what were his/her/their intentions. Second, a synopsis, one that highlights the characters and events, and also points to the major deviations from the historical record. Third, the judgement(s) – why should we care about the film, what does it contain that makes us think seriously about the past, and how might it be changed to make it more valuable as a historical work? With *Spartacus*, for example, we learn how actor Kirk Douglas, writer Dalton Trumbo, and director Kubrick managed to bring the Howard Fast novel to the screen; and that Laurence Olivier, Charles Laughton,

and Peter Ustinov changed their lines during the shoot. The film's historical
successes – created not just with story and acting, but also with camera work,
editing, colour, and music – include 'the portrayal of the gap between high
and low', slave and freeman in Roman society; the depiction of the training in
the school for gladiators; the final battle sequence with its chaotic fighting and
close combat between slaves and legionnaires; and the portrait of illegal mar-
riages and personal relationships among the slaves, taken as a fitting emblem
of resistance. Among the shortcomings are an inaccurate picture of the
makeup and functioning of the Roman Senate; a failure to mention the long
tradition of slave revolts in the Roman Empire that preceded Spartacus; and
the final speech of our hero, which exhibits an anachronistic universalism,
born of ideas from the Enlightenment rather than the ancient world. Weighed
against the historical record, Davis gives the film a 'mixed report – some successes, some missed opportunities, some failures' (Davis 2000: 36).

A similar mixed assessment holds for the other films, save that the two
works made outside of Hollywood get much higher marks for complex historical consciousness. Part of this is visual, the unsentimental eye, risky camera
movement, and offbeat editing choices of film makers (European and Third
World) willing to stretch the experience of an audience used to the comfort of
Hollywood film language, in which the location of places and people on the
screen is always clearly demarcated. *Burn!*, based on events that took place in
a dozen Caribbean and Latin American countries, but fictional in its central
story, is a 'successful experiment' that evokes the rituals and ceremonies of a
slave society, and manages to portray how events are experienced both by
groups of people and individuals. Through the personal rivalry of two men –
the native leader of the revolution and the British officer (Marlon Brando) sent
to suppress it – the film provides a splendid example of 'the micro-historical
potential of film'. The same is true of *The Last Supper*. 'Tightly linked to evidence from the Cuban past' and to its source, *The Sugar Mill*, the work is set
during Holy Week 1790 on the plantation of the Count de Casa Bayona. This
pious, elderly count who enjoys the humility of those 'rites of inversion' which
have him washing the feet of his slaves, changes quickly into a bloody tyrant
when these same slaves lead a revolt, one he suppresses with merciless
efficiency and the execution of all its leaders. If the portrait of the count is not
'nuanced' enough for Davis, she applauds its representation of a gallery of
social types – overseers, priests, technicians, slaves – and its gritty depiction of
the daily working world of the plantation and mill (Davis 2000: 52, 62).

It is no doubt a measure of our (or her) current state of mind that makes
Davis give by far the longest chapter to the films she sees as shadowed by the
Holocaust. Like *Spartacus*, the report on *Amistad* is mixed. Viewers may

come away from the film 'with a general sense of the movement of events, the interests at stake, the arguments being offered and challenged, and the popular excitement and zeal stimulated' by the trials of the Africans and the question of whether they are to be set free or sent back into slavery, but the film is not, as promised by director Spielberg, the 'mirror . . . [of] actual events as they unfold'. Like many (all?) historical films, this one, to increase suspense or add to character developments, indulges in fabrications. Davis is of two minds about such fictional moves – she has no objections to inventions seen to add depth to the story, only to those which appear to be arbitrary or unnecessary. Indeed, she occasionally makes suggestions for inventions, which to her would have been more plausible and apropos than those created by the director (Davis 2000: 79).

No inventions are called into question in *Beloved*, for as a film based upon a novel, the work is entirely an invention, thus doubly removed from the historical events of slavery. Worse yet from a traditional historian's point of view, one of the characters is a ghost of a baby girl, murdered by her mother to keep her from the slave-catchers. Yet such obvious fictions in no way prevent the film from providing a powerful, heart-rending account of the long-lasting trauma caused 'by the wounds of slavery, inflicted and then self-inflicted through resistance'. When describing *Beloved*, Davis' prose often moves from the scholarly towards the rhapsodic. Fictional they may be, but each of the characters provides us with 'historical insight' into traumatic events; each haunts us 'with the tragedies and hopes of the past' (Davis 2000: 108, 119).

What more, one might ask, can one expect of a historical film? Apparently no more than that it focus on 'Telling the Truth', the title of Davis' final chapter. But what truth? The factual truth, the narrative truth, the emotional truth, the psychological truth, the symbolic truth? For there is not a single historical truth – not on the page and certainly not on the screen. Knowing this, Davis in the final chapter has to come to grips with that topic which troubles all historians who deal with the dramatic film: the fact that such works always indulge in fabrication and invention – of characters, incidents, events, moments, dialogue, settings – and not just to make the stories more commercial or palatable to a large audience, but because both the medium and the genre insure that such invention is intimately involved in every moment on the screen. Partly this is due to time constraints, the need to compress large events into short sequences; partly to the greediness of the camera, which demands more specificity of detail than any historian could possibly know about a particular setting or incident in the past; partly to the fact that however good our actors (Davis particularly admires Anthony Hopkins as John Adams), they are impersonators who utilize a vocabulary of gestures, movements, and words to create historical figures whose voices and movements are in most cases wholly lost to us and therefore have to be wholly invented.

Ignoring the extent to which fiction is deeply implicated in all such films, Davis instead focuses on the overt fabrications that seem unnecessary or, worse, derive from a wish to make the beliefs of a past era more closely resemble those of the present (e.g. Spartacus' universalist speech). She faults film-makers for 'too cavalier an attitude toward the evidence about lives and attitudes in the past', and for 'underestimating film audiences'. To be engaged by a historical film 'spectators do not need to have the past remade to seem exactly like the present'. She also wants directors to be more honest about their sources (list them in the credits), to admit to the uncertainties of the past by finding filmic equivalents for the 'perhapses' and 'may have beens' of prose. To do so, she suggests, a director could utilize devices such as a reporter looking for a story and finding more than one version to tell; or by filling the screen with witnesses and documents that contradict each other; or by adopting the kind of experimental, multi-perspective narration used in the Japanese classic, *Rashomon*, with its four accounts of the same event, or the *French Lieutenant's Woman*, with its parallel stories set both in present and past (Davis 2000: 130–31).

Even without such devices, the argument of the book is that these five films have much to tell us about various systems of slavery across the centuries. *Spartacus* lets us glimpse the political struggles of Rome and see the development of a major social revolt against Imperial power. *Burn!* and *The Last Supper* show us a colonial system of investment, labour, and politics in the context of the customs, tales, songs, and dances of African and Caribbean people. *Amistad* and *Beloved* involve us in the horrific psycho-social conditions of the Middle Passage and the Southern plantation system, and teach us that notions of freedom can stem not just from Western but also from African roots. Though all can be faulted on some counts, these films, taken together, engage with the larger historical discourse and even add, through the powers of the medium in which they are rendered, something to our understanding of the costs of slave systems for both masters and slaves.

Despite this argument, Davis at times betrays a certain uneasiness about historical film, a feeling that peeks through her balance sheets of what individual works do right and what they do wrong, her suggestions for better inventions (which often ignore the dramatic aspect of film, the fact that a screenplay is a kind of intricate machine which, if one part is pulled out, may no longer function properly), and her repeated insistence on the traditional standards of written history. At times it seems as if her answer to the shortcoming of films would be to make them more like books – or at least to follow more closely the rules of traditional history. But we already have books, and a lengthy tradition of evaluating their evidence, arguments, and interpretations. What we don't yet have is a very good sense of historical film, and more precisely, its coordinates in the space time of our thoughts about the past; what we don't know is where history rendered in the visual media – with its movement, sound, and colour – is located with regard to traditional history.

'Historical films should let the past be the past', Davis says on the last page of the book (Davis 2000: 136). But this is certainly one thing we historians never do. It is our task precisely not to let the past be the past but to hold the past up for use (moral, political, contemplative) in the present. One is tempted to respond to Davis: 'Let historical films be films'. Which is to say that, rather than assuming that the world on film should somehow adhere to the standards of written history, why not let it create its own standards, appropriate to possibilities and practices of the medium. (Is this not what happens when one kind of history upstages another?) Better yet, why not admit that film makers have been working on such standards for a century and see it as the job of we, who do our history on the page, to investigate, explicate, and critique just what those standards are. As outsiders or theorists of historical film, we cannot prescribe the right and wrong way to tell the past, but need to derive theory from practice by analyzing how the past has been and is being told – in this case, on the screen. Davis begins to do this, and for that we are in her debt. But she doesn't take us far enough. Her judgements contain too much that derives from the standards of evidence of academic history. This puts as much a burden on film makers as one would put on historians if we were to judge their renderings of the past in filmic terms and then have to ask why are such works, compared to the colour, movement, and excitement of the screen, so slow, stuffy, measured, colourless, and silent?

In a sense, it is as if Davis has forgotten that history is not a natural process like eating, breathing, or sleeping – but a learned activity. We must be taught how to turn the past into history and how to read what we have done. A new medium like moving images on a screen with a sound accompaniment creates an enormous change in the way we tell and see the past – and think its meaning. When she calls film makers 'artists for whom history matters', Davis seems to ignore her own evidence that the best of them are something more than that. They already are (or can be) historians, if by that word we mean people who confront the traces of the past (rumours, documents, buildings, sites, legends, oral and written histories) and use them to tell stories that make meaning for us in the present. Of course the codes, conventions, rules, and practices which let them bring the past to the screen are different from those of written history. How could it be otherwise? Quite clearly, film uses data in a much looser way than academic history. Just as clearly, the past on the screen is not meant to be literal (is history on the page?), but suggestive, symbolic, metaphoric. Yet the best of historical films, as Davis herself shows, can intersect with, comment upon, and add something to the larger discourse of history out of which they grow and to which they speak. That 'something' is what we who care about the past need to learn how to read. By studying what the best historical film makers have done, we can come to better know the rules of engagement of the dramatic feature film with the traces of the past – and begin to glimpse what that adds to our understanding of history. That task will be the burden of the remaining chapters in this book.

Chapter 3

Mainstream drama

On the World Wide Web there is (at the time this chapter is being written) a site, centred at Fordham University, named 'medieval history in the movies'. It is quite a substantial site, with annotations on approximately four hundred films. True, some are mentioned more than once. And also true, its notion of 'medieval' is rather expansive, since it includes at one chronological end films set in what would normally be called antiquity (e.g. the 1980 drama *Caligula* or Frederico Fellini's 1969 *Satyricon*) and at the other end, films set in the late sixteenth and seventeenth century (Derek Jarman's *Caravaggio* 1986, and Alexander Korda's *Rembrandt* 1936). But there is no need to quibble over boundaries and periods. Whatever the temporal parameters, it is still an impressive list, for unlike the twentieth century, the medieval has hardly been a popular period in which to set historical films. Were we to leave aside works about Shakespeare (really the Renaissance) and Joan of Arc, we would rarely in recent years have seen something set in that timeframe.

The existence of 'medieval history in the movies' (and its two companion sites, 'ancient history in the movies' and 'modern history in the movies') underscores something about what has been happening in the historical profession for the last twenty or so years – historians have become increasingly interested in the visual media as both a competitor and a collaborator in their (our) attempt to convey the past not only to students but to the culture at large. This interest is also shown by the changing attitudes of our conferences and journals towards film. When I was a graduate student some 35 years ago, historical journals never deigned to mention film, and our doctoral advisers would have tossed us out of the programme and directly into the university neuropsychiatric institute were we to have suggested a dissertation on a film topic or claim a film might successfully 'do history'. Pretty much the same attitudes still prevailed in the early 1980s – and remain alive in many quarters today. Yet now virtually all major journals in the field regularly publish reviews and essays on film; panels on film are held at annual scholarly meetings, and entire conferences have been recently devoted to history and film in various countries, including the USA, the UK, Finland, Australia, Italy, Argentina, Brazil, and South Africa.

The 'medieval history in movies' website contains three fascinating lists: 'worst medieval movies'; 'best medieval movies – by historical accuracy'; and 'best medieval movies – as films'. Taken together, these provide some insights into how and what historians think about film. One can, for example, gather a good deal by looking at the criteria for judging 'the worst'. Mel Gibson's *Braveheart* (1999), is, for example, called a: 'Massively inaccurate portrayal of the life of the thirteenth-century hero William Wallace', without those inaccuracies in any way being characterized. The *Adventures of Marco Polo* (1938) is also judged a disaster because, for one thing, Gary Cooper simply is not very convincing as an Italian, and for another, the scene in which he stuffs 'dry pasta in his pocket to take back to Italy', thus giving us insight into the origins of spaghetti, seems somehow ludicrous. *The Vikings* (1958), with Kirk Douglas and Tony Curtis, fails because in the rowing sequences (and there are plenty of these) you can clearly see one Viking with a vaccination scar and another with a gold wristwatch. Franco Zeffirelli's *Brother Sun, Sister Moon* (1973), based on the life of St Francis of Assisi, makes the list because of its inappropriate 'do your own thing' soundtrack scored and sung by sixties pop singer, Donovan Leitch. And *The Conqueror* (1956) fails because John Wayne simply is not convincing in the role of the great Mongol leader, Ghengis Khan.

The best list 'by historical accuracy' contains only eight films, while the best 'as films' contains 17 films. Four works manage to make it onto both of these lists: *Becket* (1964) with Peter O'Toole and Richard Burton; *The Return of Martin Guerre* (1982), directed by Daniel Vigne and starring Gerard Depardieu and Natalie Baye; *The Passion of Joan of Arc* (1928), the Carl Dreyer classic; and *The Mission* (1986), the Roland Joffe drama, starring Robert DeNiro and Jeremy Irons. The comments as to why they are 'best' are, perhaps, even less revealing than those on the list of worst films. *Becket*, based on a play by Jean Anouilh, is called 'superb', even though the review denounces its central interpretation, for 'there is no historical data to support the suggestion' that there was a homosexual relationship between Thomas à Becket and Henry II. *The Return of Martin Guerre* is 'excellent' because it is 'based on trial records'; moreover, its director received 'solid historical advice' from historian Natalie Davis, who served as consultant. *The Passion of Joan of Arc* is also 'based on actual trial transcripts', and the actress Jeanne Falconetti gives 'the greatest performance ever captured on film'. For *The Mission* no reason whatsoever is offered as to why it is included among 'the best'.

These quotations point to something that occurs regularly when historians write about film. Judgements are made about historical value on wildly divergent grounds – accuracy of detail, the use of original documents, appropriateness of music, the looks or apparent suitability of an actor to play someone whose body language, voice, and gestures we can never know from the historical record – all of these may (or may not) be invoked as a way of praising or damning a film. Similar sorts of judgements are made about historical films in the pages of journals like the *American Historical Review* and the *Journal of American History*. They also fill the book edited by Mark C. Carnes, *Past imperfect: History according to the movies* where, in short essays, some 60 specialists assess one or more films as to their historical content. In this volume, almost none of the works come off as contributions to our understanding of the past.

Not untypical in its internal confusion (but quite untypical in its final insight, discussed below) is Gerda Lerner's essay on three films devoted to the life of Joan of Arc – Dreyer's *The Passion of Joan of Arc* (mentioned above), Victor Fleming's *Joan of Arc* (1948), written by Maxwell Anderson and starring Ingrid Bergman; and Otto Preminger's *Saint Joan* (1957), based on the play by Bernard Shaw and starring Jean Seberg. Lerner does her best to be fair to the films, but the essay keeps veering back and forth between different sorts of judgements and criteria. The Fleming and Preminger works, she says, 'adhere closely to the main historical facts'. Both 'succeed in creating a sense of historical veracity by getting superficial details right, such as the weapons and costumes of the time'. In *Joan of Arc*, Ingrid Bergman gives a 'luminous performance'; during the burning at the stake, her 'pain and terror' are wholly believable. But unfortunately the 'miraculous' ending, with a cross set against a golden sky, underscored by 'typical Hollywood music designed to signify exaltation – shatters the illusion'. The Preminger production, in following the Shaw play, gives us 'long, prescient monologues' by Joan which are totally 'ahistorical'. A framing device, telling of events after Joan's death, is clumsy, and distances the audience from the main events: 'It is as though we are seeing a film about the historiography of Joan of Arc rather than about her life and death.' Jean Seberg's performance is 'occasionally stirring but mostly unconvincing'. She plays the maid as a teenage waif and fails to convey her 'strength, drive, force' (Lerner 1995: 54–59).

Dreyer gets the highest marks – as well he should. Mostly by using close-ups, he has created, Lerner says, an atmosphere of 'horror and ravaged innocence'. The inter-titles of his silent film consist 'almost entirely of lines from the actual record of Joan's interrogation, which gives the work a spare and appropriately medieval tone'. (Its not clear if this is meant to indicate there was something 'spare' about medieval times, nor what this could mean other than the fact that castles and dungeons didn't have much furniture in their rooms.) Ultimately this film comes closest 'to conveying the historical truth'. For while the two Hollywood films 'imitate the life and times of Joan of Arc with varying degrees of success and some moments of verisimilitude', Dreyer, by using film *poetically* and *metaphorically* (my emphasis), makes us suffer the agony of the peasant girl Joan and makes us feel 'the radiance of the presence of a saint' (Lerner 1995: 56, 59).

These quotations from Lerner's essay are specifically chosen to highlight the jumble of evidence she uses to make judgements. Adhering to facts, especially details, gets pretty high historical marks. But facts alone do not in her view necessarily make for good history. Other elements are also at work. One is believability of performance, but against what, do we measure performance, other than some prefigured notion of a historical figure? Who really knows how the actual Joan looked, sounded, or gestured? How can we be sure she did not act like a waif during the trial? For Lerner, a framing device which takes us into the realm of historiography (and which some might wish to judge a good technique, at least insofar as it broadens our view and makes as aware that history does not tell itself) is judged to be clumsy and distancing. The work that she finds closest to portraying historical truth certainly uses 'facts', but draws its historical power largely elsewhere – from what she labels as poetry and metaphor.

Such apparent contradictions do not belong only to Lerner, whose essay is interesting and suggestive. But they are common to the approach taken by historians. When they (we) consider historical films, it is easy to be critical of what we see. But ask what we expect a film to be or do, and basically we historians don't know, other than to insist that it adhere to 'the facts'. This is because most of our notions come directly out of our training and practice as academics. Our basic reaction is to think a film is really a book somehow transformed to the screen, which means that it should do what we expect a book to do: get things right. This viewpoint does not belong to academics alone, but is shared by reviewers and critics. Yet as moviegoers, or anyone who lives in our media soaked culture has to know, a historical film has always been something more than a collection of 'facts'. It is a drama, a performance, a work that stages and constructs a past in images and sounds. The power of the history on the screen emanates from the unique qualities of the medium, its abilities to communicate not just literally (as if any historical communication is entirely literal), and not just realistically (as if we can realistically define realism) but also, in Lerner's words, 'poetically and metaphorically'.

The idea that works of history speak as metaphors is not unfamiliar. Historical theorists such as Hayden White and Frank Ankersmit have long argued that the metaphorical dimension in historiography is ultimately more powerful (and more interesting?) than the literal or factual dimensions. We already know, Ankersmit explains, far too much about the past to ever absorb what has been published. In the future, our relationship to the past should focus less on the acquisition of new data on the past itself and more on the language we use for speaking about the past (Ankersmit 1994b: 162–81). Though Ankersmit does not say anything about the visual media, it seems clear that one of the languages for talking about the past can be the language of film. It is a language we should (must?) learn how to read, a language which consists (at the very least) of both the possibilities inherent in the visual media and the practices (drama is one of them) which those who utilize the media have evolved.

In approaching historical film, it seems to me the best course is to follow the suggestion that Ankersmit has made with regard to philosophers who study written history. Their task should not be, he argues, to prescribe for historians the right and wrong way to write history. Instead, what they should do is to derive theory from practice by analyzing the development of how the past has been and is written. I wish to apply these sort of standards to historical film. Rather than focus on how film gets the past wrong (as do many historians), or theorize about what film should do to or for the past (which is the burden of many ideological critiques), or how it *should* construct history, we had better first study the way in which historical film makers have actually been working for the last century. Such an approach will help us to understand what is possible on the screen, given the constraints under which motion pictures function – not just those of the medium itself, but those of the economic, political, and social milieu in which such films are made. Studying the work of film makers over time can suggest just what are the rules of engagement with the past for history rendered on the screen.

Currently the problem is that historians have it backwards. Or sideways. At the very least, seriously out of alignment. What I am talking about is the relationship between the historical film and written history. Particularly the dramatic historical film. And because we can't get it straight, nobody else can either. What I mean by backwards, sideways, or out of alignment is this: for 25 years now, or ever since historians have begun to think and write about historical film, we have essentially been trying to make the dramatic feature fit into the conventions of traditional history, to force what we see into a mould created by, and for, written discourse. Such an approach ensures that history on film will come off as a largely debased and trivial way of representing the past. Those of us who have wished to make claims for the historical film have too often found ourselves on the defensive, explaining away the mistakes and inventions of film makers to skeptical colleagues, journalists, and students. It is time to end that defensive posture and to adopt a different way of looking at historical films, to suggest that such works have already been doing history, *if by the phrase 'doing history' we mean,* rather than engaging in that traditional discourse (which films clearly cannot do), *seriously attempting to make meaning of the past.* This visual form of historical thinking should not and cannot be judged by the criteria we apply to the history that is produced on the page. Essentially it exists as a separate realm, one with its own set of rules and procedures for creating works with their own historical integrity, works which relate to, comment upon, and often challenge the world of written history.

It is time, in short, to stop expecting films to do what (we imagine) books do. Stop expecting them to get the facts right, or to present several sides of an issue, or to give a fair hearing to all the evidence on a topic, or to all the characters or groups represented in a particular situation, or to provide a broad and detailed historical context for events. Stop, also, expecting them to be a mirror of a vanished reality that will show us the past as it really was. Dramatic films are not and will never be 'accurate' in the same way as books (claim to be), no matter how many academic consultants work on a project, and no matter how seriously their advice is taken. Like written histories, films are not mirrors that show some vanished reality, but constructions, works whose rules of engagement with the traces of the past are necessarily different from those of written history. How could they be the same (and who would want them to be?), since it is precisely the task of film to add movement, colour, sound, and drama to the past?

(Let me confess, as an aside, to being tired of hearing and dubious about the kind of assertions that are sometimes made in reviews or essays by academics or well-meaning critics, or on panels at conferences and academic meetings in recent years – namely, that the culture will be able to take historical film seriously when more academics are hired to advise film makers on projects, or when historians pick up the camera and begin making their own films. Either of these may or may not be a good idea, but one thing adding historians to production teams or turning them into directors will certainly not do is to remove the problematics from the dramatic historical film. Hosts of historians will not prevent history films from being works of fiction in which invented characters, situations, dialogue, and dramatic sequences will always play a major role.)

We live in a culture in which we have all been conditioned to see history as something solid, weighty, and (apparently) eternal as the thick tomes of those national and world history textbooks in which it too often gets buried. But it isn't. History is, rather, a genre of writing or, to be more precise, a series of genres, each with its own conventions and practices which serve to define the kind of past each puts on the page. A recent notion of genre, as suggested by Keith Jenkins and Alun Munslow, shows that in their histories, scholars may construct, reconstruct, or deconstruct the past, and their choice of genre (even if unconscious) will govern the meaning of their work (Jenkins and Munslow 2004: 1–18). Older notions of genre might break down into such categories as grand narrative, small narrative, case studies, micro-history, biography, and quantitative history. The point is that genres, or ways of telling the 'truth' about the past, have often changed over the last two plus millenia and certainly will do so again. The historical film is also a genre (or series of genres) with conventions, but one which has been developing for little over a century.

All these genres have as their goal the attempt to make the past meaningful for us in the present. For the historian who works in words, the process includes selecting certain traces of the past as important, 'constituting' those traces into 'facts', thus utilizing them to help create on the page a historical picture and argument. Let me be clear about this. I am *not* saying facts don't exist. I am saying that a historical narrative or argument selects only certain traces, and those traces which are chosen become the designated 'facts' as they are used as part of the historical work. For the director of the dramatic film, who must create – and it is necessary to emphasize this point – a *past that fits within the demands, practices, and traditions of both the visual media and the dramatic form*, this means having to go beyond 'constituting' facts out of traces of evidence found in books or archives and to begin inventing some of them.

This process of invention is not, as some might think, the weakness of the historical film, but a major part of its strength. Drama, Alfred Hitchcock famously said, is life with the boring parts left out. This applies precisely to the dramatic history feature. Without the enormous amount of invention, condensation, and compression undertaken by even the most 'accurate' attempt at film, the historical would not be dramatic, but a loose, sprawling form far less able to make the past interesting, comprehensible, and meaning-ful. In one sense, of course, such films are entirely an invention, a series of sequences and images of past events that are created with actors, sets, and locations precisely in order to be captured on film. This convention for telling the past on screen is certainly artificial but, if one stops to think about it, no less so than our current, accepted convention – words on the page. We must remember that such words also are not the past but only a way of evoking, pointing at, talking about, and analyzing the past – and by so doing, turning its traces into what we call history.

The 'staging' of the past is not the only fiction involved in the history film. Less obvious sorts of inventions mark virtually every frame. These include, but are certainly not limited to, the following sorts of things, to which I have given appropriate labels: *compression* or *condensation*, the process by which several historical characters or moments are collapsed into one. *Displacements*, which move an event from one timeframe to another. *Alterations*, in which a character engages in actions or expresses sentiments that may have belonged to a different historical figure or to no one at all. *Dialogue*, which in the sound film is a crucial element that allows us to understand characters and their motivations, situations, particular events and their course, outcomes and impact. Even *characters* who are based on actual historical figures become on screen an invention, for they are created by the intonations, gestures and movements of the actor who is called upon to impersonate an historical figure whose intonations, gestures, and movements are (except for those in very contemporary historical works) wholly unknown to us. Finally, all these elements come together in *drama*, a form of telling which compresses events that happened over time (days, months, years, decades) into a narrow, intense compass of usually no more than two, and in a few extraordinary cases, up to three, four or even six hours.

Taken together, all these elements comprise the fictions that allow the screen to bring us history – and to do so in the present tense. These fictions are what involve us, through the unique, embodied quality of the film experience, in the possible and proximate realities of past events and situations. They are what help to create in us the feeling that we are not just viewing history, but actually living through events in the past, experiencing (or so we think, at least momentarily) what others felt in times of war, revolution, and social, cultural, and political change. These elements, finally, are what create the contribution of the history film, which lies precisely at the level of argument and metaphor, particularly as these engage the larger *discourse of history*. By which I mean how the particular film relates to, reflects, comments upon, and/or critiques the already existing body of data, arguments, and debates about the topic at hand – and which I will later discuss in detail.

To keep this from sounding hopelessly abstract, I turn to the film, *Glory* (1989) to help illustrate my argument – how the dramatic feature, a form largely propelled by fiction and invention, can create a serious work of history. Directed by Edward Zwick, this production tells the story of the 54th Massachusetts Volunteer Infantry, one of the early African American military units in the Civil War, from its organization during the winter of 1862–3 to its disastrous assault on Fort Wagner, South Carolina the following July, when the unit sustained 50 per cent casualties in a single afternoon. Killed in that attack was the commanding officer, a 22-year-old colonel named Robert Gould Shaw, scion of a prominent Abolitionist family. Much of the story focuses on his relationship to a group of four Black recruits, men who undergo all the normal adventures and misadventures of military training that we are used to from this genre of war films. What is different here are the added complications of race. Most of the white sergeants and officers (but not Shaw) detest Blacks; many of them seriously doubt that these recruits will ever become decent soldiers or fight successfully for the Union. Shaw, who plays the strict disciplinarian in order to create a genuine fighting unit, is unpopular with his men until late in the film. In voiceover letters to his mother, we hear him poignantly describe a cultural gap between the beliefs and behaviour of the two races that, for all his goodwill, he seems unable to close.

Glory is a good film to analyze for two reasons. First, because it has been received by academics and the press as an important and largely accurate portrayal of its topic. And second, because it stands a model of the classic Hollywood or mainstream feature, the kind of film which utilizes self-effacing shots and seamless editing as it creates a self-contained, rational, and 'realistic' world on the screen in which the viewer seems to be looking directly through a window at events in the past.

By those interested in historical accuracy, *Glory* was hailed as a grand movie, a kind of corrective to the plantation, magnolia blossom and happy, loyal slave view of the war created by *Gone With the Wind* and the lengthy tradition of romantic portraits of the ante-bellum South. James M. McPherson, a leading historian of the Civil War, begins an essay on the film like this: 'Can movies teach history? For *Glory* the answer is yes. Not only is it the first feature film to treat the role of Black soldiers in the American Civil War, but it is also one of the most powerful and historically accurate movies ever made about that war' (McPherson 1995: 128). Even the testy Kenneth M. Cameron, whose book *America on Film: Hollywood and American History* is largely devoted to trashing such films on the grounds that they are full of factual errors, manages to find *Glory* an exception as it 'sets the record straight – about historical fact, about participation of Blacks in that war, about the manliness of former slaves, about their utter lack of affection for what (Thomas Wentworth) Higginson called "massa time"' (Cameron 1997: 189).

For all its reception as an accurate work of history, *Glory*, from its first images to its last, is filled with invented characters, and events for which there is no historical evidence. Invention starts before the opening credits, which are preceded by three printed paragraphs that mention Robert Gould Shaw's collection of letters at Harvard's Houghton Library, clearly implying that these historical documents have something to do with the film. Yet this stab towards historical authenticity and verification is largely bogus. The voiceover words of Shaw which tell the story – ostensibly taken from letters to his mother – are not at all direct quotations, but a kind of composite of the sorts of things Shaw wrote and observations he made during his time commanding the regiment. Moving and insightful in their depiction of the difficulty of black and white relations and mutual understanding, these invented phrases do much to provide a historical, psychological, and moral dimension to what is shown on screen.

Shaw is not the only actual historical figure in the film. Also briefly on screen are his mother, his father, Governor John A. Andrew of Massachusetts, and the great Black leader, Frederick Douglass (depicted as he was 20 years later with the long grey beard of the classic photo, and not as he looked in 1862, with dark hair and a young face). But the majority of the characters in *Glory* are wholesale inventions. This includes not just the many anonymous soldiers, black and white, who appear on screen as background to our heroes, but relatively major figures as well – Cabot Forbes, Shaw's second in command; the tough Irish sergeant, Mulcahy, who drives and torments the recruits; Thomas Searles, the Emerson-quoting, free Black man and boyhood friend of Shaw; Trip, the proto-Black Nationalist who clashes with Shaw more than once, as well as the other soldiers whose training and coming to manhood in battle are central to the message of the film.

For the most part, the sequences in *Glory* speak in a tense common to all historical films, one that we might label 'generic' or 'proximate'. The opening of the film is a perfect example. With quasi- religious, heroic music swelling on the soundtrack, we are first presented with panoramic shots, then move closer in on a tent encampment of soldiers somewhere in a green, hilly countryside. A red sun sinks behind the trees and the light is fading. A sergeant smoking a corncob pipe hands out mail, a baseball game is in progress, soldiers lounge about wearing only parts of their blue uniforms, then we begin to hear words spoken by our still unseen hero, who describes the gathering of a great army in Maryland. Cut to a daylight sequence of Union troops marching toward us along a dirt road between trees, and the camera moves close in on Robert Gould Shaw, leading his company. As Black refugees move past them in the opposite direction, our hero intones sentiments like 'we fight to free a people whose songs have yet to be written'. All these images, which set the stage for what is to come by evoking the mood and feeling of the war before the battle of Antietam, represent no more than the cobbling together of familiar (to Americans) elements from the Civil War. They certainly do not comprise a literal construction of the past, but are a kind of generic construction. The film suggests that this is more or less the way a camp looked, those are the sorts of activities that went on between battles, these are the sorts of sentiments some northerners had. Here we have a kind of proximate reality, the invention of past moments in a way typical of the dramatic film.

The parallel to this form of representation or address in written history is the general description, something like the following: 'In camps all over Maryland in the spring of 1862, union soldiers lounged about and waited, reading letters from home, playing pickup baseball games, trying not to think about the battles yet to come . . .' The difference with film is that the image cannot generalize. It must show specifics: a particular camp, a baseball game played in a specific way, a particular sergeant handing out mail. That specificity is, however, a kind of generalization, one that probably can easily be accepted by most critics of other aspects of history film. But make no mistake: to accept this kind of generalization is to become involved in a particular 'reading' of screen images that is not literal, but one that accepts the specific detail as a symbol of a larger meaning. The point: viewers who may not even realize what are they doing are in fact already involved in accepting and understanding this particular aspect of the language of the history film.

A sequence like the opening one, where specifics speak for more general realities, may have parallels in written history. But *Glory* is filled with other kinds of inventions unknown in more traditional forms. Take, for example, the sequence in which Robert Gould Shaw is offered command of the 54th Regiment. The setting is a distinctly upper-class social gathering in Boston, shortly after he has been wounded at the major battle of Antietam. Men in frock coats, women in gowns, and soldiers in uniform eat hors d'oeuvres, drink punch, and gossip. Still jumpy from the experience of combat (he spills the punch when a servant loudly slams shut a window), Shaw is brought by his mother to meet governor Andrew of Massachusetts, who explains his plans for organizing the first 'coloured' Massachusetts regiment, then tells Robert that he has submitted his name to be commander of the regiment. 'A wonderful idea', says Shaw in a flat tone that undercuts the sentiment. His lack of enthusiasm is underscored when he immediately asks to be excused and withdraws, while those around the governor, including Frederick Douglass, looked startled, even disapproving, that he has not seized the chance to take this command. Shaw then goes outside for some fresh air and is joined by his good friend, Lieutenant Cabot Forbes who, throughout the film, serves as a kind of alter ego, often playing the nice guy to the commander's martinet, raising aloud issues that

Shaw would keep buried. While Shaw silently mulls the issue, his worries about becoming the first commander of Black troops are voiced by Forbes: 'Robert, I know how much you want to make Colonel, but can you imagine the reaction to handing guns to a thousand coloureds? Can you imagine how popular that would be?' Only after these doubts are voiced does Shaw suddenly say he will take the job, and he asks Forbes to be his second in command.

The sequence is moving and dramatic – and wholly invented. Shaw was not offered the command the 54th at a party in Boston. He received the offer in a letter from the governor when he was camped in Maryland with his unit shortly after Antietam. Initially he refused the command by return mail, and when the offer came in a second letter, he refused it again. Obviously dismayed by his son's action, Shaw's father, a well known Abolitionist, travelled to Maryland and spent some time alone with Robert. There is no record of the conversations of father and son, but immediately after his father's visit, the younger man agreed to take charge of organizing and training the 54th.

One can account for this alteration in the historical record in various ways, but all are the result of the demands of the dramatic form. Letters going back and forth; Shaw pacing in his tent alone, trying to decide, or at a desk, writing; his father arriving and debating with his son – all this might have been done, but it would lack both the brevity and the drama of the sequence described above, and also bring on stage the father, who plays no other role in the work. Equally important is the fact that scenes in historical films must often do double, triple, quadruple duty. This party in Boston is the only glimpse we have of Shaw's upper-class background, something which helps to underline the great nature of his sacrifice (he is a volunteer) and to in part explain his social and psychological distance from his Black troops – its class even more than race since in this sequence he gets along perfectly well with Thomas Searles, his educated, Black boyhood friend who works for his father with freed slaves. The sequence also becomes a way of introducing other characters, such as Forbes and Searles, whose transformation to soldier will be most painful, profound, and emblematic.

What is lost in this sequence in verifiability is clearly gained in a kind of dramatic truth, one which manages to condense the doubts, the fears, and the decision into a brief encounter with Forbes. It also opens up space for the kind of ambiguities which drama is rather better at presenting than written history. The screen only has to show but not necessarily tell. A traditional historian would most likely feel it necessary to explain why Shaw refused the command twice. Film can simply depict his hesitation, let us hear Forbes' words, and make us interpret the doubts and the decision. Ultimately we are outside of Shaw as we are outside of other people, unable to really know why he hesitates or even why he finally accepts the command. Perhaps he is simply fearful after his wounds at Antietam; perhaps he fears his own abilities to lead a regiment; or perhaps his doubts are precisely the same as those of Forbes – worry, even in a good Abolitionist, over the unprecedented action of arming Blacks. The voicing of those, after all, immediately precede his decision – it is as if his moral courage conquers his irrational fears.

At the heart of *Glory* is the story of how four Black soldiers, three of them ex-slaves, go through training, enter combat, and eventually achieve a kind of manhood in battle. Regimental histories of the 54th have been written, and we know quite a bit about some of the men who filled its ranks. Yet all four characters in the film are invented. One might ask why does the film avoid building on such historical figures? Why does it not show the two sons of Frederick Douglass who were in the ranks, or tell us that the adjutant was Garth Wilkinson James, brother of William and Henry James? And why does it give the impression that most of the volunteers were ex-slaves, when in fact most were free men?

The answers are at once dramatic and historical – or what one might see as the need to speak in the specific language of the history film. The four main African-American soldiers represent four distinct types of people, and four attitudes towards the issues of the Civil War, including Black–White relations. Three are ex-slaves: John Rawlins (Morgan Freeman) a father figure, the wise elder and hard worker who rises to become the first Black sergeant; Trip (Denzel Washington), a brash, cynical, strong, angry, proto-Black Nationalist; and Country Boy, a naïve, uneducated, but hopeful lad who believes everything he is told. The fourth is a free man and the son of a free man: Thomas Searles, a well-educated, physically underdeveloped intellectual. The dramatic reason for the group is obvious, and familiar from a long tradition of American war films, which always include diverse individuals in one unit in order to create a broad range of possibilities for tension and conflict. Added to this is an historical reason. The four characters become emblems of different sides of the Black experience, standing in for the various positions Blacks could take towards the Civil War and ongoing issues of Black–White relations, then and now. Their presence also works to generalize beyond the 54th to all African-American units in the war (and by extension, to later periods of history). And while its true that most of the soldiers in the 54th were not, as the film implies, ex-slaves, but in fact free men before the war, it is equally true that most of the Blacks who volunteered for the Union Army were ex-slaves. So although it is focused on a particular unit, *Glory* speaks for the larger Black experience of the Civil War (as McPherson recognizes in his essay).

A number of incidents in *Glory* are invented to dramatize a particular historical point. Take the encounter between Shaw and a Quartermaster who so much disdains Black fighting abilities that he has 'neglected' to provide boots for the 54th. Earlier we have seen and heard racist comments from common white soldiers, who compare the 'nigger' recruits to dumb animals, but this sequence explores racist attitudes at higher levels of the military, where it was often believed that Blacks would never make proper soldiers. Only when Shaw enters the storeroom, confronts the quartermaster's lies that he has no boots, and violently begins to tear down shelves, does he win footwear for his men. The sequence not only underscores the racism in the Union Army, it does double duty by showing one of those steps by which disciplinarian Shaw gains some acceptance from his troops.

Such invented incidents and characters (and these are only a sample) help to make *Glory* a powerful work of history. They are also inextricably tied up with the argument of the film and its metaphoric thrust – that undergoing the brotherhood of arms and the risks of death on the battlefield helped African-Americans to recognize themselves and, to some extent, be recognized, at least by some elements of the white community, as full-fledged men, partners, and citizens of the United States. The moral clearly urged is that if African Americans have not yet achieved that actual equality (as we know they have not), it is certainly due to them not only as fellow human beings also for the sacrifices they have made for the country. This theme is underscored in the final image of the film as black and white soldiers are shovelled together into a mass grave (as they were historically) and the two chief antagonists – Shaw and Trip, the Black Nationalist – roll in death into each other's arms. Insofar as it is meant to suggest Black–White reconciliation, this visual metaphor is debatable. But it is one that, like the larger argument, clearly draws and comments upon the ongoing discourse about both the Civil War and race relations in America.

It is this discourse which helps us to distinguish a 'historical' from a 'costume drama'. It is this discourse which allows us to judge the usefulness of the inventions in a film. The costume drama (*Gone With the Wind* might be a good parallel with *Glory* in this regard) ignores that discourse and uses the exotic locale of the past as no more than a setting for romance and adventure. A history film, by contrast, engages that discourse by posing and attempting to answer the kinds of questions that for a long time have surrounded a given topic. During the Civil War, the issue for many white Americans was 'Will the Negro fight?' For African Americans it must have been much the same: Can we fight successfully and gain our rights? Today the historical question asked by the film may be seen as: 'What was the effect of Black military participation in the Civil War on both African Americans and Whites?' Any answer has to be contained within and must be read out of the dramatic form. Any answer must include notions of the embodied, visceral experience of the historical world which a viewing of *Glory* produces in the spectator.

The discourse of history also helps us to judge the value of the inventions. To promote historical truths, they must be apposite; that is, within the possibilities and probabilities of the given period. An invention that showed the 54th winning the battle of Fort Wagner at the end rather than being decimated would violate what we already know from the discourse (which includes data as well as arguments). But the invention in the film that shows the unit advancing on the fort from the north rather than the south – done, apparently, because of lighting problems, and setting the cameras there allowed the director to better render the difficulty of the 54th's assault – is harmless with regard to the larger meaning of the work. There is, let me emphasize, no formula for rendering such judgements. All such judgements, they must be decided on a case-by-case basis. This is equally true for the wholesale inventions in the kind of film which, instead of depicting actual historical figures, places fictional figures into actual past events or situations.

In later chapters, I will have occasion to analyze a number of other films in some detail, but for the most part, the situating of the history film within the larger discourse has yet to be undertaken. Looked at in such a way, works like *Lily Marlene* (1980), *The Return of Martin Guerre* (1982), *Gandhi* (1982), *The Night of the Shooting Stars* (1983), *Born on the Fourth of July* (1989), *Schindler's List* (1993), *Underground* (1998), *Frida* (2002), and *Kinsey* (2004), to name but a few, can be seen as comments upon, interventions into, and critiques of that discourse. *Glory* is a particularly good example because its defining characteristics – its inventions, fictions, condensations, alterations – are so widely utilized throughout the world of cinema. It is true that in some European and Third World countries, where the past weighs on the present with a heavier burden than it does in America, history films often incorporate a more tragic vision of history than one normally gets from Hollywood. A work like Gillo Pontecorvo's *Burn!* (see Chapter 1), which also deals with slavery and race relations, does not end with the kind of long-term optimistic resolution implied by having black and white in each other's arms. But the world on the screen in that film, as well as most historicals made around the globe, is constructed according to the same practices as is *Glory*.

These practices are part of a tradition, one we can label Hollywood, a tradition which is highlighted by the works of innovative directors who oppose it, and who are the subject of the next chapter. But to understand that tradition, and what such innovators are reacting against, it may be helpful to see it in terms of the following six elements:

- The mainstream feature (much like written history) tells the past as a story with a beginning, a middle, and an end. A tale that leaves you with a moral message and (usually) a feeling of uplift. A tale embedded in a larger view of history that is almost always progressive. Even if the subject matter is as bleak as the horrors of the Holocaust, the message is that things have gotten or are getting better. *Glory* may end with the death of the main characters and the decimation of the regiment, but the audience knows they died in a just cause that would (or should) eventually triumph.
- Film insists on history as the story of individuals, men or women who are already renowned or who are made to seem important because they are singled out by the camera. Those who are not already famous are common people who have done heroic or admirable things, or who have suffered from exploitation and oppression. In *Glory*, four men stand in for the experience of the 178,000 Black soldiers (and 10,000 sailors) who fought in the Union army, while a handful of officers and sergeants provide the variety of White responses to them.
- Film offers us history as the story of a unitary, closed, and completed past. Sometimes a subtle film may hint at historical alternatives, but more typical is what we see in *Glory*, which provides no alternative possibilities to what is happening on the screen, admits of no doubts, and promotes each historical assertion with confidence.
- Film personalizes, dramatizes, and emotionalizes the past. It gives us history as triumph, anguish, joy, despair, adventure, suffering, and heroism. All the special capabilities of the medium – colour and movement, music and sound effects, the close-up of the human face, the juxtaposition of images – are utilized to create the feeling that we are not watching events, but experiencing them. *Glory* allows us to feel in our gut, particularly in its battle scenes, as if we have lived moments of the Civil War.
- Film most obviously gives us the 'look' of the past, of buildings, landscapes, costumes, and artifacts. It provides a sense of how common objects appeared when they were part of people's lives and in daily use. Period clothing confines, emphasizes, and expresses the body at rest and in motion. Tools, utensils, weapons, furniture are not items on display, but objects that people use and misuse, objects that can help to define livelihoods, professions, identities, and destinies. The painful and slow process of reloading rifles in *Glory* or the close up bayonet charges become visceral lessons from the past.

- Film shows history as process. The world on the screen brings together things that, for analytic purposes, written history often splits apart. Economics, politics, race, class, and gender come together in the lives of individuals and groups. This makes history like life, itself, a process of changing relationships where political and social questions are interwoven. Robert Gould Shaw is at once a White man, a son, a resident of Massachusetts, an idealist, an abolitionist, a Harvard graduate, a colonel, a leader of a Black regiment, a Northerner, and an American.

The same elements that help to shape *Glory*, or any other film based on documentable persons and events, are at work in that other sort of dramatic feature which places wholly fictional characters in an historical setting. And both kinds of films have, by my definition, for some time been 'doing history'. Some, such as *Glory*, are recognized as contributions to historical understanding by authorities in the field, though the basis of such judgements has tended to be (such as James McPherson's, quoted above) *ad hoc* rather than systematic. Since hundreds, if not thousands of historians are now teaching courses on the historical film on topics that range from the ancient world to slavery, from the Middle Ages to Oliver Stone's America, it seems time for more of us to begin looking at such works not in terms of individual 'facts' but in terms of the *film historical language* in which the past is portrayed and against the larger discourse from which all history draws its meaning.

Some elements of that special language of film have been outlined above. The history film speaks in a language that is metaphorical and symbolic, a language that creates a series of proximate or possible realities rather than a reality that is literally true – though it also does intersect with the literal. It is a language in which film raises the kinds of questions about the past that historians raise, but one that we need to learn how to 'read', much as we learn how to read a book – not just for what appears on the surface, but for what that surface calls forth and suggests, and for how it engages what we know (or wish to know). A movie may seem simple to understand, but the best works do not simply and clearly express their meaning, as one last example from *Glory* will suggest. In a ten-second sequence, we see Shaw practising cavalry strokes by riding his horse past a series of posts and slicing into watermelons that sit on top of them. This is an accurate reflection of training practice for cavalry officers in that era, but with one significant and discordant note: the watermelons. This is Massachusetts in February, a time of the year when no watermelons can be found. Is this a mistake? No, clearly it's a visual metaphor. A fleeting moment that carries a huge load of historical meaning by pointing to a long history of racial stereotypes – in particular, that old notion that caricatures Black

Americans as folk who laze about with their faces buried in slices of water-melon. Such a metaphor, with its burden of meaning, could be missed by those not ready to read visual images. Such a metaphor is also unique to film, one of the ways the medium conveys and comments upon the past.

Here I would also like to use it as a metaphor for my argument in this chapter and this book – in which I am attempting to slice the head off our stereo-types of what constitutes historical thought. As I have tried to show here, film can provide a complicated and important vision of the past, one that renders history in a way that demands our careful attention, especially because so much of what we learn about the past is conveyed to us today in precisely this medium and this genre, on the screens large and small. What I am aiming at here is a much subtler and broader way of looking at the dramatic history film, seeing such works not just in terms of whether all their individual moments can be verified, but rather in terms of whether their overall portrait or vision has something meaningful and important to say about our past.

Chapter 4

Innovative drama

Hollywood films have dominated the world market since the 1920s, but the United States has had no monopoly on the historical. Indeed, it is not difficult for the historically-inclined to make the case that European and, to some extent, Latin American and Asian countries have over the years produced far more serious, interesting and profound explorations of the past on screen than have issued from America. The great majority of these works have, nonetheless, utilized the same six practices of mainstream historical film mentioned in the last chapter, focusing their linear and self-contained stories on individuals or small groups who exemplify or stand in for larger historical events and processes. Perhaps the two major differences with these foreign (to Americans) films has been a greater willingness to create works which place entirely fictional characters in specific historical settings, and a tendency to be more open to sad or tragic, though equally uplifting and moral, endings.

Yet another kind of film rarely, if ever made in America, has also been attempted abroad – something I labelled in the first chapter the *experimental* or *innovative history film*. Made in conscious opposition to Hollywood codes, conventions, and practices, such works are created to contest the seamless stories of heroes and victims that make up the mainstream feature (and, one might add, the standard documentary). The directors of these innovative works are often leftists or revolutionary sympathizers, people who find not just the stories but the form of the mainstream film to be suffused with individualist, capitalist values which as people working for change, they wish to combat. But the value of such films, at least to the historian, transcends their radical message. One can also see innovative historicals as part of a search for a new vocabulary in which to render the past on the screen, an effort to make history (depending upon the film) more complex, interrogative, and self-conscious.

The best of these films – works like *Ceddo* (1977), directed by Ousmane Sembene; *Zoot Suit* (1982), Luis Valdes; *Quilombo* (1984), Carlos Diegues; *Walker* (1987), Alex Cox; *Thirty-Two Short Films About Glenn Gould* (1993), Francois Girard; *Underground* (1995), Emir Kusturica – propose unusual strategies for dealing with the traces of the past, strategies that point towards new forms of historical thought, forms that need not be limited to the screen, but might, with necessary alterations due to the medium, be carried back to the printed page.

The first, and arguably the greatest director of innovative historicals was Sergei Eisenstein. His early films, clearly aimed at providing founding myths for the fledgling Soviet State, wholly ignore the contribution of individuals and instead bring the masses into history and history into the masses. This is true of his best-known work, *Battleship Potemkin*, as well as his homage to the Bolshevik Revolution, *October*. Both are often labelled works of propaganda, but the latter, at least, is something far more than that – it is also a work of history that can stand beside written interpretations of the same topic. What follows in this chapter is not only an examination of how a particular innovative film creates the world of the past and makes a historical argument, it is also meant as an extended demonstration of something alluded to in the last chapter – how a historical both relates and adds to the discourse of history out of which it comes and to which it of necessity refers.

For the historian of the modern world, 'October' can have only one meaning: that month in 1917 when the Bolsheviks ousted the Provisional Government of Russia, seized control of Petrograd, and commenced, in Lenin's words, to construct the socialist order. For the student of cinema, *October* is more likely to mean Sergei Eisenstein's film about the events of that revolution. How these two meanings of the word connect has been at issue from the moment the film was released to the Russian public early in 1928. In the more than seven decades since then, *October* has become and remains one of the best known and most enduring accounts of October 1917. So well known that it seems no exaggeration to suggest that more people have probably learned about the Bolshevik Revolution from the film than from any other single source.

But what have they learned? That is the question. *October* has often been called a work of propaganda. Just as often, fiction. Characteristic, even typical of the attitude of historians is that of Orlando Figes in his recent history of the Russian Revolution, who labels it 'Eisenstein's brilliant but largely fictional propaganda film' (Figes 1996: 484, 737). Pierre Sorlin, in a detailed chapter devoted to the film, agrees – sort of. At the outset, he calls the work 'propaganda', but then in his conclusion contradicts himself (Sorlin 1980:

159–98). Part of such a judgement stems from the fact that Figes and Sorlin, like most historians who mention the film, tend to focus attention on a single sequence, the climactic, and highly fictionalized 'storming' of the Winter Palace. (Of which more, later.) But another part of such a judgement is surely due to our intellectual tradition. Or our prejudice. We understand history to be words on a page not images on a screen. History is something we move through at our own pace, a text we can analyze at leisure, not an assault of moving images and sounds that rush by us at 24 frames a second. Yet a century and more after the invention of the motion picture, it seems time to admit that a good deal of what we learn about the past is delivered to the public in this visual medium.

The story *October* tells, and the way it tells that story, are surely part of a long tradition of explaining why and how the Bolsheviks took power. One might even argue that *October* has a significant role in creating that tradition. Images from the film – crowds scattering from the gunfire of soldiers on the Nevsky Prospekt during the 'July days' or the 'storming' of the Winter Palace – have been used in newspapers, magazines, and books to illustrate the revolution. In some more general way, the film seems to hover over all later interpretations of what John Reed labelled the *Ten Days That Shook the World*. Many historians of the Russian Revolution, even today, feel the need to mention Eisenstein's film, if only to dismiss it – usually as great art but poor history.

How does *October* relate to October? What sort of history does it propose? What interpretation of the Bolshevik Revolution does it convey? To answer these questions – and to suggest how other films might possibly be seen as vehicles for history – it is necessary to go beyond the micro-level of the individual image. Beyond the referential level of the individual fact. To answer them we must consider the film not merely as a collection of true or false individual assertions but, like all works of history, as an argument about and interpretation of the historical moments and events it describes. That means we must situate it within the larger discourse of history, that ongoing and huge body of data and debates about the causes, course, and consequences of the Russian Revolution. To evaluate *October* as history, it is necessary to see how its interpretation fits with the close to 90-year tradition of representing the Bolshevik Revolution.

We must, at the same time, do something else: see it as a film, as moving images on a screen, not as a book, as words on a page. That means to understand (and accept) that whatever it has to tell us about the past, whatever sort of history it undertakes, *October* will do so as a film. A work of moving images and sounds subject to the demands and conventions of a particular medium and a particular genre. *October* can only make arguments about the past the way a film can make arguments: through visual, dramatic, symbolic, metaphoric, and fictional forms. Like any work of history, *October* will use traces of evidence from a vanished world as a basis for staging, or creating, a representation of that world in the present. As a film, it will deliver to us a world in a narrative, a story of people, events, moments, or movements of the past in an effort to make them meaningful to us in the present. Utilizing moving (in two senses of the word) images, *October* will explain what and how and why something important happened in Petrograd in October 1917.

The well-known origins of the film can be used to lend support to those who wish to see it as propaganda. *October* was commissioned by Sovkino, a Soviet state agency for the production and distribution of films. Commissioned as part of a tenth anniversary celebration meant to commemorate the events that had brought the Bolsheviks to power. At the time, the 28-year-old Eisenstein was the most famous film maker in the Soviet Union – and among the most famous in the world. Less than two years earlier, his great revolutionary (in technique and content) film, *Battleship Potemkin*, had taken the world of cinema by storm, winning accolades for its director not only across Europe, but even in far-off Hollywood. The style Eisenstein employed in that film, a kind of heroic collectivism rather than individualist drama, and his brilliant editing techniques, were widely admired – among artists and film makers, if not the general public. His first plan after obtaining the commission was to create a huge, heroic film about the entire revolution, from the overthrow of the Czar in February to the end of the Civil War in 1921. Pressures of time (both on the screen and in the production process) led to a version that covered a smaller slice of the past: from February through October 1917. Even with this reduced version, Eisenstein did not finish editing the film in time, and only a few of its few reels were shown at the anniversary celebrations at the Bolshoi Theatre in November 1927.

Criticism of the *October*'s relationship to October began as soon as the full version of the film was screened to the public in Leningrad in January 1928. These critiques could be broad or narrow. At stake in many of them was the question: how does the film handle – or mishandle – fact? There were complaints over the omission of important facts: 'the growth of the workers' movement, the collapse at the front' (Piotovsky 1988: 216) And complaints over alterations in fact: 'The October Revolution is such a major historical fact that any playing with the fact is unthinkable' (Brik 1988: 227). For some critics, the very idea of staging or dramatizing the past was a violation:

> You must not stage a historical fact because the staging distorts this fact . . .
> You must not make millions of peasants and workers . . . think that the
> events of those great days happened exactly as they happen in . . . *October*.

> In such matters you need historical truth, fact, document and the greatest
> austerity of execution: you need newsreel (Shub 1988: 217).

For others the issue was less fact than philosophy, background, overall view or
meaning of the past:

> . . . we think that the task of a feature film consists not in the slavish imitation
> of historical facts, but in something quite different. The film must furnish
> the general background against which the events reproduced in it unfold.
> And it is against this background that some fundamental idea that infuses
> the entire script must lift, seize and lead the audience behind it. This is pre-
> cisely what is missing from *October* (Rokotov 1988: 219).

Today the same sort of complaints can still be heard:

> The film's version of events is selective and exaggerated in many ways.
> Eisenstein never details the behind-the-scenes wrangles within Bolshevik
> ranks, nor does he articulate the positions of the Mensheviks and the Social
> Revolutionaries. In accordance with Bolshevik historiography, he also pre-
> sents the 25 October coup as far more carefully planned than it was
> (Bordwell 1993: 80).

> The Winter Palace was not taken by assault: the image of a column of storm-
> ing workers, soldiers, and sailors as depicted in Eisenstein's film, *Days of
> October*, is pure invention, an attempt to give Russia its own Fall of the
> Bastille (Pipes 1991: 493).

All these criticisms seem to issue from people sceptical about more than
October. The subtext of each suggests that film is not a proper medium for
telling us about the past. One might wonder: how would Eisenstein respond?
One thing he would certainly say is: I am a filmmaker. A person who can never
forget the demands of the medium in which I work. Any film maker has to
know that no matter how much you are committed to putting the past on the
screen, and no matter how accurate you wish that past to be, the one thing you
can never do is to mirror a moment – all those moments that have vanished.
You can only create such moments with the tools and the art of your trade.
Every time you position the camera, or change the angle of a shot, or alter a
shutter opening, or use a different lense, or set up just one more light to create
a particular shadow, or ask an actor to make a certain gesture, you are inevitably creating facts and meaning about the past. Any film maker knows that
facts can never speak for themselves. We have to speak for them.

Historians, too, are people who speak for the facts (though there may still be some of us around who wish to claim that the facts speak for themselves). But when we look at the screen, we tend to want such visual history to be like a book in which the facts speak for themselves. Perhaps this is because film is deceptive. Even more than written historical narrative, film seems to speak facts directly. Unmediated. What you see on the screen is the world of the past. But it takes little reflection to tell us this is clearly not true. With film and history, it is necessary to embrace the counter intuitive. To understand that however realistic it may look, dramatic film can never be a reflection but must, like a written work, be a construction of a past. A narrative prefigured by the consciousness of the historian/film maker. A struggle over the meaning of the present and the future set in the past. An argument in the form of a story; a story in the form of an argument. An argument that is also a kind of vision of the world. One that can retain a certain strength and validity long after the data on which it is based may be superseded.

With such ideas in mind, I wish to consider *October*, place it, explicate it, judge it against the field of knowledge, data, debates surrounding its subject: October. Since this is a field filled with more voices than we could ever attend to, speaking in more languages than we could ever fully understand, I will pursue the more practical strategy of comparing the film with accounts by five well-known historians writing of those events in English. Accounts written between 1919 and 1996: John Reed, *Ten Days That Shook the World* (1934); William Henry Chamberlin, *The Russian Revolution* (1935); Alex Rabinowitch, *Prelude to Revolution* (1968) and *The Bolsheviks Come to Power* (1976); Richard Pipes, *The Russian Revolution* (1991) and *A Concise History of the Russian Revolution* (1995); and Orlando Figes, *A People's Tragedy* (1996).

The tradition begins with John Reed. American bohemian, poet, journalist, radical, and anti-war activist. He was there. He walked the streets. He listened to the speeches. He studied Russian. He collected pamphlets, books, fliers, newspapers, handwritten notes. He joined the Soviet Foreign Office and wrote propaganda directed at German soldiers saying: 'Lay down your arms, brothers'. He went home and the American government confiscated his papers. When he got them back a year later it took him six weeks to write *Ten Days That Shook the World*.

It was not the Bolsheviks but John Reed who invented the revolution as a ten-day drama; invented the notion of what a twentieth-century revolution should be in a book the author calls 'a slice of intensified history – history as I saw it . . . in the struggle my sympathies were not neutral' (Reed 1934: xxxiii). Reed may be partisan, but he sees himself as a conscientious witness/ historian, interested in setting down the truth. A truth that is dramatic:

No matter what one thinks of Bolshevism, it is undeniable that the Russian Revolution is one of the great events of human history, and the rise of the Bolsheviki phenomenon of world-wide importance ... historians ... will want to know what happened in Petrograd in November 1917, the spirit which animated the people, and how the leaders looked, talked, and acted. It is with this in view that I have written this book (Reed 1934: xxxviii).

William Henry Chamberlin gets to Moscow too late for the major events, but the afterglow still suffuses the Soviet capital and loosens the tongues of people who helped shake the world. Arriving there in 1922 as correspondent for the *Christian Science Monitor*, he is a young man who specializes in asking questions that can make people talk for days. For the next 12 years Chamberlin will continue the interviews while he also works in archives to produce, in the midst of the crisis of capitalism that we know as the Great Depression, the first great narrative history of the Revolution. One that as late as the 1960s can still be regarded by professional historians as the only broadly focused Western investigation of the October revolution based on intensive research in primary sources (Rabinowitch 1976: xvii). Like Reed, Chamberlin, sees the Revolution as:

... moving and dramatic, heroic, or tragic, or both, according to one's point of view: the panorama represented by the establishment of a new social order, based on extreme revolutionary theory, in a huge country with a vast population. . . . (Chamberlin 1935: viii).

Forty years later, historian Alexander Rabinowitch can stand as representative of a new generation of scholars. A representative, too, of what we call the New Social history. Academics who are better trained than their predecessors, distanced, sober and in the process of freeing themselves from the mentality of the Cold War that chilled American academia well into the 1960s. Some call Rabinowitch's cohort 'Revisionists'. Like the New Left of the decade in which they began to publish, they are less interested in old quarrels about the evils of Communism than in detailed studies of what happened at the local level during the revolution.

For Rabinowitch, too, the Revolution is a time of drama and monumental significance, but he tends to keep his adjectives under wraps. His focus is restrained, even narrow as he explains why the Bolsheviks triumphed in October. Back he goes to local sources, to a close study of workers in factories, companies of soldiers and sailors, sections of the party, men in the street. His aim is to give voice to the voiceless, to see the 'revolution from below'. In his pages, the Bolsheviks appear less as the united, conspiratorial, authoritarian party of both right- and left-wing mythology than as a shifting group ridden with dissension, conflicts, and splits. But as great propagandists with a great message and a savvy leader. By October 'the goals of the Bolsheviks, as the masses understood them, had strong popular support' (Rabinowitch 1976: xvii). Their seizure of power was neither 'inevitable' (the official Soviet view) nor a *coup d'état* (the conservative view): it was an enactment of the popular will that they had helped to mould.

Richard Pipes could not disagree more. A kind of 'Re-Revisionist', or simply someone who continues an earlier anti-Soviet, Cold War mentality, Pipes likes to refer to the 'so-called "October Revolution"' as nothing more than a 'classic *coup d'état*', a movement that has nothing in common with 'classic revolutions' (Pipes 1993: 498). Seeing the Revolution less as drama than disaster, Pipes roundly condemns the Bolsheviks both for gaining and keeping power illegitimately. To him the long-range causes of October are the most important. Pipes admits the blunders of the Tsarist régime, the impotence of the Provisional Government, the adroit planning of the Bolsheviks. But in his work the real causes lie farther back, in the eighteenth and nineteenth centuries, in the airy headed theorists of the Enlightenment and in the growth of a class of radical intellectuals and professional revolutionaries who harboured in their breasts the mad desire to reshape the world. Two centuries of propaganda by discontented, fanatical intellectuals translated legitimate complaints into an 'all-consuming destructive force', rebellion into revolution. It is arguably 'the most important event of the century', but October was also 'a tragedy in which events follow with inexorable force from the mentality and character of the protagonists' (Pipes 1991: xvi).

The same ancient dramatic form governs the argument of Orlando Figes' recent, magisterial history of the Russian Revolution. But his attitude towards this inexorable movement towards destruction is considerably different from that of Pipes, who can't quite decide if the Bolsheviks or the Russian people are to blame for what happened. Figes has written a 'social history' that focuses 'on the common people'. He depicts the peasantry, the working class, the soldiers and the national minorities not as victims but as participants 'in their own revolutionary drama'. The basis of his portrait are numerous recent monographs that provide what he calls a much more complex and convincing picture of the relationship between the party and the people than the one presented in 'top down' Cold War histories (such as that of Pipes?). Figes finds no abstract, single revolution imposed by the Bolsheviks on all of Russia, but a huge conglomeration of events 'often shaped by local passions and interests'. The tragedy for him is that 'what began as a people's revolution contained the seeds of its own degeneration into violence and dictatorship. The same social forces which brought about the triumph of the Bolshevik régime became its main victims' (Figes 1996: xvi).

Like John Reed, Sergei Eisenstein was also in Petrograd in October 1917. But unlike the American journalist, he had little interest in, or knowledge of, what was going on. Eisenstein was 17 years old, still living at home with his father, a reluctant student in the college of civil engineering, a closet visual artist and theatre director. On the February day when the Czar resigned, he did not even notice the end of a dynasty, and only learned about it in the evening after he walked across town to attend Meyerhold's staging of Lermontov's *Masquerade* and found the Alexandrinsky Theatre closed temporarily due to the political upheaval. Five months later the demonstrations we call the July Days caught him in the midst of an errand on the Nevsky Prospekt; he was forced to cower in a doorway at the corner of Sadovaya and watch the troops of the Provisional Government fire on unarmed demonstrators (a view he would later incorporate as a stunning sequence in *October*). On the day the Bolsheviks took power, it vaguely registered upon Eisenstein that guns were going off somewhere in the city as he made the rounds, attempting to sell some anti-Kerensky cartoons to the editors of a journal.

Not an activist, Eisenstein did for a few days join some of his fellow students who were playing at defending the new régime. But for him, a good thick book by Freud, Wilde, Maeterlinck, or Schopenhauer, was always a far better companion than a rifle. Yet he quickly came to understand the difference between a book and a film. By the time he made *October*, he knew that the film maker never has the luxury of doing what historians do. Sitting down to research, to think, and then to take years to write on a topic. And when you finish, penning a preface in which you directly announce the theme that will govern what you say, the theme that has helped to constitute all the data in the work and that suffuses the overall interpretation that you have made.

Eisenstein knew that the film maker must create history in his own way. For weeks, perhaps months, he did as much research as a pressured film maker can do. Research in memoirs, newspaper accounts, newsreels, works of history, and into the early pageants commemorating the revolution, particularly the huge 1920 event on Palace Square entitled 'The Storming of the Winter Palace'. One of his chief sources was probably – nobody knows for certain – John Reed's account, which since 1920 had borne a brief, introductory endorsement by Lenin. Eisenstein's governing theme is never directly articulated, but he puts it into every image, every movement, every camera angle, every cut. Everything in *October* points toward, and becomes part of, an argument that might be summed up this way: October was a result of the criminality and stupidity of the Provisional Government, a great dramatic movement in which masses of common people spontaneously participated. Yes, the final seizure of power was planned by a small group of Bolshevik leaders meeting in a tiny room. And yes, it is clear that Lenin is the mind behind the Revolution. But the film, in its overall argument, counters any party line notion that the Bolsheviks were the revolutionary vanguard. For Eisenstein (like Rabinowitch) shows October as the time when the masses entered into history and history entered into the masses.

I deal with overall interpretations before details because that is the way history books are structured. Prefaces may be written last, but there is simple honesty in the way they go up-front. Here is the one place the author's voice need not be veiled. No need for authorities, archives, footnotes. Here moral is all. So if you don't bother to read the book, you will still have a sense of what, when all the human struggles are described and done, the author wants it to mean. What it was that let him (for in this case they are all male) do the work to put the book together. The faith that kept the project moving over the years and that let him decide between recounting this fact and that one. For there are always too many facts from which to choose.

Some theorists sneer and call the details of history 'information'. Some people call them 'life'. You can probably get the point of the work from the preface alone, but the drama of the change we call history is in the details. Histories of the Russian Revolution tend to be long and packed with details. Reed uses almost 400 pages to cover 10 days (though his work does spill over this time boundary). Chamberlin needs more than a thousand pages for four years. Rabinowitch gives us 600 pages on the Bolshevik Party in a single year. Pipes' more than 1300 densely packed pages to take the régime into the mid-twenties; for his concise, popular edition he has boiled it down to 400 pages. Figes uses 800 plus pages to go from 1891 to 1924, with more than 500 devoted to the period beginning with the February Revolution.

Eisenstein has the normal screen time of about two hours to tell us what it was that shook the world. But measuring time against space, the screen against the page, is not an easy task. Today in a film script, the rule-of-thumb is one page of screenplay for one minute of screen time, but this is not true in the silent period when the image was far more important than the word. Eisenstein's (poetic, evocative) screenplay occupies 35 pages in the English edition (Leyda 1976). What this translates into are images and sequences that show the following: the February Revolution; the Provisional Government; fraternization with German soldiers on the front; the resumption of hostilities in the summer of 1917; deteriorating conditions in Petrograd – bread lines, falling rations and discontent; Lenin at the Finland Station enunciating the

April Theses calling for a proletarian revelution; the July days: the attack on demonstrators, the arrest of the Bolsheviks; Kerensky in the Winter Palace; the Kornilov threat to the capital and its collapse; the arming of the Red Guards; the Bolshevik decision to take power; the movement of the Military Revolutionary Committee; the Second Congress of Soviets; debates in Smolny; and the taking of the Winter Palace.

Not all of these get equal treatment. Like any historian, Eisenstein consciously plays with time. Stretches it, collapses it, gives it to us in fragments. His camera lingers over some events, passes over others in the blink of an eye. He knows how to be incredibly brief. The February Revolution that ended the Romanov dynasty lasts a little more than two minutes: Masses topple a huge statue of the Czar; rifles and sickles are raised aloft; a series of middle-class people cheer; a priest swings a censor, stands before an altar; the Czar is gone; long live the Provisional Government.

He can be even briefer. A diplomat in a frock coat bows deeply and then, in a jump cut, stands erect. Shells explode over trenches. Three or four seconds have elapsed. The Provisional Government has jumped back into war.

He can be (almost) interminable. The long, long, long evening wait before the assault on the Winter Palace. The silent statues of Petrograd brood over the Neva River. The women of the Death Battalion who defend the Winter Palace brood over the statues. Long speeches are given in Smolny. Red Guards endlessly ready themselves. We in the audience tend to snooze.

I mentioned earlier that, when looking at the film, academic historians tend to focus on a single sequence: the climax at the Winter Palace. No one quarrels about the length or brevity of any of the film's other sequences. Some covertly take issue with several of Eisenstein's other interpretations, but no more than they do with each other. Remarkably, there is little dissent over much that happens on the way to October. The February Revolution? Unanimous agreement that – as *October* suggests – it was spontaneous, popular, necessary. The Provisional Government? Inept, inefficient, stupid or criminal in its attempt to continue the war. Alexander Kerensky? Histrionic, vain, self-aggrandizing, better at making speeches than policy. When Eisenstein shows Kerensky as a would-be Bonaparte, by cutting from a closeup of him directly to a statue of Napoleon, he is hardly the only historian to suggest the prime minister saw himself in that kind of heroic role. As early as September 1917, a Congress of the Baltic Fleet passed a resolution calling Kerensky a 'Bonaparte' (Chamberlin 1935: 279). Pipes not only accuses Kerensky of thinking of Bonaparte when he restored capital punishment at the front (how does he know what Kerensky was thinking), he also mentions that the prime minister 'liked to strike Napoleonic poses' (Pipes 1995: 85) Figes mentions, in words that seem to describe a scene in the film, that Kerensky 'began to strut around with comic self-importance, puffing up his puny chest and striking the pose of a Bonaparte' (Figes 1996: 428–30).

Other topics breed strong disagreement. Not just between the film maker and the historians, but among historians themselves. These are not exactly disagreements over data. Historians use the same documents, but read different parts of them, or read them in different ways, or quote different parts of them, or link them together in a different order. Documents from newly opened archives don't change the picture all that much. They still have to be fitted into a narrative whose moral we already know.

Take the 'July Days'. The basic facts are not at issue. The Provisional Government's summer 1917 military offensive against the Germans failed miserably. Workers and soldiers in huge numbers came into the streets to demand the end of the government, some of them no doubt wished to overthrow it by force. Panicky leaders turned to the military for help. Blood was shed. The questions: Were the demonstrations planned and by whom? Was this a (failed) attempt of the Bolsheviks to seize power?

Reed, arriving two months after the events, calls the July demonstrations 'spontaneous' (Reed 1934: 5). Eisenstein shows us the masses of marching protesters, the bloodshed on the Nevsky Prospekt, the anger of the middle classes against the lower orders, the Bolshevik speakers calming the soldiers, insisting it is not time to seize power. Chamberlin agrees, saying the Bolsheviks were actually against the demonstrations. That they only took part to stay one step ahead of the masses and thus maintain their credibility as revolutionary leaders (Chamberlin 1935: 170–1). Rabinowitch complicates the picture by finding Bolsheviks on both sides of the issue, some agitating, some pacifying the crowds. Clearly, he says, it was not party policy to foment revolt. His proof? Lenin was absent in the country during the July days; this means nothing important was supposed to happen. Pipes uses that same absence as part of his evidence to show the demonstrations were part of a conscious attempt by the Bolsheviks to seize power. Lenin, he insists, always absented himself when something important was to happen. Even during the great days of October he is mostly in hiding, not from party policy to protect their leader but because he was, Pipes reiterates many times, a coward. Figes agrees that when it came things physical, Lenin was a coward, but asserts that this was not the issue in July. Had the Bolsheviks wished to seize power that day, they could easily have done so in the afternoon when 50,000 of their most revolutionary supporters, many of them armed, surrounded the Tauride Palace, seat of the Provisional Government. No less a leader than Leon Trotsky himself arrived and rather than seizing power, calmed the troops and released a leader of the Provisional Government who had been taken hostage (Figes 1996: 385, 428–30).

Controversy also swirls around the 'Kornilov Affair', that brief period in late August when the Cossack general sent troops towards Petrograd. For Reed the issue is simple: Kornilov was leading a counter revolution. Eisenstein agrees, showing us Kornilov as yet another potential Napoleon by cutting from his image to that of the same statue previously linked to Kerensky. The film shows how the general's march on Petrograd is undermined by Bolshevik agitators, who are able to convince the Cossacks of his Savage Division that the Soviet programme of 'peace, land, bread' is not meant just for the workers of Petrograd but for everyone, including them. Like Eisenstein, Rabinowitch details the way Bolshevik propagandists persuaded the Cossack regiments to refuse to march on Petrograd. Chamberlin broadens the canvas: counter-revolution was not a personal goal of Kornilov, but a move supported by conservatives tired of agitation and political upheaval, desirous of return to authoritarian ways. Pipes reads the very same telegrams between Kerensky and Kornilov that every other historian has read and comes up with this: the 'affair' was a misunderstanding due to Kerensky's misreading of the general's messages. Kornilov was no threat. He was following Kerensky's own orders to move troops to the capital to ward off a feared rising by the Bolsheviks. Figes agrees. What looked like an attempt to overthrow the Provisional Government grew out of a misunderstanding, though (as Eisenstein suggests), General Kornilov also saw himself as a kind of Bonaparte, and (as Pipes will not admit) much of his support came from people who hoped to use him to do away with the Provisional Government (Reed 1934: 17; Chamberlin 1935: 207–21; Pipes 1991: 439–67; Figes 1996: 438–53).

With October it always comes down to Lenin. Everyone agrees on at least one thing: the Bolsheviks would never have kept together, dared to move, pushed so quickly towards power, succeeded when they did, were it not for his theorizing, his leadership, his remarkable ability to drive the party towards its destiny. Eisenstein, interestingly, almost marginalizes the Soviet leader, giving him far less screen time than Kerensky. We see Lenin in a few brief flashes – arriving at the Finland Station and galvanizing the crowd with his rhetoric; arguing with the Central Committee over his insistence that it is time to seize power; surreptitiously returning to Smolny from hiding; taking the podium at the Congress of Soviets.

However you measure it, every later historian gives Lenin much more space than does the film. In books he may act behind the scenes, but his words, arguments, decisions and threats dominate every action. Reed sees the man as a strange political leader, one who leads by intellect alone.

Rabinowitch, the social historian who wants to show that Lenin both represented larger forces and did not always get his way, ultimately has to admit that there would have been no Bolshevik revolution without him. Chamberlin and Pipes twin themselves with quasi-religious descriptions of the man and his role. The former finds Lenin 'inevitably fused with the system which he brought into existence, on which the last judgement has obviously not been pronounced. He was the incarnate doctrine of militant Marxism, the revolutionary word become flesh'. The latter never quite calls him Satanic, but his description of Lenin's 'totalitarian mentality' has all the markings of a modern anti-Christ, responsible not just for a Bolshevik *coup d'état* but for the subsequent terrors and atrocities of the régime as well as a goodly number of the problems that plague Europe for much of the rest of the century (Reed 1934: 125; Chamberlin 1935: 140).

Figes too speaks of Lenin's 'towering domination' of history itself. October is indeed one of the best examples of modern historical events which 'illustrate the decisive effect of an individual on the course of history. Without Lenin's intervention, it would probably never have happened at all . . .'. Even so, the Bolshevik leader did not always get what he wanted, when he wanted it. Ideological and geographical factions within the party often were able to resist his arguments or ignore his desires. The party itself was not, as Pipes argues, a monolith strictly controlled from above, with Lenin as a puppet master. Such a view is no more than a 'myth which used to be propagated by the Soviet establishment, and one which is still believed (for quite different reasons) by right-wing historians in the West' (Figes 1996: 391–2, 456).

Maybe we should admit there is another way of looking at *October*: the film is a fiction, a creation, a text that cannot be read literally. A film that, to fit things within its timeframe, uses devices of condensation, symbol, and metaphor. *October* is no mirror to some vanished reality. None of it happened precisely the way we see it (and could we have seen it, where would we have been sitting and what would we have missed. Even the energetic John Reed saw less than we do in the film). Eisenstein can use the original settings: the Nevsky Prospekt, the Smolny Institute, Peter-Paul Fortress, the Winter Palace. He can get soldiers and political figures to recapitulate roles they played ten years before, during the actual events. He can hire Vladimir Antonov-Oveseenko to once again lead a company through the Winter Palace to arrest the ministers of the Provisional Government. But it is still fiction – made up, an illusion in black and white. At best, a series of proximate realities. But proximate to what?

The question is what kind of fiction. The question is what kind of history.

Consider this sequence: The diplomat bows and jumps to attention. The soldiers jump back into their trenches. Shells explode nearby. Soldiers crouch in the trenches, looking up. A huge machine is lowered in a factory somewhere far behind the lines. The soldiers cower. Because of the juxtaposition of images, Eisenstein's acclaimed montage, they do so apparently beneath the machine. Is this fact? Fiction? Certainly somewhere shells did explode on the front. Somewhere machines were lowered. Somewhere soldiers cowered in trenches. But the meaning of this sequence is not in some referential truth. It is in the connection of diverse details that we understand to be a metaphor.

Even verifiable historical events can become metaphors. Like any historian, Eisenstein cannot show events without showing them from a particular angle (words or images, both need a point of view), with certain lighting, movement, a connection with preceding and succeeding images (or words, or phrases). Take the scene when Kerensky, the first head of the Provisional Government to move into the Winter Palace, climbs the grand stairway toward his private rooms. Without any piece of paper to document this moment, we do know there were stairs to the family apartments and that Kerensky must have climbed them. Know too – as the sub-titles tell us as we see him climbing and climbing – that he had kept for himself three cabinet portfolios: Minister of Navy, Minister of War, Prime Minister. That, as in the film, he did like to wear a military uniform with glossy boots. That, though it is nowhere documented, must have been greeted by the same members of the palace staff who had once waited on the Czar and his family. That, as Eisenstein shows, they probably regarded him with odd, duplicitous expressions.

Such humble details could be neutral, dramatic, solemn, irrelevant. Eisenstein underlines their importance by treating them with humour. He makes us laugh. Satire is not a common trope for history, but not entirely unknown. Chamberlin, Pipes, and Figes all agree that Kerensky was a pompous figure out of a comic opera, one given to self-dramatization. The humorous sequence in the film points to more than the individual: both Kerensky and his government are depicted as equally a farce, unable to solve the problems facing the country, doomed to impotence and failure.

Others have said much the same thing. We see Kerensky in the former royal chambers as the end draws near, a leader in isolation, posturing, playing with a chess board, cowering beneath the bed covers, surrounded by the forces of the past, virtually impotent in his power to effect events. In later years, Kerensky himself will admit this. Admit he did not have force enough to stop the Bolsheviks. In life as in the film, *October* he makes a feeble effort. He phones the Cossacks. He tells them to 'saddle up' and come to defend the Winter Palace. A stableman says the Cossacks are on the way, but he is lying.

The Cossacks don't saddle up in the film. Nor did they in history. Actually, in the film we don't even see Cossacks. All we see is their horses. Or some horses on whose rear ends Eisenstein lets the camera linger. There were, presumably, horses in the Cossack stables. This is fact. Metaphor too.

Some inventions are so obviously symbolic that nobody should complain about their historicity, though some scholars do (Goodwin 1993: 84). Take the film's opening sequence: the destruction of the monumental statue of the Tsar. Knowing that this is not a statue of the deposed Czar Nicolas, but really one of Alexander III, his father, doesn't add to or subtract anything to our understanding of the February Revolution. Nor does knowing that this particular statue was really in Moscow, not Petrograd, where the film is set. Nor does knowing the real statue was not pulled down until 1921. What we do know is that the film is telling us something simple: the collective masses pulled down the Czar in 1917. During the Kornilov threat when, by reversing the film, Eisenstein has the statue reassemble itself, the meaning can only be figurative – and yet historically very clear: Kornilov's move is an attempt to restore the old régime.

Equally symbolic, and with no basis whatsoever in fact, is the most memorable sequence of the film: the brilliant montage that shows the raising of the bridges over the Neva River during the July Days. Shows them as part of the strategy by which the Provisional Government beats back a revolutionary challenge. Any viewer has to know that much of what happens on the bridges is not documented history, but historical moments created by the film maker – that macabre, and strangely sensual image of the dead girl's hair slipping into the crack between the two rising segments of the bridge; the horse hanging from the highest point of the raised bridge that plunges into the river to end the sequence.

How to explain this invention? In filmic or historical terms? Or both? Clearly Eisenstein (as he says in his memoires) was captivated by the possibilities of using the bridges to produce sheer beauty on the screen – the implacable steel geometry of the slow-rising forms played off against the frightened, scurrying shapes of humans. But he also knew that it was a common strategy of the Russian government to raise these bridges in times of crisis. Knew too that the Provisional Government would try to do so, unsuccessfully, during October (as we see later in the film). The filmic choice for Eisenstein is almost as old as cinema: to show the importance of the unsuccessful attempt to raise the bridge in October, he must let the audience in on its potential significance – by showing a successful raising in an earlier sequence. But the action also has a specific historical content. Raising the bridges demonstrates the way in which the geographic situation of Petrograd mirrors the class situation: the radical workers and soldiers live around the factories north of the Neva, the bourgeoisie and the governmental centres are south of the river – with the hands of the Provisional Government leaders resting on the levers that keep the chasm between the two impassable. Eisenstein has here provided images to convey an abstract concept: the widening split between the Provisional Government and the lower classes, a split that will lead to the October days.

The greatest piece of fiction in October, the one that critics tend to seize upon – as I have twice mentioned – is the 'storming' of the Winter Palace. So wholly fictional is this large and impressive battle that good jokes were being told about it even during Eisenstein's time. The most common: that more ordnance was detonated during the making of the film than during the original taking of the Palace. The second most common: that there were more deaths and injuries during Eisenstein's recreation than during the historical events. The former is no doubt true; the latter is probably true. Reports are wildly divergent on what really happened the evening of 7 November. Some say nobody was killed; others say as many as 16 people were killed. Most historians agree on this: there was no grand fire fight, no heroic charge across Palace Square. At the end there was no opposition to the Red Guards. They slipped into the palace to arrest the ministers of the Provisional Government.

Why then does Eisenstein give us this heroic charge and firefight?

We need to see it from the film maker's point of view. Eisenstein has a real problem: he is working in a dramatic form and must deal with the undramatic quality of what took place on 7 November. Here is the way Leon Trotsky put it:

> The final act of the revolution seems, after all else, too brief, too dry, too business-like – somehow out of correspondence with the historic scope of the events . . . Where is the insurrection? There is no picture of the insurrection. The events do not form themselves into a picture. A series of small operations, calculated and prepared for in advance, remain separated one from another in both space and time. A unity of thought and action unites them, but they do not fuse in the struggle itself. There is no action of great masses. There are no dramatic encounters with. There is nothing of all that with which imaginations brought upon the facts of history associate with the idea of insurrection. (Medvedev 1979: 50)

Try to tell that to an audience sitting in a theatre. Eisenstein desperately needs that missing 'historic scope'. He has given us a long dramatic build-up. He has drawn out the moments towards a historic climax, the advent of the Bolsheviks, the definitive change of regimes. He has shown the plans of the city in the office of the Military Revolutionary Committee, the map with its strategic sites being circled, the troops fanning out at night, the sailors coming ashore to seize the bridges, the movements towards the rail lines, the centres of communication, the fortress of Peter Paul, the cruiser *Aurora* steaming up the Neva. But he still needs something more dramatic. He needs to storm the Winter Palace.

Eisenstein's problem on the screen is much the same as that of the Bolsheviks in 1917. They could have ignored the palace. Prime Minister Kerensky had fled Petrograd. His cabinet was in the palace, but cut off from communications to the outside world. To control the country, the Bolsheviks did not need to seize the residence of the Czars. Except in terms of its symbolic importance. Lenin knew that a revolution must have a heroic symbol for the coming ages. Like the Bastille, a symbol of the bad old world the revolutionaries have conquered. Similarly, Eisenstein knew a dramatic film must have a pay-off. A release. By this point in the film there can be no doubt about the outcome. The viewer knows that the government is hopelessly surrounded. Knows that the forces on the two sides are hopelessly unequal. (This is the genesis of Eisenstein's sexist humour: only women in slips and brassieres remain ready to defend the régime.) We have seen the strategic spots circled on the map. The troops in the streets. The Winter Palace circled and encircled. But still we need a release. A catharsis. On the screen as in reality: the revolution must have a climax.

The question: does the film tell us that this climax is not literal but symbolic? Perhaps. It depends, like all reception of history, on who you are and what you already know. Certainly the battle points ahead to another historical reality that weighs on the story the film maker is telling and the world in which he has lived. A reality that he wanted to show but could not encompass within the film's timeframe: the gathering of native and outside resistance to the new régime that will plunge the country into a long, horrendous, and bloody civil war. The storming of the Winter Palace is Eisenstein's attempt to let us share in the ecstasy of revolutionary change. It is also a symbolic version of that change – and the historical consequences that would flow from it, consequences that he could not show. The taking of the Winter Palace stands in for the victories the Red Army would achieve against the four-year resistance of the Whites and the military intervention of a dozen nations which unsuccessfully attempted to crush the revolutionary régime.

These inventions and alterations, this playing loose with data, can be disturbing. Certainly to anyone who writes history by the traditional rules. But history on film, as I have been arguing throughout this book, cannot be about literal fact. The screen is a not a good medium for delivering the kind of compendious data that fills written histories. To take the model of written history for history on film is to look in the wrong place. Why? In part because we already have books. Film is another, a different way of seeing and representing the world. However literal it may look, history on film is no more than an evocation of the past and a commentary on the topic evoked. As long as we understand that, like fact and interpretation, there is no space between that evocation and that commentary. Both are present in every image we see upon the screen.

Maybe history is the wrong word. Maybe we should choose another word for the attempt to deliver and make meaning of the past in a dramatic film. Whatever we call it, *October* is certainly an attempt to convey the importance of the social and political happenings in Petrograd in the fall of 1917. To argue that October was a moment when the Bolsheviks embodied the spirit of the Russian masses who had overthrown the Czar in February and had become wholly disillusioned with the Provisional Government in the months since then. That the Bolsheviks did no more than lead where the Russian people wished to go. This interpretation, this argument comes in a presentational form different from that of we historians who work with words on the page. So different that one might say the film's meaning lies somewhere in the narrow land that separates history and poetry as Aristotle defined them. To make its argument, *October* tells us neither *what happened* nor *what might have happened*. Instead it presents a cunning mixture of the two – a mixture that (not completely different from written history) creates a symbolic or metaphoric expression of what we call the Bolshevik Revolution.

Let me take this one step farther and say that, however much written history depends upon facts to underpin its argument, its meaning too lies in its larger symbolic expressions. The tropes, the shape, the overall thrust of the histories we write is prefigured by the values of the historian and the demands of narrative form. Eisenstein, prefigures his story of October as a dramatic and heroic tale, then finds (and creates) appropriate images in which to tell it. He well knows that his truth is not referential but metaphorical. John Reed, whose earliest writings depicted the revolution as a implacable natural force, works much the same way; his ten-day structure, one that marks much subsequent thinking about October, is a dramatic, not a historical device. So in their own ways do Chamberlin, Rabinowitch, Pipes, and Figes. All, in prefaces, lay out the arguments that allow them to look at the same material and find very different meanings. For however true the congeries of data that each presents to us, the shaping of that data into an argument, the meaning of that data as we (are supposed to) absorb it, is not, ultimately, literal, but metaphoric and moral. After all the facts, what we are left with is the argument. Or vision. Not with the details but with broad evaluations of what those details mean. For

Reed the revolution is 'a beacon for mankind'. For Pipes a horrendous tragedy perpetrated by a lawless minority. That Eisenstein provides an image of Revolution closer to Reed (and Rabinowitch) than Pipes has less to do with research or the accuracy of individual details than his personal experience, his beliefs, his value system.

One more important difference between *October* and the other accounts: save perhaps for Reed, who had also written drama, the other historians point to rather than involve us in the drama of those days. None has the emotional impact and excitement of *October*, which involves us, thrusts us into October as a time of human movement, action, hope, struggle, tension, humour, triumph, defeat, change. Like any film, it indulges in the kind of historical emotion that our written forms usually avoid. Part of this is due to the medium. Part is tradition: as academics we must be measured, distanced, objective, uninvolved – even if we wish to depict October as world shaking drama, tragedy, necessity, the story of one year in the life of the party or 30 years in the life of a nation. To accept *October* as history is to accept emotion as part of reading history. Accept, too, the idea that the metaphoric is better than the literal as a way of judging the work of the historian. The time has come for us to be willing to evaluate the forms and metaphors as well as the content that the historian produces. Doing so will allow us to gather the best of historical films, such as *October*, into our historiography.

Chapter 5

_____

Documentary

W hat does the documentary document? That is the question. And it's not just mine. The documentary is a problematic form to all those who in recent years have tried to define and theorize it, and the history documentary is, if anything, even more problematic. Ostensibly, the documentary directly reflects the world, possessing what has been called an 'indexical' relationship to reality – which means it shows us what once was there, in front of the camera, and in theory, what would have been there anyway were no camera present. This as opposed to the dramatic film which must elaborately set up and stage a world that is then filmed specifically for the camera. Certainly there is some truth to this notion that the images in documentaries often do have some indexical relation to the world, if only – as with the 'fact' in the work of written history – on the level of the individual moment or scene: that politician did stand up before a crowd and make that inaugural address; those soldiers did leave that trench and charge across that open field into machine gun fire; those workers did picket that factory and were rousted by those baton wielding police; that is Adolf Hitler, riding in an open car past cheering crowds at Nuremberg in 1935.

Part of the problem is with the word itself – 'documentary'. with its implication of a direct relationship to reality. But the common alternative, the 'non-fiction film', does not provide a much more satisfactory description – and it, too, is equally debated. Like the work of written history, the documentary 'constitutes' facts by selecting traces of the past and enfolding them into a narrative. Like the written history, the documentary ignores the overall fiction – that the past can be fully told in a story with a beginning, a middle, and an end. Indeed, in some ways the documentary is so much like written history that, far less than the feature film, it hardly seems to point towards a new way of thinking about the past. The parallel or closeness between traditional history and the documentary undoubtedly accounts for the fact that historians, journalists, and the general public are rather more trusting of the documentary than the dramatic feature. But this is a mistaken form of trust. For the documentary also shares much with the fiction film. Like that form, it sometimes uses images that are proximate rather than literal realities (a landscape today for the way it looked at some time in the past, generic images of soldiers for specific images), occasionally dramatizes scenes, and regularly structures material into the conventions of drama, with a story that begins with certain problems, questions, and/or characters at the outset, develops their complications over time, and resolves them by the end of the film. To this it adds a kind of (at least implied) mystification – the notion that what you are seeing on screen is somehow a direct representation of what happened in the past. In that sense, the drama is more honest precisely because it is overtly a fictional construction. With a drama, you know – or you should know – that what you see is a construction of the past.

The documentary has, in short, always done something more than simply reflect the real world, save perhaps in the earliest days when the Lumière brothers and their hired cameramen turned the cinematograph on street scenes in various parts of the world (and even so, it is likely that the camera and/or the cameraman had a considerable influence on the people and things involved in the moments they filmed). Certainly in the classic world of documentary story-telling, like that of the esteemed pioneer, Robert Flaherty, the reality delivered was staged as much as found. In his masterpiece, *Nanook of the North*, an account of Eskimo (the word in his day for Inuit) life, Flaherty had to teach his subjects how to hunt seal with harpoons, a skill they had long ago lost. Just as, in that same film, the director could only obtain those intimate shots of the native family inside their igloo by in fact constructing a special igloo for them with one wall cut away, through which the camera could record their 'traditional' life. In his effort to bring the world an accurate picture of a culture in a film that lies right at the intersection of anthropology and history, Flaherty had to stage reality – create a fiction in the name of truth. The truth in this case being about how primitive peoples coped with the hardships of their lives.

If the documentary has never simply reflected the world as it is, but has always been what the great British practitioner John Grierson called 'a creative treatment of actuality', this is especially true of those that focus on history – for these works have the added problem that the actuality has long since vanished (Plantangina 1997: 10). Yet it has left traces, and like the historian whose task it is to find ways of turning those traces into historical discourse, documentary film makers must do the same. The results of their efforts (and such documentaries date back to the work of Esfir Shub in the 1920s) have been of so little concern to academics devoted to film studies, that books on the history and theory of documentary mention historical works only in passing. The solitary attempt to deal with the genre has been undertaken in a dissertation at Uppsala University. Picking up on and adding to Grierson the more recent ideas of scholar Carl Plantinga, David Ludvigsson calls the historical documentary a film about the past which involves '*creative treatment that asserts a belief that the given objects, states of affairs or events occurred or existed in the actual world portrayed*' (italics in original) (Ludviggson 2003: 65). Such a definition encompasses both the notion that the documentary refers to an actual world of the past, and is at the same time always positioned, ideological, and partisan. Even if wholly made from actuality footage or other traces of the world, it is never a neutral 'history lesson', but a cunning work that must be as carefully interpreted by the viewer as the dramatic film.

So far I have been using the word documentary, as if it refers to a single kind of visual format, but in fact such films create their on-screen worlds in a variety of modes of representation. Among six different types named by Bill Nichols in his writings on documentary – the *expository*, the *observational*, the *interactive*, the *reflexive*, the *poetic*, and the *performative* – it was the first of these which dominated the historical documentary for many decades (Nichols 1991: 32). The *expository* has generally been a compilation film, one which utilizes old, actuality footage and a voiceover narration (Voice of God) to tell the viewer what the images mean and to make the larger argument of the work. Often it also contains stirring music to underscore and punctuate that argument. Originating in the films of Shub (in her films the voice has to speak in the inter-titles), this form reached a kind of apotheosis (at least in the United States) in the 1950s and 1960s in such television series as the 26-part *Victory at Sea*, a highly nationalistic and patriotic chronicle of America's participation in World War II.

Because it depended upon actuality footage, the *expository* was for a long time limited to very recent history, but its horizons began to expand backward into the nineteenth century as film makers created techniques for blowing up and panning over old photographs in a way that almost made them seem to come alive. Using the same sort of precise and meaningful camera moves over drawings, posters, etchings, paintings, and other artifacts, allowed the history documetary to chronicle even earlier eras. Shortly before the Second World War, Swiss director Curt Oertel was able to create a narrative piece called *The Titan*, a biography of Michelangelo in which we see no live humans but, rather, piazzas, palaces, landscapes, pieces of sculpture, and other works of art, while the soundtrack of words and music tells the story of the Renaissance master. In a similar fashion, *The Norman Conquest of England* (1955), made by director Roger Leenhardt, uses images from the Bayeux tapestry to show the eleventh-century invasion of the British Isles by William the Conqueror (Barnouw 1983: 200–202).

The invention of lightweight cameras and recording equipment in the 1960s were part of the impetus that moved the documentary towards the forms named as *observational* and *interactive*. Now it became much easier to go out to film historical sites, as well as to set up and interview talking heads – either historical witnesses who had lived through events which they recalled and described, or experts such as historians, who were used not only to help create a narrative, but also to provide an overview of and context for the story being told. Among early landmarks of this new genre are two works from France: Marcel Ophuls' *The Sorrow and the Pity* (1970), a four-hour, twenty-minute portrait of France under the Nazi occupation, told for the most part by talking heads, some famous, some infamous, and some obscure; and Claude Lanzmann's *Shoah* (1985), which contains nine-and-a-half hours of inter-active interviews with survivors of the Holocaust (Lanzmann is often on screen prodding his witnesses, even into strong emotional states), punctuated by observations of contemporary trains of boxcars, clearly meant to be reminiscent of the 1940s, rolling across the Polish countryside and in through the gates of Auschwitz.

The *reflexive* and *performative* modes may be rare among historical documentaries, but not unknown. The first two tendencies inform such works as Jill Godmilow's *Far From Poland* (1984), which frames its story of the Solidarity movement with the personal, ideological, and aesthetic problems the film maker has in creating the work (among other things, she can't get a visa to travel to Poland), and along with actuality footage, also uses re-enactments based on the texts of interviews reported in Polish newspapers; and Michael Rubbo's *Waiting for Fidel* (1974), in which the camera mostly documents the days of the Canadian film maker and his crew as they wait vainly in Havana for a promised interview with the elusive Cuban leader. The *poetic* may be the rarest form for a historical documentary, but the term well describes a group of films by Peter Forgacs which, taken together, constitute a kind of private history of European families from the 1920s to the 1940s. Based on home movies made by amateurs, these works alter the originals with zooms and pans, tinting and toning, freeeze frames, titles, laconic commentary, and suggestive music by composer Tibor Szemzo to create a poetic view of the past that can also be terrifying to contemporary viewers – just how, we are forced to think, can these folks play so light-heartedly, how can they enjoy this outing, vacation, or wedding when the Holocaust is just around the corner? Why don't they get out while the getting is good?

All six forms of historical documentary continue to be made, along with hybrid works that draw on more than one of these traditions. The well-known American director Ken Burns, for example, mixed together old photos with contemporary images from battlefields; a voice of god narrator with quotations, read by actors, from the letters and diaries of participants; talking head experts, with composed music full of nostalgic melodies, in order to create his highly popular, eleven-hour, made for television series, *The Civil War* (1990). When that proved to be an enormous success, Burns went on to use much the same formula for a variety of other subjects in American history, including *Baseball* (1994), *The West* (1996), and *Jazz* (2001).

All forms of the documentary contain lots of information about the past, though some tend towards macro- and others towards micro-historical data. All use that information to make an argument about the topic at hand, though in the *expository* the argument is always much more direct and clear (even heavy handed) than in, say, the *reflexive* or the *poetic* (in a film like *Victory at Sea* the audience is left in little doubt as to the heroic and patriotic meaning of all the battles shown; in *Far from Poland*, the message contains some ambiguities, even doubts about its own depiction of Solidarity, and in a Forgacs film such as *The Family Bartos* the theme can be subtle to the point of elusiveness). All historical documentaries also are made in such a way as to induce strong feelings in the members of the audience, to provide what one scholar has called an 'emotion-laden' experience (Ludviggson 2003: 65). This is done in a variety of visual and aural ways – not just through the images used, but also in the way they are framed, coloured, and edited; as well as through the sound track, the quality of voice of both narrators and witnesses, the words spoken, the sound effects, the music from found sources, or composed, to heighten the impact of the images. Like the dramatic film, the documentary wants you to feel and care deeply about the events and people of the past.

Whatever form the historical documentary takes, it inevitably inserts itself into the larger historical discourse, that field of data and debates that surrounds its subject. To give some sense of how documentaries can relate to a field, I want to show how several of them approach a single topic with different modes and with a different sense of history. For my purposes, a perfect topic for this study is the Spanish Civil War. Perfect for me because I have both written a book on the war and helped to make a film about it. Perfect in a larger sense because a large number of documentaries have been made on the war over a period of more than half a century. Perfect because the war involved so many political parties and ideological positions that no consensus has ever been achieved on its major topics.

The Spanish Civil War has long been seen as a kind of dress rehearsal for World War II. It began in July 1936, with a military uprising (led by four generals, including Francisco Franco) against the recently elected Popular Front government (a coalition of liberals, socialists, communists, and anarchists) of the five-year-old republic. What the leaders of the revolt expected to be a classic pronunciamento or *coup d'état* which would be over in a week, turned into a long, drawn-out affair that wracked the Iberian Peninsula for almost three years, and led to over half-a-million deaths. Part of the violence was due to the always-bloody nature of civil wars, in which old scores are often settled, and part to the sharp ideological split between left and right both in Spain and throughout Europe. For the war quickly became internationalized, with Nazi Germany and Fascist Italy intervening heavily on the side of the rebels (the so-called Nationalists), and the Soviet Union on the side of the Republic. Hitler's contribution was the Condor Legion, some 8,000 men equipped with the latest weaponry, including the new Stuka dive bomber, as well as the heavy Junkers and other planes of the Luftwaffe that helped to destroy the ancient Basque town of Guernica; Mussolini dispatched over 100,000 troops, including armoured divisions; Russia sent aeroplanes and tanks, officers and political operatives, and underwrote support for what was initially a spontaneous flow of volunteers from other countries into Spain to fight for the Republic (which had lost most of its officers and trained military personnel to the Nationalist generals). A total of some 45,000 foreigners, leftists, union members, and refugees from fascist countries joined together under the banner of the International Brigades and the slogan 'Madrid will be the tomb of fascism'.

It wasn't. After two-and-a-half-years of a war of attrition, the Nationalists entered the last holdout, Madrid, in March 1939, taking complete control of the country. By then, the native fascist party, the Falange Espanol, had been marginalized by Franco, who welcomed support from the fascist powers, but was himself an old fashioned military dictator with little interest in creating a corporate state. Yet if the military struggle of the war concluded in 1939, the battles over its history have continued until today. This is true of all wars, indeed of all historical topics. Which is why we are still asking and answering the old questions: Was slavery the cause of the American Civil War? Or was it economic disparities between North and South? Was the war the American colonies fought against England a revolution or a war of independence? Was the French Revolution the cause or the consequence of social change? Did Alexander the Great over-extend himself and undermine his own cause by invading India? Consensus is never fully achieved on such topics because they always involve political, ideological, and moral considerations which can never ultimately be settled by appeal to data.

The battles among academics over the war have been vigorous. Little wonder. The conflict involved the three great, opposing ideologies of the twentieth century (fascism, communism, democracy) as well as some lesser ones (anarchism and traditionalism), which means that for historians the issues are hardly dead. Equally important, the régimes which embraced and fostered these ideologies have all vanished, as has the Spain of Franco, into the dustbin of history. In Spain, itself, the issues of the war and its aftermath – first in the Franco régime's major reprisals against the vanquished, then in the long-running (almost forty years) repression of civil and political rights – are still so alive that while localized studies or particular topics have been done, no general history of the conflict has ever been undertaken by a Spanish academic. The three most important ones have been produced by a British scholar, an American, and a team of two French historians, and these works are at odds over the causes, course, and consequences of the conflict (Broue and Temime 1961; Thomas 1961; and Jackson 1965). Did the growing civil chaos of the Second Spanish Republic justify an uprising? Was the revolution in the Republican zone after the war began a positive or negative development? Which side was responsible for more atrocities? Did the Republic lose the war because a Non-Intervention Agreement, signed among the major countries and followed by the United States, prevented it from purchasing arms to which, as the legal government, it was entitled to do? Or was the loss due to ineptitude, fascist intervention, or because Soviet agents created an internal reign of terror in the Republic that suppressed the Anarchist and Trotskyist parties of the Popular Front and demoralized a larger public?

Such questions also hover over all documentaries on the war. Yet it is only the rare, long film, such as the five-hour, twelve-minute work made for Britain's Granada Television that can even begin to address in breadth such complex issues. Entitled *The Spanish Civil War* (1983), this mini-series is divided into six chapters. Each addresses a major aspect of the conflict: 1. The historical origins of the war. 2. Revolution, counter-revolution, and terror. 3. The international contribution on both left and right. 4. The growth of the Nationalist state. 5. The nature of the Republic, its revolution and internal conflicts. 6. Victory, defeat, and subsequent history under the Franco régime. With this amount of time, the work can explore topics in some depth. Chapter two, for example, can extensively document at both the macro- and micro-level the charges and evidence of atrocities on both sides. Through interviews with former foreign journalists, government ministers, Nationalist leaders, and common workers and peasants, one gets multiple and sometimes contradictory perspectives on the issue. Some witnesses claim the difference in atrocities is that Republicans killed in the heat of passion, while Nationalists systematically purged their enemies – and the narration seems to agree. Yet a British journalist implicitly contests this notion by saying that in Madrid, Anarchist and Communist committees for justice vied with each other over how many Nationalist supporters they could kill. This story sounds like one of those urban legends raised to the status of fact – yet again the narration seems to assent.

Beyond giving the gross figures, the claim of historians that perhaps half of the war's half-a-million deaths were due to vigilantism or terror, the film is able to bring such statistics down, much as does a written work of history, to a local and individual level. It does this through extended (up to five-minute) examinations of events such as the Nationalist slaughter of Republicans in the Badajoz bull ring, the way right-wing prisoners from the Model Prison in Madrid were systematically disappearing (we see their graveyard) during their supposed removal for safety to Valencia, or the terrorist bombing of Guernica by German aeroplanes, which the Nationalists then attempted to blame the Republicans. In one exemplary case study, we are introduced to images of a farming village in Andalucia, then and now; hear locals who were children at the time of the war describe how impoverished workers took control of the town, imprisoned the landowners, seized and killed their fighting bulls, and enjoyed eating meat for the first time in years. When Nationalist troops marching out from Seville approached the town, all those in prison were hastily shot – and the names in the prison record book that we see matches those on the headstones, all dated 1936, that the camera pans over in one section of the graveyard. The Nationalist capture of the town is documented with a few photos, then we again see the prison book, now filled with the names of peasants and local workers, as the camera dollies to a corner of the same cemetery, to a mass grave where only recently (the film was made after the Franco régime ended) a monument to the slain has been erected.

Such relatively even-handed detail on historical questions only seems possible in this kind of documentary mini-series. The more common strategy for the film maker who has the usual one or two hours of available screen time, is to make a (conscious or unconscious) decision on such questions and then, within the body of the work, to highlight images, interviews, and narration which support that particular interpretation. What this means is that a great number of documentaries are as much polemical as they are historical. This is the case with the first and probably the best-known of all features on the war, Frederic Rossif's *Mourir à Madrid* (1963). Mixing actuality footage from archives in Paris, Moscow, the United States, and East Berlin (including unedited images of the Condor Legion never before been used in a film), the film frames the story of the war with images of what might be called 'Eternal Spain' (the bogus title given by the director to get permission to shoot some contemporary film in Franco's realm) – a long, poetic section of a peasant leading sheep over hills and through valleys in a misty dawn. The story of the war is told with a highly stylized narration that explains the causes, course, and consequences of the conflict, and that is regularly intercut with poetic quotations from writers, artists, and historical figures, read by professional actors. With such materials, *Mourir à Madrid* makes a historical argument that, while providing evidence on both sides, clearly embraces the Republic and its defenders, both native and foreign; denounces the rebels and their fascist allies abroad; and makes bitter fun of the democracies which supported non-intervention. Its opening phrases, voiced over images of a barren landscape, set the stage for what is to come: 'Spain 1931. 503,061 square kilometers, almost the size of France. Twenty-four million inhabitants . . . half the population – twelve million – are illiterate. Eight million live in poverty. Millions of farmers own no land. Twenty thousand people own half of Spain. Entire provinces belong to a single man. The average salary of a worker is one to three pesetas a day. The country has twenty thousand monks, thirty-one thousand priests, sixty thousand nuns who reside in five thousand convents, and fifteen thousand military officers, of which eight hundred are generals. There is one officer for each six soldiers; one general for each one hundred soldiers' (Chapsal 1963: 7).

These words – and words are what inevitably drive the meaning of the images in Voice of God films, and in most other documentaries as well, to the point where one might describe such films as, essentially, lavishly illustrated lectures – clearly are meant to make the audience applaud those who defend the Republic and all the progressive elements in Spain. Opening with newsreels that show the abdication of King Alfonso XIII in 1931 and the immediate proclamation of the Republic, the film shows that a first, mildly leftist government moved to reform some of the country's great inequities by separating church and state, establishing schools, and working towards agrarian land reform. Such actions create horror and a backlash among the old guard landowners, military men, and church leaders, who begin to organize themselves to take back what they believe to be their country. Civil unrest, protests among industrial workers and peasants, and an anarchist uprising in the Asturias which is brutally suppressed by the army – all these lead to an election in early 1936 that is won by a Popular Front coalition (comprised of liberals, socialists, Trotskyists, communists, and anarchists). This victory is followed by more social turmoil and violence, as gangs from both right and left wing parties clash in the streets. The assassination in July 1936, of the leader of the right wing faction in parliament, Calvo Sotelo, becomes the excuse and the trigger for the generals to rise against the régime. The army seizes some large areas of the country, but in the major urban centres (Madrid, Barcelona, Valencia, Malaga) unions and leftist parties, bearing arms distributed by local leaders, beat back the military threat. A few days after the uprising, the country is divided into two roughly equal zones – and the real war begins.

The rest of *Mourir à Madrid* closely follows the military campaigns of the next two-plus years, detailing the offensives and battles (Jarama, Brunete, Belchite, Teruel, the Ebro), as well as the intervention by foreign powers. If the screen is filled with actuality footage, the history is driven by a narration that, while it certainly deploys many facts (as in the quotation above), makes them part of a highly evocative rendering that ultimately shows the war as a kind of romantic drama, a great lost cause, a last ditch attempt to stop the fascist powers before they launch Europe into the Second World War. This attitude allows *Mourir à Madrid* to slide by major topics that would detract from this overall theme. Fewer than a hundred words of the narration deal with the complex internal contradictions of the Republic, and these only in the most general terms:

> The parties are numerous and divided. The POUM, on the extreme left, wants both victory and revolution. The anarchists of the CNT and FAI, who have the majority of workers, want a victory without discipline, a people but no state. The socialist party and the communist party are the ones who hold power, the socialists because of the number of their deputies, the communists because of their activism and the arms provided by Russia. The conflicts between them are settled by arms and demonstrations in the streets (Chapsal 1963: 94).

All this is true enough, but it seems a very oblique way of describing the bitter warfare among political parties, especially the deadly street fighting among anarchist and Communist militias in Barcelona in May 1937 (a so-called war within a war). This was followed by a stepped-up campaign of terror launched by Communists against the Anarchists and member of the POUM (so-called Trotskyists), which led to the imprisonment and deaths of both leaders and rank and file. (It was this campaign that made British author, George Orwell, flee the country for his life after having fought with a POUM unit, as detailed in his book, *Homage to Catalonia*.) And as for the important question (posed at the time and ever since) of whether or not this campaign weakened the Republic and aided the Nationalist triumph, the film refuses to raise it or even to enter the debate. Why? To represent the bloody internal conflict would surely serve to darken the portrayal of the heroic Republic, which is the director's theme.

If *Mourir à Madrid* exemplifies the traditional, *expository* documentary, *The Good Fight* (1982), represents the *interactive*. This film about the Abraham Lincoln Battalion, the military unit of Americans who fought with the International Brigades, creates a history through mixing actuality footage with the recollections of eleven volunteers, who appear on screen to tell their own tales. Initially the three directors of the film, Noel Buckner, Mary Dore, and Sam Sills, hoped that, as in some such works, the story could be told wholly through the voices of these historical participants. But the interviews did not provide enough of an historical overview or a rich enough context to knit the individual tales together and make the battalion history fully comprehensible, so a narration had to be added. (In the interests of full disclosure, let me say that I was co-author of this narration, as well as one of historical advisers on the project.) The lecture from on high aspect of the voiceover is modified because of the speaker's rather folksy approach, underscored by his identity: this is Studs Terkel, at the time the film was made, a well-known journalist with a national reputation for his socially conscious oral histories. His informal delivery makes it sound not as if God, but your favorite uncle, is describing the war.

Framing and bringing to life the history of the battalion are the stories of the eleven volunteers, who become emblems for the 3,200 Americans. Even before we see an image, with the screen still black, we hear the sound of a hammer, then see a middle-aged, bearded man at work on a building while the narration says 'Abe Osheroff was a carpenter in 1937 when he decided to volunteer as a soldier in the Spanish Civil War'. Cut to a white-haired woman describing combat, and we learn that this is Evelyn Hutchins who was a photographer before she went to Spain to drive a truck. Quickly we meet all the others in brief shots and an accompanying narration which stresses their impulses as basically anti-fascist – seamen Bill Bailey and Bill McCarthy; nurses Ruth Davidow and Salaria Key (who is Black); student Ed Balchowsky; unemployed Tom Page (also Black); labour organizer Steve Nelson; aspiring artist Milt Wolff; and magazine writer, David Thompson. The names and faces provide a sense of the diverse backgrounds of the Lincolns, even as they misrepresent the composition of the battalion. No more than 30 of the volunteers (less than 1 per cent) were Black and fewer were female, while at least 50 per cent were Jewish (here I take it that two of the eleven, Davidow and Wolff, are Jewish). Yet the opening sequence makes the message clear (as clear as in those suspiciously and conspicuously diverse military units in Hollywood's movies about World War II) – the Lincolns represent America, and to underline the point, David Thompson ends the pre-credit roll by saying it directly: 'a lot of guys went over there from all walks of life'.

The war as a struggle against fascism – this theme, enunciated in the opening moments, threads through the film, accounting for its strengths, its shortcomings, and its erasures. Two separate sorts of sequences alternate to create
the story. Events in Europe, Spain, and the USA, the larger history into which
the volunteers enter, is shown through actuality footage, newsreels, and photos,
and explained by the narrator, while the story of the Lincolns comes in the
personal tales of the eleven witnesses, all of whom speak movingly of their
experiences before, during, and after Spain. From the former we learn about
the growth of fascism in Europe and the manoeuvring of governments on the
world stage, about armies in the field, and bombs falling on cities for the first
time in history, and the slowly increasing support for the Loyalists in neutral
America as the war continues. From the latter we get a chronology of the battalion and learn about the human face of war. The veterans tell us why they
went, how they went, and what they did in Spain, naming the battles –Jarama,
Brunete, Belchite, Teruel, and the Ebro – in which they fought. From them
were learn of the difficult night-long hike over the Pyrenees (France had closed
its border), the insufficient training with wooden sticks rather than rifles, the
horrors of going into combat and seeing buddies blown to bits, the rigours
of living for months in the field, the camaraderie that grows among those
who face death each day, the growing weariness as the war turns against
the Republic, supplies begin to run out, and everyone realizes that defeat
is near.

What we don't learn is equally significant. Leftist politics, other than the
generalized anti-fascism, is absent from *The Good Fight*. We are never told that
the International Brigades were organized and directed by the Comintern,
and dominated by officials from the Communist Party. Nor that at least 70 per
cent of the Americans were members of either the party or the Young
Communist League (a much looser organization during the late 1930s). The
word, Communist, is connected to the battalion on a couple of occasions, but
obliquely. Once Steve Nelson is described as a labour organizer for the
Communist Party. Once we are told that the commissars, assigned to each unit
to ensure discipline and explain the political context of the war, 'usually followed the Communist Party Line', but not the whole truth, that they always
did. (I had written the line without the word, 'usually', which was added by
the directors.) From the most self-reflective and critical of the volunteers, Abe
Osheroff, we hear that there were too many boring political speeches, and that
when some Communist leaders from the US visited the troops, they talked a
lot of 'bullshit'. But that's about it. Never does the film touch the deadly splits
within Spain that had resonance within the American ranks, where socialists
and liberals could feel outnumbered and stifled. Nor is there any mention

of the terror against anarchists and Trotskyists which spilled over into the International Brigades and may have touched the Americans. Certainly the troops knew about the terror, even if they would not have called it that (Rosenstone 1969: 373–75).

The reasons for these erasures are clear enough. The title itself explains them: *The Good Fight* is history as homage, a film meant as a warm historical tale of commitment and courage, a lesson for the current generation. If this isn't clear already, the final sequences over the end-credit roll underscore the notion – we see the aging Lincolns, carrying the battalion banner to various political demonstrations through the decades, including protests against the Vietnam war and the contemporary (to when the film is made) movement against American involvement with the Contras in Nicaragua. Such a theme necessitates, or so the film makers think, no shadows darkening the portrait. A new generation which knows something about the horrors of the gulag might not understand that left wing movements in the United States, including the Communist Party, had a broad base of support in the 1930s, and that large sections of the American public did not yet see the Soviet Union as an 'evil empire'. So a decision is made to downplay the all-important role of the party in the organization and leadership of the International Brigades. Among the eleven volunteers, only one, Osheroff, expresses anything mildly negative about the leadership – and then without naming it. Occasionally Bill Bailey or one of the others describes himself as 'political' before Spain, without any unpacking of this codeword for member of the Communist Party. As for the (admittedly few) veterans of Spain who came home and claimed there had been a stifling of dissent and even some terror in the ranks – they are wholly absent, for their presence would take away from the affirmative message the directors wish to create out of the remnants of the past.

No doubt the rarest form of history documentary is the *poetic*, yet that is the label one must use for *El Perro Negro* (2004), directed by Peter Forgacs. As suggested earlier in this chapter, the Hungarian director has in the last 20 years made a series of films that fit into this category. The basic materials with which he works are home movies, images shot by amateur film makers who were not intent on documenting, as do news cameraman, major public or apparently historical events, but were more concerned with their families and friends, with weddings, births, parties, sports, vacations, and other leisure-time activities, all of which may be put under the rubric of private history. Forgacs is not the only film maker working with such materials. In America, Alan Berliner, among others, has made use of such home movies to create portraits of generational experience in such works as *A Family Album* (1987). But nobody has pursued this form more assiduously, and nobody has taken on bigger historical topics than Forgacs, who has turned out more than 30 titles in the last 20 years, a large number of them dealing with the European experience from the 1920s to the 1940s.

The growth of Nazism in the years between the World Wars, and in particular, the horrors of World War II and the Holocaust, are so generally well known that their huge, brooding presence over the lives of people in Hungary, Holland, Greece or Germany in that period, allows Forgacs to get away with minimal explanation as to how the private lives he displays on screen are threatened, even doomed by events in the larger political world. In *The Maelstrom* (1997), he can show you a Dutch family calmly packing suitcases and being playful on the night before they are to be shipped from Amsterdam to the East, and we in the audience feel weighted with our knowledge of the fate that awaits them. But with the Spanish Civil War, the subject of *El Perro Negro*, Forgacs cannot assume much understanding on the part of his audience. In today's history texts, and in our general knowledge, that conflict, if remembered at all, is largely seen as a bitter prelude to the great World War that followed. What remains are no more than a few catch phrases – Guernica, Franco, International Brigades, La Pasionaria, the Toledo Alcazar. Which means that in this film Forgacs must find a way of creating the historical context to let us understand the import of what we see.

The majority of the images in *El Perro Negro* come from two amateur film makers, themselves characters in the film and emblems of the larger conflict. The one with the most screen time is Joan Salvans, son of a wealthy Catalan industrialist, whose family lives at La Barata, a vast, hilltop estate near Barcelona. The other is Noriega, a student from Madrid whose background is never fully explained. Through the home movies of the former we see moments in the lives of an upper-class family – weddings, births, dinner parties, dances, outings in the country, trips to Paris – beginning in the late 1920s and ending abruptly in late July, 1936, when during the second week of the war, Joan and his father are murdered by an anarchist named Pedro the Cruel, who was possibly an employee in one of their textile factories. Through the movies of the latter, we see flashes of the revolutionary chaos of Madrid in the first months of the war, then learn a bit about military life on both sides, since Noriega serves briefly in the Republican army, and then is captured and made to join the Nationalists ranks. He lives to film the Nationalist victory parade past cheering multitudes along the Castellana in Madrid in May, 1939, during which Francisco Franco puts the sash of state over his own chest, and the airplanes of the Condor Legion roar over the ranks of marching troops.

In the first half-hour of the film, images of the high life of the Salvans clan are counterpointed by a laconic narration, spoken in the soft voice of the director, which describes the increasing troubles of the political world – the abdication

of the king, the onset and then the problems of the Republic, the street violence between parties of the right and the left, the growth of anarchism (which
has an effect on the Salvans textile factories and leads Joan's father to stand as
a candidate for a right wing party). Occasionally other images and voices break
into the world of the Salvans. An obviously wealthy man seems to discipline
some employees; hungry peasants stare at us from barren fields, and voices –
whose? we don't know – explain how these rich people exploited us, how
much they seemed like devils. (The voices are actors reading segments from
Blood of Spain, an oral history of the war edited by Ronald Fraser, but there is
no way for the casual viewer to know that.) We hear too of Pedro El Cruel,
one of the hundreds of thousands of landless who came from impoverished
Andalucia to work in the factories of Catalonia, an anarchist who spent time in
jail but was released during an amnesty proclaimed by the Republic. We even
see him, or do we? Is he that figure, circled in white, amidst the mass of workers
leaving a factory? The film suggests this but doesn't confirm it. Then the
murder of Salvans senior father and Joan are reported by the voice of the latter's
daughter as we are shown an image of a road, perhaps the one on which they
were ambushed. Perhaps not.

This sort of vagueness continues in the sections on Noriega, who is camp-
ing with a girlfriend in the mountains near the capital when the war breaks
out. Both of them are arrested, held in jail, and then sent Madrid, where he
narrowly avoids being shot. Why this treatment? Perhaps to local radicals he
seems like a conservative, a supporter of the rebellion – but we aren't told and
probably neither was he. For more than a year Noriega avoids military service,
by hiding in his apartment, yet we get images of and reports on life in Madrid,
where wearing a necktie or even spectacles might get you shot as a bourgeois.
Or so the voice that relates his story lets us know. It also describes his own,
divided family, one brother a liberal, one a conservative, one a communist, one
a Falangist. Can this be true? Or is it an obvious metaphor? Perhaps it's
another voice, another family – it's difficult to tell. The same questions hang
over his military service. Somehow after hiding out he is caught and sent to the
front in Estremadura, where he is captured by the Nationalists, put in a camp
for three months, then given a choice of being killed or joining one or another
branch of the military. He chooses the Falange because the pay is higher, and
spends the rest of the war in Estremadura, never engaging in any activity more
hostile than firing his rifle into the air. Some of the images are of Noriega himself, in uniform, with other soldiers. Obviously he has given the camera to a
comrade. He does the same thing on the day he is mustered out, and we are
treated to an evocative scene of him, shot from behind, running away from the
camera, down the empty street of a small village carrying two suitcases, joy in

his stride and the way he swings the bags. All of it seems to say: The war is over and I'm alive.

The description of *El Perro Negro* in the previous two paragraphs can make it seem far more linear and traditional a work than it is. This problem stems from the fact that I am using expository sentences to explain a fragmented, poetic, and often mysterious work whose images are often punctuated or contested by the spare, evocative score of composer Tibor Szemzo, or the haunting sounds of flamenco and other traditional Spanish musical forms. It is not just that the stories of Salvans and Noriega are to some extent intercut, but also the intrusion of those many images in the film that are beautiful and moving, yet inexplicable – moments that perhaps may be metaphors, if only we learn how to read them. What are we to make of the glorious movements of a horse, galloping in a barnyard, then circling back and slowing into a stately trot? Other images seem to be obvious similes – the film cuts from General Millan Astray, a one-armed, one-eyed veteran of the Spanish foreign legion who was best known for his public pronouncement, 'Viva la muerte' (Long live death), directly to the image of a pig. Clear enough, but what of the sequence that follows – a man lifting one pig out of a bunch of them in a pen and tossing it over the wall, with the frame freezing just as the animal leaves his hands. Is this what will happen to Astray? To all of Spain?

In its last third, the film becomes increasingly accelerated, diffuse, even chaotic. Having concluded the story of Salvans and mostly finished that of Noriega, *El Perro Negro* takes on some of the characteristics of a more traditional documentary, but in a hurried and fragmented form which can be difficult to comprehend. The film begins to chronicle military campaigns, touching on battles such as Belchite and the Ebro, using images taken from a plane of the Condor Legion as it bombed Republican lines during the Brunete offensive, letting us hear the words of one of the pilots describing the deaths of the enemy below, depicting captured International Brigaders who are about to be executed, showing naked Italian troops on horseback wading into the Mediterranean (this occurs right after the offensive that cut Spain in two in the Spring of 1938, but we are not told that, nor that the soldiers are Italian), following the flight of Spanish refugees across the French border, letting us see Nationalist soldiers reach that border and give the fascist, stiff-armed salute to the French police. This latter part of the work can be confusing to those who don't already have a knowledge of the events. It's almost as if the form of the film has begun to mirror the growing chaos of the Republic as it lurches towards collapse in the final months of the conflict.

Given this description, someone may wish to raise the question of why *El Perro Negro* should even be considered a history documentary rather than, say, just a work of visual poetry that utilizes images from the Spanish Civil War to evoke general feelings about war, destruction, and the inhumanity of mankind. Put bluntly: how can a work so abstract, poetic, and fragmented in its narrative be considered history? What does it really tell us about the conflict? Such a question points directly to a much larger one: before we give the label history to something, what is it that we do need to know about the past, why do we wish to know it? If history is a matter of piling up traditional data, then *El Perro Negro* doesn't do a very good job. If history is the creation of some sort of clear argument about vanished events, then *El Perro Negro* falls short. Certainly it fails to deliver the kind of straightforward story that one finds in both *Mourir à Madrid* and *The Good Fight*. Even *The Spanish Civil War*, for all its attempt at even-handedness, creates a kind of implicit moral argument about its subject. For its makers cannot help knowing that simply by depicting the Nationalist régime as it was, with its fascist allies, its stiff-armed salutes, and its glorification of traditional Spain of the church, the military, and the dictator as leader, they can count (for the most part) on negative assessments from a contemporary audience suffused with democratic values.

To name *El Perro Negro* (or similar works) as history is to claim that history can include forms beyond the discourse that tries to understand the past, and can include the notion of encountering the past as a site of the sublime, something which may be experienced in flashes but never explained. Yet this is a sublime that arises from a particular historical scene, as the narration and many of the images make clear. This is Spain in those three years of war. These are images of people who lived at that time. At one moment they danced, gave birth, took part in rallies, stood before burning churches, fled from bombs dropped from on high, huddled in trenches, and fired weapons in a war whose causes they may or may not have understood and may or may not have believed, but which thrust them into this dangerous moment of time that we now observe from afar. *El Perro Negro* presents us with bits of lives, mini-narratives, fragments of voices, horrendous images, even moments of humour and good cheer, and says all these different worlds existed at once, and this too was the Spanish Civil War. In a way, the film creates a kind of counter history, a challenge to the viewer to make sense out of its disparate elements. Perhaps this makes it an esoteric history, one intended for people who already have some knowledge of the war. Yet of all the documentaries I have seen on the conflict, this is the one that, after years of study, I find the most startling and provocative, a commentary on the others and all that I know about the war. If one of the tasks of history is to make familiar events of the past strange, that is, to make one see them anew, then *El Perro Negro* is definitely history.

Implicit in films like *The Spanish Civil War, Mourir à Madrid*, and *The Good Fight* is the notion that each is conveying *the* story, the *true* story of its subject. My critique, especially of the latter two, is not simply that no single film or book can create *the* true story because, as we well know, the evidence from the past can be used to produce a variety of true stories depending upon how we interpret that evidence, but that these particular documentaries ignore evidence that runs contrary to their theses. Such a practice is, let me suggest, common in history documentaries, which are far more likely than written works (certainly academic books) to erase rather than explore inconvenient moments, events, and ideas. By contrast, the narrative strategies and the aesthetic of *El Perro Negro* work against any such claim. There is a modesty in this sort of history, a willingness to allow the viewer to decide what lessons to take away from the many events depicted. The contemporary viewer will likely be more sympathetic to the Republic than to the Nationalists, who can harbour a figure like the death-loving General Millan Astray. Yet this same viewer will have to wonder: what did Joan Salvans and his father do to get themselves killed? Is being a factory owner an excuse for a death sentence? The personalizing of history by home movies – this is not a rich industrialist but a particular man and his family – seems to raise moral questions that other films can subsume into abstract categories (how easy it can be for a film to not say but simply suggest that 'rich industrialists' who exploit workers deserve to be removed).

To make this critique is not to suggest that the documentary is not capable of creating works of history that tell us something valuable about the past, it is only to suggest something about the limits (and perhaps strengths) of the form. Elsewhere I have written of *The Good Fight* as a kind of history as homage, and *Mourir à Madrid* clearly belongs in that same category (Rosenstone 1989). Which is only to say that the history documentary can tell us, as both of these films do, a great deal about the past, but in viewing them it is necessary to understand that whatever their claims, the real aim is a particular sort of truth, one calculated to make the viewer feel strongly about some aspect of the past. However serious the intent, the documentarist works with a different set of rules and expectations than the academic historian. The best statement of the aim and practice of such film makers comes from the experienced documentary director, Alan Rosenthal: 'I want to put my viewers in touch with historical reality. I want, using a certain artistry, to convey important ideas to people who know little of the subject. I want to encourage the viewers to ask questions after the viewing. I want to tell a good story that will engage both the head and the intelligence, and the heart and the emotions. I want to put viewers in touch with the past in a way that academics can't do.

I want to help them keep memories alive. And I want to recall a forgotten history or an overlooked piece of history that seems to me important. Obviously . . . I can't give them reality but I can give them a credible representation of reality and tell them certain things about it which may affect who they are and how they view the world' (Rosenthal 2005).

Is this not the real task of history? Certainly it is for any and every sort of history that is put on film.

Chapter 6

Telling lives

Nobody ever has anything good to say about the biographical film – a form usually dismissed with a kind of sneer as the 'biopic'. Though over the last 45 years, 14 of the Academy Awards for Best Picture have gone to such films, these have presumably been given for dramatic excellence rather than historical insight or truth. Critic Ronald Bergan expresses a kind of common wisdom when he writes (appropriating a line from Roland Barthes): 'the biopic is a fiction that dare not speak its name . . . (it takes) people's real lives and transforms them into the realms of myth' (Bergan 1983: 22). The only scholar to investigate the topic at length, George F. Custen, puts the negative case in stronger terms: 'Hollywood biography is to history what Caesar's Palace is to architectural history: an enormous, engaging distortion, which after a time convinces us of its own kind of authenticity' (Custen 1992: 7).

These judgements refer to the products of Hollywood, and largely to films made in the era of the studio system, and they ignore independent films or those shot in the rest of the world. Custen's book, *Biopic*, focuses on the years 1927–60, though in a later essay he brings the study up to 1980 (Custen 2000). If the subjects of biographical films change somewhat in the latter period, with the lives of more women and more people born outside the United States depicted on screen, the author finds little change in the overall shape and meaning of the form. The biopic is 'based on the cosmology of the movie industry . . . In this view of history, the greatness of the individual figure becomes that set of qualities that made a producer great or powerful in Hollywood rather than those traits that characterized the famous person in his or her own lifetime' (Custen 1992: 4–5).

One problem with this assertion is that while Custen deals extensively with the mores and practices of Hollywood, he never gets around to actually testing to what extent the latter half of it may be true – that is, he fails to place biopics into the larger discourse surrounding particular figures. Given his overall aim as a Professor of Communications, which is to chart the patterns of such films over time, this may be an understandable lapse. But a lapse that is certain to leave unsatisfied anyone interested in the problems of shaping biography, of just how one can render a life – either in words on the page or in images on screen (or in any other way). If Custen is uninterested in the contents of biography, Bergan takes a particularly narrow view of its traditions and practices. He warns that we should not go to the biopic 'as we do to a literary biography, to learn the facts of lives under scrutiny' (Bergan 1983: 22). But is that the reason we go to biographies – to learn the facts? Interesting as they may be, facts could be delivered with chronicles and lists of data. If facts were the aim, we would have no need of the literary form of the biography as it has developed for over two millenia.

The life story, as delivered in words, has a long history and a longer tradition. To begin to understand the biographical film – its shape and structure, the way it handles data, the way it creates the world in which its subject thinks, feels, and acts – one must attempt to see the form within the larger issues of biography. To do biography is to make the case that individuals are either at the centre of the historical process – or are worth studying as exemplars of lives, actions, and individual value systems we either admire or dislike. But exactly how you do biography has been a matter of debate as long as the telling of lives has been a literary endeavour – for more than two millenia in the West. Over this span of time, notions of the aims and purposes of the form have often shifted, and one looks in vain for some consensus across the ages. Is biography the story of great people (for most of history, men) we wish to emulate, or great villains we wish to condemn? Should it focus on public life or (as more recently) personal life? Should it show its subject as a creature of the times or someone whose rises above history and helps to create the times, or somehow split the difference and have it both ways?

Today, decades after literary theorists have turned their critical eyes upon the genre, little about biography has been settled. Ultimately it seems to be an elusive, perhaps even an undefinable form. Both those who write biographies and theorists (many of the latter are also the former) have a great deal of trouble reaching any consensus, or explaining in any systematic (or even non-systematic) way, exactly what elements make for a good biography. To read in the field is to understand that biography possesses no hard and fast rules. The one thing you can say is that it is always a highly interpretive act, a work that inevitably includes fictional components – here using 'fiction' in its original meaning from Latin, in the sense of 'formed'. Yet many who write on the topic also are willing to admit that the genre often contains doses of fiction in the more modern sense of 'an imaginative creation'.

Roland Barthes put it simply, calling biography (in the phrase that Ronald Bergan lifted) 'the fiction that dare not speak its name'. Others have elaborated on this insight. Carolyn Heilbrun asks, 'Who can write a biography without inventing a life? A biographer, like a writer of fiction, imposes a pattern upon events, invents a protagonist, and discovers the pattern of his or her life' (Heilbrun 1993: 297). Paula Backscheider expands upon this notion: 'The best biographers know that they are inventing through their selection and arrangement of materials; they are establishing cause and effect and other relationships, and they are determining what was most formative and important for someone else, someone they do not know. They must choose what to include, leave out, emphasize, and subordinate, and when they do, they have constructed a narrative that, whether they are aware of it or not, partakes of cultural stories with expectations for resolutions and interpretations built in. Narrative becomes the life and the basis for the judgements that will be rendered about the subject' (Backscheider 2000: 18).

It may seem surprising to start an essay on biography with its fictional elements, since common wisdom see facts as the basis of a life. But the relationship between fact and the *story* of a life has always been tenuous and shifting. Too much fact, too many details, and you are likely to bury your subject by smothering the larger interpretive patterns that make us understand (or so we think) a life – as we can see by looking at the three- and four-volume lives which entombed so many nineteenth-century politicians, statesmen and military leaders. True, the importance of fact in, and to, biography has grown over the last two centuries, paralleling the growth of empiricism in the human sciences as well as larger changes in the cultural and historical climate. Yet most theorists of the form understand, as Ira Nadel points out in *Biography: Fiction, Fact, and Form*, that facts alone cannot explain the configuration that constitutes a life. Often biographers depart from facts or bend them in order to create a particular atmosphere or mood or a more consistent figure of a historical person. The aim in such cases, which Nadel traces back to the 1830s, has been 'Boswellian understanding rather than Baconian data' (Nadel 1984: 6).

Ultimately the relationship between fact and fiction, content and form in biography becomes what Hayden White has called a problem of the writing: 'we make sense of the world by imposing on it the formal coherency that we customarily associate with fiction'. It is this fictive power which explains how biography translates fact into literary event. According to Nadel, we resolve our own sense of fragmentation through the unity or story of the lives of others'. (White 1978: 99) For him it is precisely this fictive story which provides us with a coherent vision of life.

Questions of the boundary lines between fact and fiction in the representation of past lives also mark the literature on the historical novel. Without making a real excursion into that field, I simply wish to draw on Sir Walter Scott, the major figure in that genre in the English language, for some insight into problems of telling lives. Scott was an author who well understood that it was impossible to reproduce the past as it really had been, that part of his task involved a great deal of 'translation' (his word) in order to make a long vanished world accessible to his audience. In the dedication to *Ivanhoe*, he confronts this question directly by explaining he is not, after all, writing in Anglo Saxon or Norman French (the languages of the period in which the story is set) but in modern English – which is a first and basic sort of translation. But there are others as well. For example it is impossible, Scott admits, to confine his vocabulary, ideas, and sense of life entirely within limits of timeframe in which the story unfolds because part of his task is to convey this lost world to a modern audience: 'It is necessary for exciting interest or any kind that the subject assumed should be, as it were, translated into the manners as well as the language, of the age we live in . . .' (Scott 1900: xlvii; Lukacs 1983: 62).

The imposed fiction of a story, the creative use of fact, the translation necessary to make a life comprehensible and interesting – all these elements that are part of traditional biographical writing (and the historical novel) also mark the biographical film (where part of the translation involves the use of the visual media and sound.) The latter, in short, belongs to a long tradition. What this means is that the written biography and the biographical film are less different than they may appear to be. The overall project of telling a life is similar in both media. Biographer and film maker both appropriate some of the trace details left by a life and weave them into a story which has a theme that infuses meaning into the days of their subject. The resulting work is ultimately based less on the raw data than on that data incorporated into a vision created by the literary (or filmic) skills of the biographer. That is why very different bios can be made about the life of the same individual, without any new data having been found. (Like the director of the historical film, the biographer on film also must 'invent' fact to meet the double demands of the dramatic form and the timeframe of film. For an explication of this notion, see Chapter 2.)

As the major sub-genre of the history film, the biofilm represents an enormous field. Custen enumerates 396 such works produced in Hollywood between 1927 and 1980. This is but the tip of a huge iceberg, for not only does his study omit the last quarter century, it wholly ignores works made in other parts of the world (including countries like Britain, Germany, France, Italy, and

Japan, which have rich film traditions), and never mentions a single one of the vast number of biofilms that have been produced for television all over the globe in the last half century. Given the size and the universality of the genre, and the difficulties of locating or viewing more than a tiny fraction of them, generalizations about the biofilm must be tentative. Yet years of tracking such works suggest to me that the form can be seen in terms of three (admittedly) baggy and arbitrary categories: the biopic of Hollywood's studio era; the 'serious' biofilm which has for a long time been made in Europe and other parts of the world, and has more recently come to Hollywood; and the innovative or experimental bio, which presents a life in the form of a fragmented or achronological drama rather than a traditional linear story. (A fourth form, the documentary film biography, follows the formal properties I have mentioned in Chapter 4 and will not be dealt with separately here.)

In each of these categories, significant works have been created – films that provide knowledge of, insight into, and interpretation of the lives of individuals; films that let us see, hear, and understand a great deal about not only the person but, in many cases, his or her historical milieu. In each category, we can find works which fulfill Nadel's definition of biography as 'fundamentally a narrative which has as its primary task the enactment of character and place through language . . .' (Nadel 1984: 8). A major difference here is that the word, 'language', must be made to include notions of 'image', 'colour', and 'sound'. Those additions, along with the changes that occur when biography is turned from a literary narrative into a dramatic production, ensure that the biofilm will always deliver a rather different figure from what we get in a written biography. This difference means that such films may not only be seen as a new form of biography, but one that at its best can also serve to highlight some of the shortcomings of the written genre.

The contribution of the biofilm, at least to historians, may seem most obvious in the second category, what I have labelled 'the serious biofilm'. By this I mean films in which the director has either worked closely with an historical consultant and/or adhered faithfully to events as recounted in one or more written biographies, and in doing so has indulged in a minimal amount of invention with regard to characters and events. Into this category we could place such films as director Margarethe Von Trotta's *Rosa Luxemburg* (1986), a portrait of the pre-World War I, Polish-born leader of the German Social Democratic Party; Andrzej Wajda's *Korczak* (1990), which tells the story of the famed medical doctor and educational leader who could have left the Warsaw Ghetto but instead stayed with the school and went off to Auschwitz with his children; or Julie Taymore's *Frida* (2002), which tells of the life, loves, and art of Mexican painter Frida Kahlo. All three have been criticized for their portraits, but such has had more to do with their emphases than with invention. Objections have been voiced to the intrusion of Luxemburg's stormy love relationships into the intensely political world of the German left-ist leader; to what has been called an apparently upbeat ending that has Dr Korczak leading his students off the boxcar bound for Auschwitz and into a summer field, where they disappear into bright sunlight; and to the downplaying of Kahlo's activities as a committed member of the Mexican Communist Party (which went alongside those of the painter of her own tortured body and soul).

The response to such critiques is not difficult to make. First, love relation-ships were, as Luxemburg's published letters show, not something marginal to her career but exceedingly important to her both personally and theoret-ically, as part of the exploration of one's full human potential which she advocated. Second, since it is well known (at least by the presumed Polish audience) that Korczak went to his death with his students, the upbeat ending of the film is not meant literally but is better seen as a metaphor, to indicate something about the overall character of the man, the courage and strength of his self-sacrifice, as well as, perhaps a belief in an afterlife. Third, since Frida Kahlo is known primarily for her paintings (which have a great deal of personal but little social content) as well as her relationship with Diego Rivera, the downplaying of her political beliefs, however fervently held, is no more than part of a strategy to highlight what is her real contribution to the world of art. These responses are not meant to put an end to criticism, but only to illustrate that at least these biofilms (and, obviously, others) can be debated for their overall portraits in much the same way as one would debate any traditional biography – less over the accuracy of individual bits of data than over the whole interpretation.

More surprising than the claim that such 'serious' biofilms present plaus-ible portraits of their subjects may be the assertion that even in the standard Hollywood biopic, it is possible to find an important interpretation of a life – and even suggestions about a different sort of biographical thinking. Drawing on the scholarship of J.E. Smythe, I wish to make such an argument for direc-tor John Ford's *Young Mr Lincoln*. This 1939 film was hailed on its release by the well-known critic and early film historian, Terry Ramsaye, as a unique biographical work which went beyond a mere recording of historical events. But enthusiasm for the film as biography has not been shared by later scholars – least of all, historians. Lincoln experts see it as 'a historical travesty and folksy perversion'. Mark Reinhart, author of a book about Lincoln on screen, writes: 'It is unfortunate that *Young Mr Lincoln* has come to be regarded by many as one of the greatest portrayals of all time, because the film's script and Henry Fonda's performance do not accurately reflect the Lincoln of History' (Smythe 2003: 194).

The problem for such critics is twofold: first, that Ford's film is full of invented or imagined situations (Lincoln standing down a lynch mob or settling a case between two clients by threatening to bang their heads together); and second, that it completely distorts chronology by bringing into temporal proximity events which happened years apart. Most egregiously, the film moves Lincoln's famous legal victory, the 1858 William 'Duff' Armstrong murder trial, back to a much earlier point in his career. And while the film remains true to the dramatic climax of the trial, in which Lincoln famously uses an almanac on the phases of the moon to show it was too dark for a witness to have seen what he claimed to have seen, the film drastically alters many of the specific events and circumstances of that trial.

Young Mr Lincoln is a long way, however, from being a complete invention. Nor does it wholly ignore data. The dramatic opening scene shows the young attorney making his first electoral speech in 1832, in the precise words recorded by his law partner, William Herndon: 'My politics are short and sweet, like the old woman's dance.' But it's not solely the words that create the character. The body language of actor Henry Fonda as the lanky frontiersman, slouching on the porch railing of a store before his talk, moving awkwardly into position in front of the small crowd, fiddling with his hands, and speaking in a high, mid-western drawl – all these elements perfectly exemplify how film can create a kind of dimensional, almost tactile historical figure in a way that is beyond the capabilities of the written word. Here a skilled performer takes what we know from historical accounts (that Lincoln started out as an awkward, country rube and never fully shed those characteristics) and embodies that knowledge into movements and moments which allow the audience to feel as if they are (apparently) witnessing the past.

By studying the production history of *Young Mr Lincoln*, Smythe is able to show that these changes and fictions were neither mistakes nor attempts to make the film more commercial, but deliberate strategies on the part of producer Daryl Zanuck, screenwriter Lamar Trotti, and director John Ford (all of whom were to some extent versed in Lincoln studies) to compare the 'human' Lincoln with the 'monumental' Lincoln that in the 1930s dominated both textbooks and the national mind. In doing so, they created a 'more subtle engagement with the past' than one finds in most historical films of that era. The 'sense of history' in this work 'does not depend upon reflecting or transcribing the standard version of the past with the careful arrangement of dates and documents, but rather *attempts to compare the conflicting sources of knowledge* (my emphasis) about Lincoln's life and image.' This is a bold move by Smythe to stake out a new role for the traditional biopic. Indeed, she goes on to suggest (unfortunately with little evidence, for it's a choice idea, and one worth serious investigation) that *Young Mr Lincoln* is part of a larger movement in which 'certain Hollywood film makers during the "classical" era were generating a new approach to American historical cinema' (Smythe 2003: 207–8).

Without necessarily accepting this larger claim, one can certainly celebrate *Young Mr Lincoln* (though clearly a 'fictional biography') as a work that fulfills Nadel's definition of biography as a narrative which well enacts 'character and place'. The film gives us a story of a poor man on the make, trying to get ahead in the commercial and political world of Springfield, Illinois, a town not that far removed from frontier days, but one that already boasts an upper class given to airs about their superiority over the likes of him. The portrait of the future president is largely positive, but no more so than the ones drawn in the standard biographies, such as the most recent work by David Donald. Like the written versions of his life, this Lincoln may be slightly idealized, but he is hardly a stainless hero. When Abe settles that case by threatening, in a half friendly, half hostile manner, to knock his clients' heads together, or when he cheats at the 4 July tug of war, helping his team to win by tying the end of the rope to a horse, we see something of the origins of the shrewd, calculating, ambitious politician who manoeuvred himself to the White House – hardly a place where you end up by accident. The Lincoln of this film may be admirable, but he is no icon. Indeed, the final sequence, a direct cut from the young attorney who has emerged victorious from the trial to the image of the marble Lincoln of the Washington memorial, suggests much about the difference between frail flesh and blood and the monuments we make out of our heros.

More provocative as portraits and perhaps more suggestive in terms of the possibilities of biography are those works that can be placed at one end of the spectrum – innovative or experimental biofilms. Elsewhere I have devoted an entire essay to one of these, *Walker*, direct by Alex Cox, a film about the monomaniacal American buccaneer who invaded Nicaragua with a small army in the 1850s, stayed on to become that country's president, and upon being pushed out by armies from other Central American countries, burned the capital city of Granada to the ground. Cast as a kind of black and absurdist comedy, and full of overt anachronisms (Mercedes automobiles, *Time* magazine, and computer terminals in the 1850s), the film nonetheless both absorbs and comments upon a long tradition of representing the man and his adventures. Through the acting of Ed Harris, *Walker* also provides a stunning portrait of what we might call the 'democratic imperialist', the fervent believer in traditional American values who, under the guise of exporting them to less fortunate people, becomes a monstrous figure who helps to destroy other countries (Rosenstone 1992).

Also suggestive is *32 Short Films About Glenn Gould*, a portrait of the great Canadian pianist, which to a certain extent follows the form of his most famous recording, Johann Sebastian Bach's *The Goldberg Variations*. The film takes as its themes Gould's creativity and eccentricities, and puts them alongside his musical genius. While there is a vaguely linear overall structure – the first of the 32 films deal with his childhood, the last ones with his decline and death – the variations break into discrete, disconnected segments that ultimately form into what might be called a multi-perspectival or cubist portrait of the pianist. Lengths of the segments vary widely; so do the genres. Some sequences are acted moments in the life by professionals (to call them 'dramatized' would be to suggest more intensity than any of them possesses); others are talking head interviews with associates and friends of the pianist; a few are wholly abstract, the dance of hammers along the strings inside a piano; or sequential close-ups of the enormous number of strangely beautiful pills Gould took daily; or animated abstract forms moving in time to one of his recordings. If these fragments purposefully do not coalesce, they certainly work to create a strong sense of a character and place – Gould the man obsessed by music; the loner and extreme hypochondriac; the person who so disliked close human contact that he communicated with friends over the telephone, who retreated from public performance to the recording studio and proclaimed the concert hall is dead, who loved the isolated purity of the frozen north so much that he created a radio series about its wilderness, yet who understood the world of finance well enough to exhibit a great genius for playing the stock market. The lack of a linear narrative does not prevent, but is crucial to, the creation of a deep and dimensional portrait of a complex and talented human being.

To explore the potential and reach of the biofilm, to see the form in a larger context, I want to examine three dramatic features about the life of a single figure, John Reed, the American poet, journalist, and revolutionary, whose book, *Ten Days That Shook the World*, is the classic account of the Bolshevik Revolution. That these films – *Reed – Insurgent Mexico* (1973), by Mexican director Paul Leduc; *Red Bells* (1982), by Soviet director Sergei Bondarchuk; and *Reds* (1981), by American director Warren Beatty – are the products of different traditions and film makers with clearly different ideologies will help to suggest something about the range and possibilities of the genre.

[In the interest of full disclosure, I must explain another factor that has helped to determine this choice: I published a biography of Reed – *Romantic Revolutionary: A Biography of John Reed* (1975) – and later served for eight years as historical consultant in both the pre-production and the filming stages of *Reds*. This sort of insider knowledge can only help my analysis, for as I have argued elsewhere, historical films are best evaluated against the discourse of the topic with which they deal, and I have been immersed in the discourse on Reed for decades now. On the release of *Reds*, I wrote an essay that was critical of certain aspects of the film. Twenty plus years later, I find that my criticism fails to take into account something important – that *Reds* speaks not in literary but in film language (Rosenstone 1982).]

The three biofilms may be devoted to the same subject, but they are quite different in their approach and aesthetic qualities, as well as in the period of the life which they cover. One thing they do share is a similar theme, a theme which also tends to drive biographical books about Reed – the desire to explain how and why this privileged young man from a wealthy Portland, Oregon family, this Harvard graduate who in his twenties became one of the highest paid reporters in the United States, ended up not just writing about two revolutions (Mexico and Russia) but ultimately embracing the Bolsheviks, helping to organize the Communist Labour Party of the United States, attending as a delegate the Second Congress of the Communist International in Moscow in 1920, and going off to the Soviet-sponsored Congress of the People of the East in Baku, where he contracted the typhus that led to his death. His body lay in state as a hero of the revolution before Reed was buried alongside other Russian notables in the embankment in front of the Kremlin wall.

My own book on Reed carries him from the cradle to the grave in some 400 pages or 130,000 words. This gives ample space to elaborate on everything from family antecedents (his maternal grandfather was one of the richest pioneers in Oregon), to early psychological development (he was a sickly child who had to struggle to overcome some early physical handicaps and fears), to the multiple contexts in which he lived – from the social movements of his childhood (his father was a militant progressive who exposed corruption in the Oregon timber industry); to the battles for political and educational reform in early twentieth-century Harvard (he was active as a journalist and member of the Socialist Club and various international societies); to the artistic and sexual ferment of Greenwich Village in the teens (where modernism in the arts, personal liberation, sexual experimentation, and political radicalism were the norm); to the desert and mountains of Northern Mexico where he rode as a correspondent with the troops of Pancho Villa (he sympathized with the peons exploited by large landowners); to the trenches on both the Western and Eastern fronts during the early years of the First World War (a senseless slaughter for no purpose, as he saw it, other than to benefit capitalism); to the excitement of Petrograd during what he would label as the great Ten Days (which seemed a culmination of the radicalism espoused in Greenwich Village). If the film makers do not have the luxury of detailing all these phenomena as a way of explaining Reed's movement towards revolution, each is able to evoke a number of them. (And one can certainly question whether these factors do ultimately explain that decision, or are they simply the necessary but not necessarily sufficient conditions? Indeed, to what extent is any written biography a real explanation of the person rather than an educated hypothesis about the meaning of a life.)

Unlike written biographies, biofilms rarely attempt to cover the entire span of a life. To this general rule, the Reed films are no exception. The one with the narrowest timeframe, the hour and forty-five minute *Reed – Insurgent Mexico*, deals with no more than half of the four-month period the young journalist spent in Mexico, and focuses on three segments: his weeks with the horseback troops of General Tomas Urbina, his meetings with Pancho Villa in Chihuahua, and his days in the front lines during the battle to seize the strategic city of Torreon. *Red Bells* (1982) actually consists of two two-hour films – the first devoted to Reed in Mexico and the second to his weeks in Petrograd before and during the Bolshevik Revolution. Unlike *Insurgent Mexico*, each of these films encompasses Reed's relationship with a woman – in the first case, his wealthy lover, Mabel Dodge; in the second, his wife, Louise Bryant. *Reds* (1981), save for a one-shot, opening sequence, begins after his Mexican adventures and takes three hours and fifteen minutes to follow Reed from his first meeting with Louise Bryant in Portland Oregon in 1915 to his death in Moscow in the fall of 1920. Unlike the other works, this film devotes a great deal of time to his personal life, particularly the relationship with Louise, as well as to the milieus in which he flourished – the radical sub-culture of Greenwich Village in the teens, the world of professional journalism, the Socialist sects out of which the Communist Labour Party grew, and the revolutionary environment of Petrograd and Moscow.

Insurgent Mexico, shot in sepia tone no doubt to emulate the photos of the early twentieth century, is a film in which the personal is stressed more than the public life. Reed is the focus of attention in every sequence, and though the visual and verbal languages (point of view shots, cutaways, conversations) provide glimpses of larger issues of exploitation, injustice, and revolution, the camera always returns to events seen and experienced by Reed – his tentative entrance into Mexico against a flow of refugees; his journey south in a peddler's wagon to the hacienda of General Urbina; the challenges from and friendships with the uneducated, fearsome horseback soldiers of what he calls *La Tropa*; the cross-country trip to the front lines at the hacienda of La Cadena; the flight for his life when the enemy attacks and decimates Urbina's troops; the reunion with the remnants of *La Tropa* in another town; the evening when he saves a girl from being violated and allows her to sleep in his bed while he curls up on the floor; the interviews with Pancho Villa in Chihuahua; and the journey with the revolutionary army to the major offensive on Torreon.

The story recounted plays with chronology for dramatic effect (e.g. Reed actually got to know Villa before joining Urbina). But then Reed's own auto-biographical report, *Insurgent Mexico*, does the same thing and often in much the same way (Reed 1959). Most of the incidents and a good portion of the dialogue come directly from its pages. One way to read the book is as a coming-of-age story, a tale of a naïve young American achieving manhood and political insight through his companionship with the men of *La Tropa* and his encounters with Villa – what is subtext on his pages becomes the organizing theme of the film. At first the youthful Reed seems to be a cool, collected sort who, when asked by soldiers why he doesn't carry a gun, makes the argument that for the revolution to succeed, words are as important as deeds. That these attitudes are something of a façade becomes clear when, at a fiesta, a drunken Reed confesses his fears to a close comrade that he is not the man his father was, a true battler who died in his struggles against corrupt power. He sees himself as a dreamer, someone who never goes all the way, who is afraid to plunge fully into the fray, who remains a reporter because, even though he loves the revolutionary cause, he fears death on the battlefield.

Personal troubles intersect with social issue when he raises the question of journalistic 'objectivity' with a group of American reporters just before the battle of Torreon. Reed wonders aloud if, when one sees injustice, conveying the facts to the world is enough. In such a situation, isn't there a need to act? He comes close to doing just that during an evening assault, but as Jack prepares to toss a primitive grenade, Pancho Villa shows up on horseback and takes it away from him, shouting 'You're a journalist, not a soldier. I need journalists more than soldiers!' The climax comes the next day when Reed walks through the streets of a liberated town. As the victorious troops ride by, yelling and firing their guns in the air, he takes off his jacket, wraps it around his right hand, and smashes the plate glass window of a store – and the frame freezes, ending the film, save for a voiceover which links Mexico to his later time in Russia. This final action, invented and gratuitous, is not from the book. Clearly, it is the director's attempt to create a visual metaphor that expresses Reed's commitment to the revolution, as well as foreshadowing future actions which would not transfer well to the screen within this narrative – his passionate articles in favour of the Mexican revolution; the interview with President Woodrow Wilson in which he urged military backing for Villa; the writing of *Insurgent Mexico* itself, which turned Villa into a hero and Reed into one of the most highly visible journalists in the country; and finally, his involvement three years later as a partisan in the Bolshevik Revolution.

Red Bells lies at the far end of the biofilm spectrum from *Insurgent Mexico* – in scope, style, and vision. The two-hour segment dealing with Mexico is an epic, a spectacle in colour and widescreen in which our hero disappears from sight for long periods of time while we watch thousands of horseback and foot soldiers engage in bloody military actions, riding across vast, desert land-scapes, attacking huge, walled haciendas, and battling their way through the narrow streets of adobe villages. Large portions of the film depict events that Reed never witnessed; this includes two long sections devoted to the struggles of Emiliano Zapata's revolutionary forces in Morelos, hundreds of miles south of his location. (Reed did have a strong desire to cover Zapata, but this move was vetoed by his editors in New York.) Some of the historical detail and con-text is delivered in voiceovers from two different sources – Reed's own writ-ings on Mexico, and a god-like 'voice of history', which moralizes, explains the significance of what we see on screen, and flashes forward to his later career.

Unlike the more intimate Mexican film, *Red Bells I* provides a series of flash-backs to earlier events in Reed's life. A couple of sequences suggest his grow-ing political consciousness – Jack gets arrested during a labour dispute; or he hotly discusses the Mexican Revolution with other editors in the offices of the *Metropolitan Magazine*. But the majority of them provide visions of the world of glamour, celebrity, and ease which he left behind. At the centre of that world is Mabel Dodge, the wealthy hostess of a Manhattan salon, who after becoming Reed's lover, whisks him off to her villa near Florence, where leisure activities are the order of the day. Together they attend lively fiestas in nearby villages, black-tie piano recitals in the villa's elegant public rooms, or make love in Mabel's sumptuous bedroom. Representing a world in which Art (with a capital letter) is the highest value, she keeps trying to make Jack forget the world of social concerns, abandon journalism, and return to his earlier forms of creative writing – 'You are a poet', she says over and over. 'This is a marvellous place to forget the world and write poetry.'

The film relates many of the same events as does *Insurgent Mexico* (but depicted far more lavishly – not one woman making tortillas as the troops pre-pare for battle, but ten women; not fifty soldiers in La Tropa, but five hun-dred), and the flashbacks do the same work as the confession in the earlier film – they let us see the young man's internal struggles. In *Red Bells I* Reed finds himself tugged between two sorts of worlds, the lavish but effete life style of Mabel and the more urgent, rugged life of front line journalism – a life which also suggests commitment to the downtrodden of the world. The choice has really been made before the film begins, but to drive home the point the film depicts a nervous Reed, huddled with Mexican troops in the trenches near Torreon, who suddenly overcomes his fear, charges up a hill into gunfire alongside Villa's troops, and stops to toss a hand grenade at the enemy. His joy in the explosion indicates that he has joined the revolutionary movement.

Red Bells II has the same epic qualities as the first, only here the mass movements involve sailors, soldiers and factory workers who play out their revolutionary drama on the huge stage of Petrograd, with its broad boulevards, huge squares, and lavish palaces, its churches, fortresses, canals, and bridges that span the wide Neva River. Once again Reed disappears for long stretches of time as we watch the unfolding of revolutionary events, many of which he only learned about through rumour and report. This time his female companion is his wife, Louise Bryant who, unlike Reed, never fully embraces the revolution. Even less than *Red Bells I* does this film attempt to explain much about the man before his arrival in Petrograd. No wonder. It was aimed at a Russian audience for whom Reed was a schoolbook hero, a legendary foreigner who, like the Marquis de Lafayette in America, helped to support the fledgling Soviet Union in its hour of need, and for that was buried as a hero in front of the Kremlin Wall. To Soviet citizens there was as little need to explain Reed as there was for the makers of *Young Mr Lincoln* to explain young Abe's later career. But familiarity in this case leads in the opposite direction – not towards the personal but towards the social. Reed in *Red Bells II* is largely an emblem, an eyewitness to history, a man whose biographical importance is that he was there, he saw the great events, recorded them, and embraced the cause.

The opening sequence has Reed on his deathbed, delirious from typhus fever, while Louise hovers over him. Her voiceover reminiscences lead to the extended flashback which constitutes the remainder of the film, the story of the revolutionary events through which they lived together. Most of the incidents are taken directly from the pages of *Ten Days That Shook the World*, but the accomplishment of *Red Bells II* lies less in its dramatic story than in its filmic qualities of movement, production design, and montage. Events set in original settings – Smolny Institute, where delegates to the Second Congress of the Soviets debate while members of the Military Revolutionary Committee plot the takeover of the country; the Marinsky Palace, where the representatives of the doomed Provisional Government indulge in passionate but ineffectual speeches; the Winter Palace, where Prime Minister Alexander Kerensky manoeuvres and confers with diplomats and ministers; the Nevsky Prospekt, where speakers harangue crowds and the masses mysteriously ebb and flow – convey the multiple, clashing worlds of Petrograd in October 1917, the confusion, uncertainties, plans, counter plans, doubts, plots, arguments, threats, and rumours that roiled the city. One extended sequence, enormously evocative of the clashes and contradictions of the revolutionary situation, cuts back and forth between a ballet at the elegant Marinsky Theatre – Louise and Jack, wearing formal dress, are in attendance – and the restless streets of the city, with the young American always on the move through the crowds, asking questions, listening to debates, talking to workers, eavesdropping on conversations, watching the newly formed Red Guards drill, trying unsuccessfully to find out what groups have ordered particular roadblocks in front of the Kazan Cathedral – the Provisional Government, the Soviets, the military? Nobody seems to know.

The climax for Reed, the Bolsheviks, and the film is the taking of the Winter Palace. Unlike the sequence in Sergei Eisenstein's *October*, this one does not depict a huge battle, but something more like the token resistance that historians record (though once the Palace is entered we see literally tens of thousands of people streaming through Palace Square). Reed and Louise are there – as they were historically. Twice, earlier in the film, she has turned to him and asked: 'Jack, are you now a Bolshevik?' Each time he has equivocated, saying words to the effect, 'I like what they're doing', or 'I'm beginning to think so'. In the final sequence, as he starts to follow the troops towards the Winter Palace, she asks him once again. This time his answer is clear: 'I'm with them.' A minute later, as he watches Red Guards climb a barricade before the Palace door, he punctuates his statement by pumping his fist in the air and shouting: 'Hooray. Hooray. Hooray.'

Compared to a traditional written biography that follows a subject from birth to death, *Reds* focuses on a short period in the life of its subject. Yet compared to the other films discussed here, it covers a rather large portion of his life – the last 5 of his 33 years. Its geographical canvas is also broad, with American sequences set in Portland, Oregon, New York City, and Provincetown, Massachusetts, and foreign ones in France, Finland, Petrograd, Moscow, and Baku. If *Insurgent Mexico* may be seen as a coming-of-age tale, and the two chapters of *Red Bells* as epics in which the individual is less important than great events, *Reds* is a love story or domestic drama in which almost as much screen time is devoted to Louise Bryant as to Jack Reed. One might even see it as edging towards a double biography, though for all its attempt at gender equality, the film leaves little doubt that without Reed's career there would be no story to tell.

Despite the longer span of life depicted, *Reds* fails to tell us very much about Reed's background. Only the first few sequences, set in his hometown of Portland on one of his rare trips home, let us see that he is from a wealthy family and a conservative social milieu whose members clearly don't understand his politics. (When Jack says he is collecting money for *The Masses*, perhaps the leading leftist and modernist magazine in the United States, a relative asks: 'Is that a religious publication?') The film begins with Reed in his late twenties and at the height of his fame – an acclaimed journalist due to his reports from Mexico, an admired leader of the radical Bohemian subculture of Greenwich Village, and something of a ladies' man. Louise, a married woman who has been attracted to Portland's famous son from afar, initiates their relationship by requesting an interview following a public lecture on the World War that he delivers at the Liberal Club. At her studio, they have an intense, political conversation that lasts until dawn. During their second meeting, as they stroll in a park at night, she pushes things along by saying: 'I'd like to see what you look like with your pants off, Mr Reed.' He obliges.

The remainder of the first half of the film (it is divided by an intermission) intertwines their stormy relationship (she has a love affair with his good friend, Eugene O'Neill) and subsequent marriage with the political events which draw Jack, first as a reporter and then, increasingly, as a participant. Following their first sexual encounter, Louise leaves her husband and follows Reed to Manhattan. Her introduction to the cultural and political *avant-garde* of Greenwich Village becomes our own. In one extended sequence, the poles of the world they inhabit are brilliantly juxtaposed as the film cuts back and forth between close, crowded shots of Jack and Louise dancing at the Liberal Club, the different steps they attempt and the different, seasonal costumes they wear marking the passage of time; and close, crowded shots of the two of them, with various friends who are artists, writers, and radicals, lounging in bars or sitting in their apartment's living room, arguing over social theory and politics, tossing around names like Marx, Engels, Freud, Jung, and Debs. There is little real explication of ideas here – just enough of a gesture to indicate that radical notions are very much part of this subculture.

Reed's path to revolution takes him from labour sympathizer, to anti-war activist, to chronicler of the Russian Revolution, to organizer of the Communist Labour Party. He is arrested while covering a meeting of the Industrial Workers of the World, and arrested again after he makes a public speech against America's entry into the World War. Magazine editors begin to trim his radical reports, and when he objects, they refuse to print his stuff. Sensing that the first, February Revolution in Russia is only the beginning of something bigger, he gets Louise to accompany him to Petrograd (its also a move towards reconciliation since they have been separated over infidelities). They arrive during the volatile month of September 1917, as Russia teeters on the brink of revolution. The shift from reporter to activist takes place on the day when the couple enter a factory in which the workers are heatedly debating whether or not to support the Bolsheviks. Called to the platform to speak on behalf of the

American workers, Jack, at first tentatively, then with more force, says that they are waiting for the Russians to lead them towards world revolution. Amidst thunderous cheers, he tries to get back to Louise, who is still in the audience, but he is mobbed, and the crowd comes between them – as the revolution will for the rest of their lives. Their gaze across the shoulders of working men lead into a montage in which scenes of the Bolshevik takeover (troops marching, seizing key points in Petrograd, entering the Winter Palace) are intercut with silhouetted images of Jack and Louise making love – and all of these are bridged by a powerful chorus singing the *Internationale*.

The overall meaning in this sequence seems clear (if a bit strange) – the uniting of the couple and uniting of the Russian proletariat in the Revolution are somehow acts of love. But there is a more specific metaphor here too – that of Reed's personal commitment to the revolution. Unlike the invented moments in the three other films, this one is based upon a real incident in which he was called to the front of a factory meeting, and where he pledged American solidarity with Russian workers. But the notion of a moment in life as a turning point is a dramatic idea, not a historical one. It is the film maker who has decided to turn this incident into a metaphor for Reed's conversion. In truth it is impossible to pin down personal change in this way. But because *Reds* is a dramatic work, the director shows us the man changing rather than doing what I could do in my biography, that is, generalize his change as the product of many causes over a long period of time.

The second half of *Reds* deals with the consequences of Reed's commitment to Bolshevism. When the ship that brings them home docks in Manhattan, government officials seize his papers. Soon both he and Louise are called to testify before a Congressional committee investigating the revolution. When she goes off on a lecture tour, he stays home to write *Ten Days That Shook the World*, then begins the tedious business of organizing a Communist Party. Secretly he travels (there is an Allied Blockade) to the new Soviet Union to get recognition for his party (one of two new Communist parties in the US) and when he tries to return home, Jack is captured and held in prison by the anti-Communist government of Finland until an exchange of prisoners is worked out by the Soviets. Back in Moscow, he begins to see some of the uglier aspects of the revolution – the lies, the repression, the propaganda, the growing gap between its ideals and its practices – but the typhus he contracts in Baku kills him before any real disillusionment occurs. It also brings him closer to Louise than ever before; on his deathbed they agree to call each other 'comrade'.

Reds is constructed very much like the classic Hollywood historical drama – the film delivers a linear, closed and emotional story with a strong moral message, which might be summarized as follows: commitment to changing the world through politics is both admirable and very American, but you must change the politics of the personal as well as the politics of the world. But there is another part of the film, one that turns it into a more complex and interesting work. For the dramatic world is both framed and penetrated by another historical realm, one created by the voices and faces of witnesses, elderly folk who lived through some of the same events of the period, knew (personally or by reputation) Jack Reed and Louise Bryant – and are willing to talk about them and the historical period in which they were actors.

The witnesses both provide a context for and a commentary on the dramatic scenes. They speak about broad social and historical topics (Greenwich Village, labour unions, free love, the arts, the anti-war movement, the hopes stirred by the Russian Revolution) as well as more intimate ones such as Jack and Louise's affairs. In bringing together dramatic and documentary genres as it does, *Reds* becomes a kind of experimental film. It is not a work that attempts to change the form of filmic (and historical) discourse in the way, say, Eisenstein tried to change the conventions created by Hollywood, by radically altering them with fast and obtrusive editing, or doing away with individuals and personal psychology. *Reds* keeps the traditional modes of documentary and dramatic address, but (in a move one might be tempted to call post-modern) it juxtaposes these two worlds without insisting that the story in one of them is somehow more real than the story in the other. It is true that the length of dramatic, as opposed to the documentary elements – perhaps 10 to 1– and the presence of big Hollywood stars on screen (Warren Beatty as Reed, Diane Keaton as Louise, Jack Nicholson as Eugene O'Neill) may seem to give that world more weight. But ultimately the drama is bracketed by the craggy, seamed faces of a chorus of elders and their documentary voices, which literally have both the first and the last words in the film.

The addition of the documentary elements to *Reds* creates a second historical world and a second level of meaning – one might say that in the film, two different discourses continually play against each other. Sometimes the drama illustrates the remarks of the witnesses, sometimes it contradicts them, If anyone supposes that people who lived through the events are more reliable than a Hollywood screenwriter and director who are merely re-staging the past, the film calls that supposition into question. From the outset we learn that these folks are not only very old, but exceedingly forgetful, self-contradictory, and even capable of remembering things which never happened. This raises the question of which is more fictional and which more accurate – the dramatized past or the remembered past, history or memory? *Reds* doesn't settle the issue. What it does is to create a biographical portrait which calls into question some of its own historical assertions, and leaves viewers having to decide between them. Ultimately the dual discourses in *Reds* pushes upon us the simple idea which all biographers and historians (should) by now understand – that there can be no single historical or biographical truth. That biography, like history, is always a story created by competing voices.

Of all the John Reed biofilms, *Reds* is the one which indulges most frequently in such fictive moves as condensation, alteration, and outright invention. With a few minor exceptions, the others are content to take characters and incidents directly from Reed's own books, though none of them questions to what extent those works were the product of the writer's own inventiveness. All the films also draw to some extent on other historical sources – this is equally true of the major sections in *Red Bells I* devoted to Zapata's war, and to the intimate scene in *Insurgent Mexico* when Reed confesses to his lifelong doubts and fears. Since such a moment does not occur in his own book, it has to be based on a larger reading of his life – as well as on the nature of the medium and the dramatic form. One can read the coming of age story of *Insurgent Mexico* as an extended personal confession – so what the director has done is to translate that confession into a dramatized moment on screen.

If the other films stick more closely to written texts and to verifiable historical fact, it may be because their time span is short and their geographic reach not very broad. *Reds* not only covers the events of five years, but takes upon itself the task of depicting multiple social worlds and political movements. Some of its factual errors are flagrant: Jack and Louise riding on a single train from France to Petrograd in 1917 without encountering German armies. Others involve the kinds of condensations and displacements one finds in every historical film. Take the opening sequence, in which a nude photo of Louise causes a scandal at a Portland art exhibition. This invention instantly shows that she was a highly unconventional woman – and can be linked historically to a series of photos of herself naked on a beach which she sent to Jack the following year. Or take the subsequent sequence, Reed's speech to the Liberal Club. Asked by the man who introduces him to answer the question, 'What is this war about?' he answers with a single word: 'Profits.' In truth, Reed spoke to the club in 1914 not 1915, and spoke at length. But that one word brilliantly encapsulates the message of his earlier speech and, indeed, everything else he had written for the last two years about a conflict that he called in the title of his first article on the topic, 'A Trader's War'. Another major condensation, this time of characters, may be seen in the depiction of Reed as buddies with the celebrated anarchist leader, Emma Goldman. Certainly they did know each other, but not nearly so intimately as depicted in

Reds. Yet in the film, Goldman clearly is meant to stand in for an entire older generation of radicals who helped educate Reed into leftist world view and politics. Her early disillusionment with the Bolsheviks (historically accurate) towards the end helps to show that Reed himself, despite some difference with Russian leaders, is still ultimately a partisan of the revolution.

In the introduction to *Ten Days That Shook the World*, John Reed calls his book, 'a slice of intensified history' (Reed 1934: xxxiii). On the following pages he successfully captures the confused, even chaotic feeling of Petrograd in the crucial days of revolution, as he cuts from one site to another, breaking an already jumpy narrative with the texts of speeches, newspaper articles and the contents of posters. In doing so, he was helping to invent a new kind of journalism, termed by one scholar 'a narrative immediacy . . . that makes the reader a vicarious participant in the historic event' (Lehman 2002: 190). He was also anticipating to some extent the way films would create historical – and biographical worlds. If the biofilm can never achieve the richness of detail or depth of analysis of a long, written biography, it can, as we see in the examples above, give you a slice of a life, intensified by the genre of drama and the power of the medium. Film may lack the ability to provide deep psychological insight, or extensive descriptions of particular intellectual or political milieus, but it can suggest with a terrifying immediacy how the past looked, and how people moved, felt, spoke and acted – in time. Unlike the written word, the biofilm, even in its flashbacks always functions in the present tense, suggesting, even making you feel as if you have lived through those moments yourself.

As in reading or viewing history, what you take away from a biofilm depends upon what you bring to it. The readings I have done of the three films are obviously informed by the years of study a specialist devotes to a topic. How they would have been read by their target audiences is difficult to discern, as is the question of how they would be understood by audiences in those same countries today. In the United States, to judge by reviews when it came out or comments made by my students in recent years, some viewers of *Reds* don't understand the dimensions or radical doctrines of that Greenwich Village subculture in which Reed lives, though they do obtain some notions of his social conscience and quest for personal liberation, both of which are threaded through the action and highlighted by the witnesses. People not raised in the Soviet Union might have some difficulty understanding why this young American in *Red Bells II* races around Petrograd so ferociously in October 1917, though they could hardly misunderstand his role as a witness to history. Foreigners who don't know about Mexico might not realize that in embracing Pancho Villa, Reed is identifying with the more radical wing of the revolution, though the most casual viewer could not miss his transformation from reporter to activist in both films that deal with this period of his life.

What I am suggesting is that biofilms, like all works that deal with the past, are entities with unstable meanings that shift over the years, that they are read and understood according to specific viewing audiences or individuals. Less than full-blown portraits, they should be seen and understood as slices of lives, interventions into particular discourses, extended metaphors that suggest more than their limited timeframes can convey. Each of the films about Reed certainly engages the traces of his life that one can find in research collections, as well as the figure portrayed in history books. As do all biographies, the films reconfigure him, comment upon the other works, enter into the debates over his life, and revivify some of its moments in an effort to make him meaningful to a new audience. To show, for example, Reed, himself just beginning to have some questions about the Bolsheviks, telling Emma Goldman in *Reds* that she doesn't understand revolution in practice because she's only known it in theory, and to cut from that directly to Reed withdrawing his resignation (submitted over political differences) from the governing board of Communist Internationale (both true incidents) is to make an interpretation, to argue against those who think that Reed was disillusioned and ready to forsake Communism at the end, and to make it *in the language of film* – a juxtaposition brought on by the direct cut.

None of the Reeds presented on screen is quite the same one that I created in *Romantic Revolutionary* in 1975, nor the one created by Granville Hicks in 1936 or Eric Homberger in 1990. Yet each in its own way certainly fulfills Nadel's definition of biography as 'fundamentally a narrative which has as its primary task the enactment of character and place through language' (Nadel 1984), though the language here is visual, aural, and dramatic. The Reeds in these works are presented at different times of life and through a different aesthetic, but they can be seen as built on the same historical figure – the ambitious writer and reporter who became first a chronicler and then a partisan of revolution. The strategies of these works differ greatly, but an argument can certainly be made in favour of each as a genuine biographical form – the intimate, psychological portrait of a fearful man who grows to radical commitment by his encounter with the Mexican revolution; the person whose individuality is less important than his symbolic or emblematic role, a figure less remembered for his particular predilections and tastes and more for the larger historical events he witnessed and chronicled; and the man torn between love and activism, who spends much of his life trying to balance the demands of the personal and those of the political, the private world of love and the public world of social change. These three works riff off the same set of historical and biographical data used by all biographers of Reed, and all are valid ways of drawing meaning out of his life, and carrying that meaning to a new generation. None could be called definitive, but then again no biographical interpretation ever is. If we learn how to read them, each of these films has much tell us about John Reed, the man, and about his personal struggles, and each suggests something about the larger issues of the times in which he lived. What more can one ask of a biofilm – or for that matter, of a written biography?

Chapter 7

Film maker/Historian

For anyone who lived through the 1960s on a campus, there has to be a shock of recognition on seeing the anti-war demonstration in *Born on the Fourth of July* (1989), Oliver Stone's film based on the life of Vietnam veteran Ron Kovic. A feeling that you were once present at this very scene, saw these very students on the steps of a university hall, with their long hair, Afros, beards, levis, bandannas; witnessed these very gestures, the raised arms and clenched fists; heard this very speechifying by Blacks and Whites, the denunciations of war, the shouted words *Nixon, On strike, Shut it down, Right on.* Even that middle aged figure on the steps, wearing a dashiki and calling for a March on Washington, looks strangely familiar – but at the same time somehow too old and out of place. Before the tear-gas bombs explode and the cops descend with swinging clubs we (who were around in the Sixties) may realize: that is Abbie Hoffman, King of the Yippies, saying precisely the kind of things he had said at such demonstrations 20-some years before the film was made.

The sequence is based upon a real event. The film lets us know that this is Syracuse University shortly after the Cambodia 'incursion' and the killings at Kent State, that moment in early May 1970 when hundreds, thousands, of college and high school campuses went on strike. Syracuse was among them, but the demonstration there was far different from the one we see on the screen. At Syracuse the words might have been violent, but the afternoon was peaceful; the police did not shoot off tear-gas and they did not wade into the crowd with clubs. Nor was the demonstration there attended by Ron Kovic, the hero of the film, and author of the book on which it is based. Nor by his girlfriend, for he did not have a girlfriend. Nor was it addressed by Abbie Hoffman.

A creation of director Oliver Stone, this sequence is not exactly a complete fabrication but, rather, a cunning mixture of diverse visual elements – fact, near fact, displaced fact, invention. It refers to the past, it prods the memory, but can we call it history? Surely not history as we usually use the word, not history that attempts to accurately reproduce a specific, documentable moment of the past. Yet one might see it as a generic historical moment, a moment that claims its truth by standing in for many such moments. The truth that such demonstrations were common in the late 1960s. The truth of the chaos, confusion, and violence of many such encounters between students and police. The truth of the historical questions the sequence forces viewers to confront: Why are these students gathered here? Why are they protesting? Why are they so critical of our national leaders? Why do the police break up the rally with such gusto? What is at stake on the screen for our understanding of the 1960s? Of recent America? Of the United States today?

No American film maker in the last half-century has been more obsessed with historical questions or has raised more public controversy than director Oliver Stone. And it is precisely because he deals with history that his films have been so controversial. Except perhaps for his first Vietnam film, *Platoon*, each of the six works that, taken together, can be seen as charting, or at least suggesting, a history of the United States from the assassination of President John F. Kennedy in 1963 to the involvement in the civil war in Salvador in 1980, has been attacked as a violation of its subject, with the chorus growing from the vigorous debates over *Born on the Fourth of July* to the denunciations and vilification of the director which were part of the response to the two films about presidents, *JFK* (1991) and *Nixon* (1995) (*Salvador*, 1986, and *Heaven and Earth*, 1993, are the other two of the six films). Some small portion of the criticism has been of the film-making itself, with words like 'bombastic' or 'simplistic' used to describe Stone's plot lines, characters, and aesthetic. But the overwhelming majority of the attacks have had to do with his supposed misrepresentation not only of history but of himself: how dare Stone, some critics say, call himself a 'historian' or 'cinematic historian', when he is nothing but a Hollywood film maker.

   The question of whether Stone can or cannot, should or should not be considered a 'historian' also haunts the pages of a volume entitled *Oliver Stone's USA*, a collection of essays written mostly by scholars and edited by historian Robert Brent Toplin. (I have a contribution in it entitled 'Oliver Stone as Historian'.) Almost every piece in the book at least considers the question and most try to answer it, though many of these answers are somewhat equivocal. The issue is complicated by Stone's own statements and writings, both in this volume and prior to its appearance. Although everyone seems to think the director has claimed the title 'historian' or 'cinematic historian', he denies the charge and points to a single 1991 interview with journalist Stephen Talbot in

Mother Jones magazine as the source of the allegations. In that article, he is quoted as calling himself a 'cinematic historian'. But, according to Stone, the journalist did not actually quote him but simply made up the term. Either way, from that single remark, picked up by the *Washington Post* and spread throughout the media, seems to stem all the allegations about Stone's desire for membership in the history community, and the denunciations of that claim. Now he wishes to make himself absolutely clear: *I do not think of myself as a cinematic historian now or ever . . .'* (italics in original) (Stone 2000: 40).

Too bad. Because I do. It's a claim I want to make not only for Stone but also for a number of other film makers – though to do so we will have to broaden our definition of the genre. That is something all the authors of essays in *Oliver Stone's USA* refuse to do. Admittedly, each essay (other than my own) focuses on a single film rather than a larger body of the director's work. In each, the issue is not whether the author likes or dislikes the films, but what are the proper rules and procedures for historians. Whether it's the charge that he 'blurs almost beyond distinction fact and fiction, historian and subject', or that he 'fails to maintain the spirit of objectivity that historians must respect', or that he has 'crossed the line between artist and scholar by combining film with history, by projecting onto the silver screen his highly subjective version of actual persons and events and enlivening them with colourful imagery, concocted dialogue, and imaginary people', or that he obliterates 'what most historians think is necessary for good, bias-free history writing – a critical distance between the historian and his or her subject', or that he 'wants to participate in the historical debate on the character of Richard Nixon without conforming to the canons of history', the consensus among admirer and critic alike is that whatever Stone is doing on screen, it's certainly not history (Farr 2000: 165; Kurtz 2000: 164–6, 171; Ambrose 2000: 202).

To these generally negative feelings there are at least two exceptions – the essay by diplomatic historian Walter LaFeber on the history and politics expressed in *Salvador*, who says that in this work Stone realized his (apparently unclaimed) ambition of becoming a 'cinematic historian' (LaFeber 2000: 109). And the analysis by Jack E. Davis that terms *Born on the Fourth of July* a work of 'revisionist history', and revisionist in two ways – of the normal Hollywood view of American combat and in the sense of allying itself with the work of the New Left historians, who saw the past 'from the bottom up'. Davis is also clear that this history arises out of the unique qualities of the medium: 'Aided by the visual power of film, Stone's non-traditional theme carries an emotional force not enjoyed by the scholar historian, who typically has only the dubious aid of academic prose and sometimes a small selection of grainy photographs' (Davis 2000: 139).

This furore over Stone may be unique in the annals of film history. Certainly it has no real parallels in the United States, and while there have been controversies over individual historical films in France, the UK, Spain, Argentina, and Japan (and no doubt elsewhere), none seems to have centred around the question of whether a film-maker could claim the title 'historian'. It's true that the 'history' in films is regularly debated by the press, as in the 2004 controversy over *The Passion of the Christ* or the earlier journalistic and scholarly flap over whether or not *Schindler's List* did justice to the experience of the Holocaust, but the question of Mel Gibson or Stephen Spielberg as 'historians' was not the issue. Indeed, it is the rare director who has wished to seize that title. Among Americans, you have to return to D. W. Griffith to find someone making such a claim – and for him it was not just personal, but part of a larger theory that saw film replacing books in the future as the primary medium for conveying knowledge of the past.

One film-maker who did come to think of himself a historian was Roberto Rossellini. An originator of the influential *Neo-realismo* movement of the mid-forties, the Italian director during the last years of his life, from the mid-1960s to the mid-1970s, made more than a dozen historical films (mostly for television). Believing that 'film should be a means like any other, perhaps more valuable than any other, of writing history . . .', his late contributions included some multi-part series, such as the twelve-hour *Man's Struggle for Survival* (1964–70), which carried the human story from pre-civilization to modern times; the three-chapter work, *The Age of the Medici* (1972); and a number of individual films that were often based around the life of a 'representative figure' of an era in which Rossellini found a major shift in human consciousness (Brunette 1987: 255). Among the latter was the best-known of his historical works, one considered by many critics to be among the director's major accomplishments, *The Rise to Power of Louis XIV* (1966); as well as works centering on Blaise Pascal, St Augustine, Socrates, René Descartes, and the Apostles.

Earlier in his career, Rossellini had directed a couple of more traditional historical dramas, but these late films were different – consciously didactic, they attempted, in words he wrote at the outset of these efforts in 1963, to 'tell the story of the great events of nature and history in the simplest and most linear fashion' (Brunette 1987: 255). Rossellini saw history as a kind of science, which meant his task was the presenting of 'pure information' about the past on the screen. Yet at the same time he was a leftist who wanted to unmask the sins of capitalism. Never did he seem to understand (or at least he never admitted it in public) the basic contradiction in his ideas – that information cannot be conveyed neutrally, least of all by someone with his agenda. To make the past linear is already to interpret it; to tell from a Marxist perspective is to add another layer of interpretation.

The underlying theory of Rossellini's history films may involve some self-mystification, but his practice was indeed an attempt at a new way of conveying the past. Containing minimal camera movement and montage, little plot, and no suspense, these films are what I have called, 'dedramatized' – designed to be distanced from viewers almost in the manner of Bertold Brecht's 'alienation effect', raising no emotions and thus allowing the audience time to think (supposedly) about what is happening on screen (though snoozing is a more likely reaction to these works than thinking). While the settings can be sumptuous as a way of conveying the sheer materiality of the past, the actors (often amateurs) do not use gestures, movement, or even voice inflection to create their characters. Indeed, characters is probably the wrong word, for the figures in Rossellini's historical films are no more than emblems of particular groups or classes; certainly they are never individuals who attempt to make us understand who they are or what they feel. In these works we see, but we don't share, the past; we look on and watch characters in costume stand around and, essentially, deliver lectures to each other. *The Age of the Medici*, for example, contains an enormous amount of talk about the Florentine economy, the cloth industry, banking, the new art works by Masaccio. The result of Rossellini's theories are works that seem less to be films than a series of tableaus in which movement is slight, and the lack of action seems meant to let us focus on the historical lectures the director wishes to deliver. Aside from *Louis XIV*, which embodies a materialistic thesis about how the king came to control his unruly nobles through building Versailles and making them dress lavishly as he did, none of these movies achieved more than minimal success with critics and virtually none with audiences. They remain as an interesting, sustained attempt by one director to become a historian by refusing to utilize the practices of dramatic film.

If almost no film-makers have wished to claim the title, historian, it may well be that they, as much as the public and the scholars, have been acculturated into traditional notions of history as a written discourse. Reviews of films in the press continually make directors aware of the sharp boundary lines drawn by the culture between what might be dubbed 'proper' history and the dramatic film. Despite this, certain directors in various parts of the world have been burdened enough by history to make them repeatedly turn to the past as a setting for films in which they try to raise significant historical questions. Most of these directors have worked outside Hollywood. With lower budgets, often government support, and a deeper sense of the constraints that history place on the present generation, film-makers in Europe and parts of the Third

World have a more continuous and better record of dealing with historical issues on the screen. Among them I would include such people as Andrzej Wajda in Poland, Ousmane Sembene in Senegal, Margarethe Von Trotta in Germany, Miklos Jancso in Hungary, Theo Angelopolous in Greece, Carlos Saura in Spain, Maria Luisa Bemberg in Argentina, Hsou Hsien in Taiwan, Vittorio and Paolo Taviani in Italy, and Emir Kusturica of Serbia (to name just a few).

Claims for directors as historians have already been advanced by some scholars in cinema studies. In a book-length analysis of the films of Theo Angelopoulos, Andrew Horton not only devotes the second of nine chapters to the director's obsession with the past of modern Greece, but continues to point to the historical questions and themes in the work as part of the analysis of individual films in other chapters (Horton 1997). Angelopoulos's historical vision is described by Horton as a broad one. His consciously created trilogy (*Days of '36*, 1972, *The Travelling Players*, 1975, and *Alexander the Great*, 1980) traces the history of his homeland from the turn of the twentieth century through the civil war of the late 1940s, while in two later films (*The Suspended Step of the Stork*, 1991, and *Ulysses Gaze*, 1995), the director has expanded his vision to encompass the devastating conflicts of the 1990s that have roiled and helped to re-draw the map of the Balkans.

For the most part these works are not based on the lives of actual figures. Angelopoulos sets fictional characters into historical situations. He focuses not on the rulers of the country but on more common people, their indirect victims, those who must live and suffer the results of the decisions made by governments and revolutionaries for war, peace, revolt, resistance, development. What is acknowledged by many as his best historical film, *The Travelling Players*, follows the movements of a peripatetic theatre company in its cross country trials and tragedies over the course of almost two decades. Through the individual experiences and destinies of its characters we are given a view from below of Greece, starting with the dictatorship of General Ioannia Metaxas in the 1930s, and going on to the Italian invasion, the German occupation, the Partisan resistance, and finally the Civil War of the late 1940s and early 1950s – the first time that controversial war was depicted on screen.

Angelopoulos may provide a kind of invented history, but taken together his films are, in Horton's words, 'narratives that reflect his perspective on the complex web of Greek history', works of enormous complexity that are at once meditations on the past and explorations of what has been repressed by official discourse (the Civil War being a case in point). His body of works represents 'an attempt to see clearly through the dark window of Greek history

. . . with all of its internal conflicts, external pressures, and ancient baggage from past empires and eras so that we experience . . . how individuals and their destinies are absolutely woven into and form the fabric of their culture and their times' (Horton 1997: 57).

Less concentrated on a single era, the Taviani brothers have made films which straddle a period in Italian history from the early nineteenth century to the mid-twentieth century, but the questions they deal with in their dramatic works are similar to the kinds posed by historians. As scholar Marcia Landy points out, their works are germane to the issues of national history and culture as raised by the well-known Marxist theorist, Antonio Gramsci. Whether dealing with the age of the *Risorgimento* (*Allonsanfan*, 1973), World War II (*La notte di San Lorenzo*, 1982), or the recent past (*Padre padrone*, 1977, *I sovversivi*, 1967) – the brothers repeatedly raise questions of subalternity, regionalism, and class struggle while dealing at length with the country's political, economic, and cultural divisions between north and south (Landy 2000). Often they take on the conventional historical wisdom. *La notte di San Lorenzo* challenges one of the country's sacred and deeply imbedded myths – that of the breadth of Italian Resistance, and the notion of a nation united against Nazism and fascism (Sorlin 1995: 77–87). In this film, through the eyes of a female narrator, we see a young girl's view of the deceptions, cowardice, and complicities that marked a particular town (San Miniato, where the Tavianis were born) during the brief period between the retreat of the Nazis and the coming of the Americans. Such historical re-enactments, as Landy points out, consistently portray 'the struggle for cultural self-expression and engagement on the part of both their upper-class and peasant protagonists'. They also manage neither to sentimentalize nor monumentalize the past, for the Tavianis' 'treatment of history is predominantly interrogative, analytical, and ironic . . .' (Landy 2000: 165).

What makes the directors mentioned in the preceding paragraphs into historians? It seems to me they are a different breed from those film makers who during the course of a career turn once or twice to the past as the setting for a movie. What these directors have in common is some sort of personal stake in history. All seem *obsessed and burdened by the past. All keep returning to deal with it by making historical films, not as a simple source of escape or entertainment, but as a way of understanding how the problems and issues that it poses are still alive for us in the present.* Throughout their dramatic films, these directors ask the same kinds of questions of the past that a historian asks – not just what happened or why it happened, but what is the meaning of what happened to us today. Such questions are obviously answered not as an academic historian would, but within the possibilities of the dramatic genre and the visual media. In the totality of their works, the best of these film maker historians provide a broad interpretation of, or larger perspective upon, some topic or aspect or theme out of the past – the civil war in Greece (Angelopoulos), the meaning of modernization in Italy (Tavianis), the shadow that the lingering legacy of colonialism casts over modern African nations (Ousmane Sembene), the struggles of a country with fascism and communism as well as the experience of living in the Third Reich (Margarethe Von Trotta).

To call their accomplishments those of 'historians' is, as mentioned earlier, to broaden and alter the notion of what we mean by that term. Perhaps a new word is necessary, but 'cinematic historian', as used (or not) by Oliver Stone, and more recently in the writings of Robert Toplin, seems to indicate a historian of the cinema, not someone who uses the visual media to tell the past (Toplin 2002: 34–9; 2004: 8–57). My own preference is to keep the word 'historian' and define it as someone who devotes a significant part of her or his working career to making meaning (in whatever medium) out of the past. Obviously on screen this entails different conventions for rendering history than those we traditionally use. History on film is largely about emotion, an attempt to make us feel as if we are learning about the past by vicariously living through its moments. And this experience comes in stories that, like the work of more traditional historians, both engage the discourse of history and add something to that discourse. In doing so, the directors make the past meaningful in at least three different ways – they create works that *vision, contest*, and *revision history* (Rosenstone 1995b: 8–13).

To *vision* history is to put flesh and blood on the past; to show us individuals in life like situations, to dramatize events, give us people to identify with, make us feel to some extent as if we have lived moments and issues long gone. It is to give us the experience and emotions of the past – in this it is very different from the distancing and analyzing of a written text. To *contest* history is to provide interpretations that run against traditional wisdom, to challenge generally accepted views of particular people, events, issues, or themes – personal, national, or international. To *revision* history is to show us the past in new and unexpected ways, to utilize an aesthetic that violates the traditional realistic ways of telling the past, or that does not follow a normal dramatic structure, or that mixes genres and modes – all these towards the end of making the familiar unfamiliar and causing the audience to rethink what it thinks it already knows.

With these categories in mind, I want to examine the works of Oliver Stone, in recent years (perhaps in all of American history) the director who was from the mid-1980s through to the mid-1990s persistent in the practice of rendering history on film. In half-a-dozen works, he wrestled with the agonies of

American society during and after the era of Vietnam, making three films directly about the war, two that deal with the Presidents whose lives bookend the war, and one about US involvement in the civil war in Salvador – which can be seen as an extension of the foreign policy themes of Vietnam. In these works, Stone has not only brought alive the issues of the past, but in one of the two presidential films, *JFK*, has raised the issue of to what extent the past is knowable and representable. This film also stands as a perfect example of what can be seen as another possible task for the historical: to be provocative. To create a past on the screen so outrageous or controversial that it forces a society to openly debate an important historical issue. Not only did *JFK* refuel the controversy over who killed President Kennedy, it also forced Congress to pass a law declassifying tens of thousands of documents relating to the case.

To analyze Stone as historian is to be faced with a dilemma surrounding chronology. Does one deal with the films in the order in which they were made, or in the order of historical events they depict? The latter would seem to make the most sense, save for one thing – such a chronology will not reveal how his views on the past have shifted, even hardened over time. Stone's beliefs, particularly about historical causation, grew more murky and conspiratorial over the passing years. The motivation for US involvement with the Central American right wing leaders (and death squads) that is depicted as fairly straight forward imperialist militarism (and the overcoming of the 'Vietnam syndrome') in the first film, *Salvador*, has morphed by the last film, *Nixon*, into a view of the course of history being caused by something the President and other characters refer to as 'the Beast' – an apparent metaphor for the military–industrial complex which, since President Eisenhower first used the term in 1960, has metastesized into a vast cancer that infects all of American policy, domestic and foreign.

Perhaps the best way into Stone's historical works is through what he sees as the central experience of that era, the war in Vietnam. Central both in terms of personal growth, artistic and historical vision, and national developments. As a patriotic young American, Stone volunteered to serve in the army in Vietnam, where he was twice wounded and awarded a Bronze Star. His tour of duty in that war without front lines – a war in which the elusive enemy was nowhere and everywhere, where body counts rather than strategic points seized became the supposed measure of military success, and some of the American military were exposed as guilty of committing atrocities – left Stone, as it did many soldiers, disillusioned about the American mission and highly sceptical about the gap between official rhetoric and on the ground reality (body counts regularly proved that the US was winning the war). As the conflict dragged on and on, those attitudes grew into a larger critique of the whole American effort. What were we doing in Vietnam anyway? Were we really fighting communism? Or were we attempting to put down a national liberation movement? What was so vital to American interests in this land eight thousand miles from home?

Stone's personal encounter with Vietnam infuses his three films about the war. It also seems to lend a kind of authenticity to his depictions that other films about the conflict never quite achieve. At least that was part of the reaction from film critics and veterans alike. *Platoon*, the first Vietnam film, left many ex GIs claiming that the confusion, terror, arguments, mixed motives, poor morale, deadly firefights, atrocities, and widespread use of marijuana that Stone put on screen were precisely what they had experienced in Nam (Roberts and Welky 2000: 66–90). The film was, in fact, a thinly-disguised autobiographical work that drew not just for atmosphere but also for incidents, directly on Stone's own tour of duty. The second film in the trilogy, *Born on the Fourth of July*, derives from Ron Kovic's autobiography of the same name, but the director identifies so closely with the author – 'Ron and me, we're like brothers' – that he merges his own story as soldier and veteran (along with those of other GIs) into the film (Kagan 2000: 145). The third film, *Heaven and Earth*, which tells the story of a Vietnamese woman, seems to draw on Stone's experience not of the battlefront but of the towns such as Saigon, where soldiers went for rest and recuperation, as well as on the guilt he must have felt over what how the American presence warped the culture and economy of Vietnam – the bars, the prostitution, the drugs, the GI treatment of young girls as hookers and chattels, the arrogance of the foreign soldiers towards the natives.

Platoon, as many critics have pointed out, is a film that on the surface omits any historical, political, or military context. What we see is the initiation of a young volunteer, Chris Taylor, into battle through experiences and encounters that, for the most part, could have taken place in almost any war. With a story that is less a fully formed plot than a series of incidents, the film nonetheless raises historical questions because of its inevitable insertion into the ongoing debate over American involvement in Vietnam. It was released in 1986, just 11 years after the fall of Saigon, and if the war was not still a daily topic of conversation, its shadows and trauma, its costs and consequences for the nation, still were very much part of the American landscape. The first image – new recruits exiting from the hatch of a transport plane while plastic body bags are being loaded onto it – and the first ironic words, spoken by hollow-eyed, returning vets to the newcomers, 'Gonna love the Nam', already suggest that something is amiss, especially to an American audience, raised on war films that stress the triumphs not the costs of our military undertakings.

The tone set at the outset continues throughout the film. Chris Taylor does not just enter combat, he enters a culture of grunts who are shrewd, hip, wary, and highly sceptical about the leaders and issues which have brought them here to the Central Highlands of Vietnam. Unlike American soldiers in other films, these soldiers do not talk in agitprop phrases about the coming glorious victory but, seeming to know the war is unwinnable, mostly speak about how best to survive to the end of their tours of duty. This culture of GIs is, like the United States itself, divided, at war with itself. In Nam, the conflict is between the juicers and the dopers, those who get drunk to the strains of Country and Western music, and those who smoke marijuana and listen to psychedelic rock, with the latter – in an echo of the culture wars at home – including both the Black and the more sympathetic of the soldiers. In the sequences of combat, the intense firefights during the day or night, another historical lesson emerges, though one that might be a bit more difficult for an audience to read. Here the mountainous terrain and dense jungle work to highlight the miscalculations of those who planned the war as winnable through American technological superiority. For the landscape and foliage nullify air power. On the ground it is the skill of the soldiers which wins skirmishes – and the Vietnamese know how to use the terrain and brush far better than do the Americans.

More than anything else, the depiction of atrocities mark *Platoon* as something new – if not in the national experience (for atrocities have been committed by US soldiers in other wars) then in American films. In a particularly horrifying sequence, the soldiers respond to the murder of one of their own by going berserk in a native village, shooting innocent civilians, clubbing children to death, attempting rape – and the mayhem only stops when their lieutenant gives orders to burn the food supply, poison the wells, and torch the village. In other words, the random atrocities are ended by officially sanctioned ones. Only after this does Chris realize the war is unwinnable. So does the other hero in the film, the highly moral Sergeant Elias, who comments: 'We been kickin' other people's asses so long, I guess it's time that we got our own kicked.' What might be considered treasonable words in any other film (or in life) make perfect sense in the world of *Platoon*, which in the words of one critic 'has told the familiar young soldier's story without copping-out on the ineradicable bitterness and confusion of the Vietnam war' (Kagan 2000: 107).

Born on the Fourth of July, Stone's second go at Vietnam, works on a much broader canvas than the first. As if assuming we have already seen *Platoon* and understand the pain and confusion of the grunts in the field, this film spends only 20 minutes of its two-and-a-half hours on combat scenes. The rest of the time goes to the home front, as witnessed through the lens of one person, one family, and one community. In telling the story of Ron Kovic of Massapequa, Long Island, partly before and largely after his two tours of duty in Nam, Stone explores some of the causes and consequences of American involvement in the conflict. But not on a geopolitical level. This film represents a kind of history from below, a micro-history that deals with the human cost of the war. For this purpose, Kovic is the perfect subject, a living metaphor. The product of a competitive, hyper patriotic family, a young man prone to repeat 'love it or leave it' every time someone voices a criticism of the United States, Kovic joins the marines with the notion that he can help to stop communism from reaching American shores. In Nam, he is shattered psychically and physically – first by accidentally killing one of his own men, then by sustaining major wounds that leave him with a body dead from the waist down, a paraplegic in a wheelchair who will never again be able to walk or to father children.

Kovic's return home degenerates into a harrowing journey through a period of shame, guilt, fear, darkness, and despair, before he finally begins a turn towards some vision of hope for the future. While the focus on the film remains steadily on Kovic, the way he is treated by family, friends, the community and the nation helps to shed light on larger historical issues. Honoured as a hero, he is ignored and mistreated as a human being. At the under-funded Veteran's Administration hospital where he spends many months, conditions are horrendous (men forced to lie in their own urine and excrement) due to the fact, as one nurse explains, that the government is spending its money on the war. Back in his home town, the members of his family don't know how to deal with his grief and anger at his condition – some of his siblings are against the war, while his highly patriotic parents turn away in disbelief from his stories about killing civilians and babies. A friend who managed to avoid the draft offers him a two-bit job as a cashier at his successful fast food restaurant, callously saying of the lowly position, 'You have to learn to walk before you can run'. His former girlfriend, now at Syracuse University, is too occupied with the anti-war movement to have much time for him. When in full dress uniform, he rides alone as a local hero in a convertible during Massapequa's annual Fourth of July parade, some of the younger members of the crowd boo and give him the finger. Later that day, at a public gathering where he is supposed to speak in support of the troops in Vietnam, he falls mute, his mind crowded with flashback images and sounds from the battlefield. Here at home, the war continues to take a physical and mental toll not just on our hero, but on him as a symbol of America.

His reaction to this uncomprehending reception at home (after the 4 July parade, he and an old friend who also was in Nam have a poignant discussion over how nobody understands or cares about what they actually went through out there) involves a descent into near madness, a period of drunkenness, fights in bars, brutal quarrels with his family, dope smoking, a move to Mexico, an attempt to romance a whore, and finally a physical struggle in a wasteland with another wheel chair vet over who really killed more babies in Nam. This is the nadir, the point at which a kind of redemption begins, one that involves two moves: first, seeking out the family of the man he accidentally killed and confessing what he considers to be his crime, and second, joining the Vietnam Veterans against the war. As a leader in that movement, he is among the demonstrators who break into the Republican Convention in Miami that renominated Richard Nixon in 1972. At the conclusion of the film, clean shaven and wearing a tie and jacket, he rolls out to address the 1976 Democratic Convention on behalf of the Vets, after telling a reporter, 'Just lately, I've felt that I'm home, like maybe we're home'.

This upbeat ending has been widely criticized as Stone's attempt to soften the sting of the sharply negative picture of the United States that pervades the rest of *Born on the Fourth of July*. Some point out that the confession to his victim's family is not part of Kovic's autobiography, but only an invention of the film maker – without seeing that the entire book is the confession, and the sequence only an attempt to visualize that confession in a dramatic form. Other critics complain that this film, like *Platoon*, ignores the big questions of economics, politics, and empire – why the United States got into war, why the ideology of anti-communism was so pervasive, how the administration of the military draft ensured that it was the sons of the lower, not the middle classes, who preponderantly fought and died in Vietnam.

That such charges are largely true does not diminish the real accomplishments of *Born on the Fourth*. It only means that Stone is making a particular work of history with its own thesis and claims on our attention. As historian Jack Davis put it:

> *Born* is more honest and forthcoming than the typical institutional history, and it rejects the ancestor worship pouring forth from public history. Stone's film can be seen as an actual inquiry rather than a mere presentation. He frames the movie around a historical problem, addresses critical questions about the American experience, and offers an interpretation of the recent past than approaches that found in academic scholarship (Davis 2000: 136).

The 'historical problem' is set not at the national but the individual level: why did Americans go and how did the war effect them? The answer in part comes in an unusual thesis, one, perhaps unique to Stone. From the early sequences which have the Ron Kovic playing soldier in the woods near Massapequa, batting on the Little League baseball diamond, and competing on the high school wrestling team, the film roots the aggression of Vietnam in a kind of competitive masculinity linked to blind patriotism – what might be called the John Wayne syndrome. The link, interestingly enough, comes through President Kennedy's bellicose inaugural address, with its warning to all foes and its demand that Americans ask not what their country can do for them, but what they can do for their country. The Kovic family gathers to listen to the speech, and we see them clearly taking this call to heart. In later films, especially *JFK*, Stone will mark America's troubles from the assassination of the President, who will be portrayed as the good king struck down prematurely. What this suggests is that like other historians, Stone has the ability to alter his interpretations over time, but whether this is a sign of growth and maturity, or mere intellectual skittishness, is something for the viewer to decide.

The ultimate contribution of *Born on the Fourth* is less that of a biography than of a metaphoric history of America in the Vietnam years. In the film we encounter a small, American community both before and during the war; undergo the harrowing experience of battle with its atrocities; suffer the degradations of a handicapped veteran's life; and confront the gap between the rhetoric of patriotic justification and the reality of events on the battlefield and after the war itself. To this vision can be added elements that are very much part of traditional history. *Born on the Fourth of July* recounts, explains, and interprets a single life, and by extension, a whole period – the experience of Vietnam. In depicting the actions and attitudes of Americans in Vietnam and afterwards, the film engages and adds to the body of evidence we have from the war as carried in other books, essays, films, works of history. The film also makes an original and interesting interpretation of American involvement in Vietnam by linking the high cost of blind patriotism to a certain kind of American masculinity. Finally, it generalizes the experiences of one man to be those of a nation, showing the way war touched not only other veterans but also civilians who lived outside the circle of experience of the war. By giving us images of a painful split in the Kovic family, the film suggests the split in the family of the nation itself.

The third film in the Vietnam trilogy, *Heaven and Earth*, deals with America more indirectly. Here Stone does what few historians of the United States would dare to do – attempts to render the Vietnamese experience of not just the war but the entire struggle for liberation. The work is based on the autobiography of Le Ly Haslip, daughter of a peasant family who farm rice in a beautiful valley and live in a traditional, Buddhist way, in harmony with nature. Into this Eden, history erupts, first in the form of French soldiers, who burn the village; then as Vietcong guerrillas, who take away the sons of the peasants; and finally in the combination of South Vietnamese troops, their American advisers, and the ever present helicopters which turn the sky to thunder and flames. Le Ly becomes one of the victims of history – raped and beaten, her home destroyed, she finds her way to Saigon where she becomes pregnant, works as a dope dealer, and occasionally as a prostitute. A marine sergeant falls in love with her (largely out of guilt over America's actions in Nam, it turns out), eventually marries her, and brings her back to San Diego, where over time the cultural differences in expectations and social roles ultimately tear the marriage apart. Years later, after she has founded a business and prospered, she returns to Vietnam with her three children and finds her mother and one brother still alive, back in their old village. But now there is a huge gulf between them, for her family treats Le Ly more or less as a foreigner, as the American she has, without knowing it, become.

The portrait of traditional Vietnam in the film may be sentimentalized (though Haslip herself thinks it remarkably good), but that of the American invaders is no more of a caricature than that of the revolutionary Vietcong. Both can be brutal in the course of military or intelligence operations (active on behalf of the Vietcong, Le Ly is interrogated by the South Vietnamese and Americans, and raped by a Vietcong). The GIs we see in Saigon are for the most part decent enough, yet they are young men in an alien land in search of the pleasures that young soldiers generally seek, and inevitably their money works to corrupt and coarsen the natives. What is rare is that *Heaven and Earth* does provide a picture of Vietnamese villagers as real people, not just part of the backdrop for American actions. The broader interpretation of history has to do with the cost to other lands and people of America's involvements abroad.

A similar theme runs through *Salvador*, the story of Richard Boyle, a once famous photographic journalist who has through drink and drugs become a kind of deadbeat, living on the margins in San Francisco. When his wife walks out on him, Boyle decides to redeem his reputation by returning to Salvador, a country where he formerly lived and worked, and where he has left Maria, a woman he once loved. Using the lure of drugs and promise of beautiful women, he convinces a disk jockey friend named Dr Rock to drive him to El Salvador. Soon Boyle finds Maria and proposes marriage. He also finds evidence of the growing right-wing power in a country where leftists in the jungle are threatening revolution and a middle-of-the-road government is caught between the extremes of right and left. Boyle's journalistic nose leads him to photograph the freshly dead bodies at the garbage dump of El Playon, people murdered by right-wing death squads, headed by Major Max, a leading politician, candidate for president, and a man who has a good deal of support among the personnel of the American embassy. Dr Rock, who starts out as a naïve tourist, slowly begins to learn about the thuggery and chaos that are beginning to overwhelm this Central American world. They and we witness the growing arrogance of the right – their rape and murder of four American nuns; and finally the crushing of a leftist uprising with the aid and complicity of the incoming American administration of Ronald Reagan.

Central to the film is the assassination of Archbishop Oscar Romero, the leading figure in Salvador's fight for social justice. From the pulpit of the cathedral after a Sunday mass he delivers a powerful speech (the film version is close to Romero's own words) aimed at the military establishment, ordering them to stop supporting the right by killing their peasant brothers and sisters, saying 'Violence on all sides is wrong. I order you in the name of God to stop this oppression'. Minutes later, immediately after Boyle and Maria have taken communion, Romero is gunned down by one of Major Max's men – and then all hell breaks loose as the worshipers in the packed church flee out the door, only to be met by squads of soldiers who wade in to disperse the crowd with clubs and guns.

While these events are documentable, they happened not, as depicted in the film, in a single day, but over the course of a week. Archibishop Romero's speech denouncing right-wing death squads was made in the cathedral on a Sunday. His assassination came the next day while he was saying mass in a small neighbourhood chapel. At his funeral service a few days after that, the crowd of 100,000 mourners outside the cathedral was attacked with clubs and guns by the military, leaving at least 50 people dead. By condensing these three events – the sermon, the assassination, the military action against the people – into one passionate sequence, Stone is able to make clear the connections between Romero's views and his assassination, as well as to underline the complicity between the death squads and the military.

As with the Vietnam films, there were critics who found *Salvador* simplistic, a film which failed to delineate the perilous socio-economic conditions of Salvador (or Central America) that created the political situation, a study in black and white which ignored the moderate centre in the country in the form of President Jose Duarte, a work too sympathetic to the leftist revolutionaries. Yet while he admits there is some truth in those charges, diplomatic historian Walter LaFeber argues that in this work Stone becomes a 'cinematic historian' because the film catches much of the atmosphere of the period so well, and gets 'the political debate accurately . . . There could be no political resolution in El Salvador because, as Stone correctly argued, during the 1980s there was no viable middle ground . . . the United States continued its all-out support of the Salvadoran military even as Washington officials hoped that in some miraculous way the more moderate Duarte could control the politics' (LaFeber 2000: 108).

In *Salvador*, the story of Boyle and Rock becomes symbolic not just for what happened in that country in the early 1980s, but for the whole thrust of American anti-communist foreign policy, with its long history of overt and covert actions in Central America. By telling the story obliquely, through the eyes of these two Americans, Stone engages the debates about American foreign policy since World War II. The critique made by the film is rarely heard outside history books written by leftists such as LaFeber or published in the small radical press – that anti-communism was a cover for profits for American corporations and power for our military and secret intelligence services; that the US has in the name of this anti-communism played a basically anti-democratic role throughout the Western hemisphere, supporting killers and thugs who masquerade their own self interest behind anti-communism. Agree or disagree, this is at once a legitimate and exceedingly contestatory interpretation of US history rendered for the general public.

Up to this point my treatment of Stone has been largely in terms of characters and stories – as if the filmic qualities of his work were not important. But nothing could be further from the truth. Stone is a master of his medium, with a particular talent for rendering the visceral on screen, the tangible feeling of reality, very close up and very 'in your face'. This is true in the earliest film, *Salvador*, in such a grisly sequence as the one in which Boyle is pistol whipped by border guards and dragged off to be shot (the rifle misfires and he is saved); true in the shocking realism of *Platoon*'s terrifying firefights that led veterans to say: 'that's the way it was in my Vietnam'; true of the VA hospital when Ron Kovic spends months screaming for nurses to clean away the vomit and feces that stain his bed. Stone is also superb at rendering the confusion of battle and mass movements of crowds – the military attacking the worshippers fleeing the site of Romero's assassination, the chaotic disorder of the battle in which Kovic shoots one of his own men, the struggle between anti-war demonstrators and police described at the outset of this chapter.

Stone's aesthetic in these films is powerful and confrontational, the very opposite of subtle. It is the film-making of excess, with sequences that are strong, bombastic, over the top – noisy with sound effects and loud voices, bright with primary colours, underscored too often with swelling orchestral music or the pounding beat of hard rock. If a character screams 'fuck you' once in a Stone film (as Kovic does to his mother), he will probably scream it a hundred times. If one character is full of light and a beacon of goodness, like Sergeant Elias in *Platoon*, then another will be full darkness, a black hole of evil, like Sergeant Barnes. If a man commits suicide, as does Le Ly's American husband, he shoots himself while naked in a van in a public place. Stone always goes for the jugular, using every effect of the medium to emotionally heighten the audience's experience, as if to make certain that as much as the characters, you feel the pain (there is little joy in his films) of history.

All this said, there is a definite change over time, a growth in Stone's mastery of film technique and language, one that both helps to propel and strongly inflects the meaning of his histories. The narrative in an early work like *Salvador* is straightforward, the colours bright and primary, the set-ups and editing standard Hollywood realism, with perhaps just a touch of the grotesque that one associates with expressionism. But by the time he makes *Born on the Fourth of July*, the director's palate has broadened considerably to include what might be called the odd, hyper-realism of the Massapequa's two Fourth of July Parades, or the smoky oranges, jerky hand-held camera images, disorienting swish pans and odd angles that characterize combat in Vietnam. Visible as are these changes, at least in retrospect, nothing prepares one well for the quantum leap in film-making that Stone will take when he makes *JFK* (1991), a change in visual historical language so radical that its lessons have yet to be absorbed by other directors. Indeed, Stone himself will not go so far again in an historical film, though the experiments in expression with colour and editing that start in this film will continue in *Natural Born Killers* (1994).

JFK is a superb example of a film which doesn't tell history so much as revision it – through both its form and its message, with the two of them inextricably linked. (The violent objections to the work, which began long before its appearance, have had to do with both.) The film does not, of course, tell the story of President John Fitzgerald Kennedy in office, but of his assassination and its aftermath. Rejecting the Warren Commission findings that Lee Harvey Oswald was a lone assassin, the film explores the question of who was really responsible for the President's death. The driving investigative force on-screen is the real life character, New Orleans District Attorney Jim Garrison, whose book *On the Trail of the Assassins* serves distantly as the source of the story. Garrison, who actually brought an alleged conspirator named Clay Shaw to trial, and lost that trial, plays the role of surrogate historian in search of truth. Clearly he is also meant as a stand-in for all people of goodwill who believe in democracy and want the real story of the assassination to be uncovered. Following Garrison's search, the film recounts the events, real, possible, and imagined, that lie behind the assassination; explains them as part of a major conspiracy at the highest levels of the US government, and interprets this conspiracy as one set in motion by various people, groups, agencies, and companies that had much economic gain to make from the continuation of the Cold War and the hot war (in Vietnam) against communism.

To put a label on it, *JFK* may be seen as a work of modernist or even post-modernist history. It presents events from competing perspectives, mixes film stocks (black and white, colour, and video), idioms, genres, and period styles (documentary, Soviet montage, Hollywood naturalism, domestic melodrama) to represent the variety of contexts in which the event occurs. It tells multiple stories and creates many interpretations of the assassination, including some which contradict each other. These competing possibilities for what happened, all asserted with the same degree of possibility, tend to emphasize the artificial and provisional reconstruction of any historical reality. What seems to be happening here is that *JFK* both questions history as a mode of knowledge (the multiple interpretations) and yet asserts our need for it (Garrison's closing address in the Shaw trial, in which we in the audience are put in the position of the jury trying a supposed conspirator). The district attorney questions witnesses, ferrets out documents, and tries out theories seeking a truth, yet at the same time seems to show that ultimately truth is impossible to find. The past in the film, the possible history, becomes an unstable mix of fact, fiction, truth, illusion, a fragmentation of contexts, motives, beliefs, rumour. Yet the theme is clear enough, for the work leaves us with the feeling that we live in a dangerous, national security state that is out of control of the people, a hidden state with power over national and international events – including the assassination of the president (Burgoyne 1197: 88–103).

A similar mood hovers over *Nixon* (1995), where – as mentioned earlier – references to 'the Beast' point to a government run by hidden powers. Like *JFK*, this film abounds in government conspiracies, yet these are far better documented than the ones hinted at in the earlier film. The attempts of the CIA to assassinate Fidel Castro with the help of the Mafia (using such bizarre methods as poisoned cigars); the burglary of the office of the psychiatrist of Daniel Ellsberg, who leaked the Pentagon Papers to the press; the Watergate break-in of the McGovern campaign headquarters – all these are a matter of public record. But *Nixon* is not really a film about conspiracies. Nor, surprisingly, is it a film about politics but, rather, one that centres on character – a portrait of the president as a tragic hero. The model for the film is, at some distant removed, Shakespeare – somewhere between the histories and the tragedies. Essentially this is an attempt to understand why this obviously smart and talented politician undertook criminal acts that led to his humiliating downfall.

In so far as it is political, the film gives a fair picture of Nixon as a moderate conservative on domestic affairs and a visionary in international relations, a president who withdrew from Vietnam so slowly that more Americans died after he came into office than before his election, but who also, over the objections of right wingers, sought *détente* with the Russians and reopened relations with China, going to Beijing to meet with Mao Tse-Tung. Stone's portrait is flavoured with insights drawn from quasi-Freudian psychology. In flashbacks from the White House days, we see Nixon's poverty-stricken background and his difficult relationship with his harshly religious parents – the father who beat him, the mother who controlled him through an almost erotic combination of love, punishment, and guilt. Such sequences don't quite add up to a convincing argument that childhood traumas are responsible for the paranoid and rather dishonest man who became president, but they do create some sympathy for the president in his trials and downfall.

In keeping with its theme, Nixon highlights drama rather than film-making. Stone is still a stylish director, but unlike *JFK*, here there is no attempt to expand the formal boundaries of historical film. Once again we have some razzle dazzle editing, unusual intercutting of colour film, black and white, and video; inventive mixtures of documentary footage and drama. But by now it is familiar, part of a visual brilliance that has become part of Stone's normal repertoire. A major motif in the film concerns Nixon's rivalry with John F Kennedy. Or, to be more specific, his rivalry with Kennedy's image – the young, handsome, rich, smooth, sexy, smiling politician was always envied by this stiff, awkward boy whose poverty clung to him like an ill-fitting suit. In disgrace and on his way out of the White House, Nixon looks up at a portrait of Kennedy and says 'When they look at you, they see who they would like to be; when they look at me, they see who they are'.

In this chapter I have been making claims about the film maker as historian – about what such a phrase can and might mean. Earlier in the book I have argued that certain historical films are able to render the past in a meaningful (if fictional) way, render it well enough so that the issues surrounding the history of race in America, or the Bolshevik Revolution, or the life of one American radical, are brought before us anew. Here I have been trying to take this idea farther by explaining how certain film-makers have over their careers created a large enough body of works to be considered not just as one shot historians of a single topic, but as historians in a broader sense – ongoing interpreters of a nation, an era, a field.

To suggest that film makers can be historians is to reach for a meaning of that word that long predates our current idea, which dates from the nineteenth century, that history is a matter of telling the past as it really was – or in the case of film, showing us the past as it really was. It is to accept the notion that history is no more (and no less) than the attempt to recount, explain, and interpret the past, to give meaning to events, moments, movements, people, periods of time that have vanished. Clearly that has been an aim of Oliver Stone in *Salvador*, *Platoon*, *Born on the Fourth of July*, *Heaven and Earth*, *JFK*, and *Nixon*, works which consciously confront some of the major historical issues of the recent US past. As much as any historian who works in words, Stone has wrestled with the late twentieth-century history of the United States – the 1960s, the war in Vietnam, the Kennedy assassination and what followed: the presidency of Nixon, the scandals of Watergate, intervention in Latin America. Doing so, he has created a powerful interpretation of contemporary American history.

This engagement of Oliver Stone with history is hardly accidental. He is a man who was obsessed (I write in the past tense because in the last decade Stone's work has moved off into realms other than history) with historical questions and the search for answers. Each of his films has a conscious thesis about the past, almost always stated right at the outset in a montage, or a speech, or a sequence of images (often documentary footage) which let us know that what we are about to see involves the great public issues of our time. *JFK* opens with President Eisenhower's farewell address, with its warnings about the dangers to America of the growing military industrial complex. *Salvador* begins with a montage in which peasants are beaten and slaughtered by the military in an act of terror that comes to symbolize the betrayal of democratic elements in that country. Early in *Born on the Fourth of July*, Ron Kovic's family gathers to hear President Kennedy's inaugural address, with its call for Americans to bear and burden, pay any price to defend democracy. The subsequent dramatized history in such works plays out the early thesis, showing how the events provide a context for the actions of, for the most part, ordinary Americans.

As with other historians, in Stone you can also find a larger, cumulative body of meaning. Taken together, the six films mentioned above create a kind of collective historical argument about contemporary America. Central to his historical vision is the assassination of President Kennedy as a pivotal event in America's problems (but as mentioned, like any historian, Stone can be contradictory, for *Born on the Fourth of July* seems to point to Kennedy's rhetoric and stance as the cause of the Vietnam War). His larger interpretation has in some quarters been called paranoid – that the US government is out of control, or in the hands of secret agencies; that lots of things being done in the name of the American people are criminal; that our democratic heritage and institutions serve as a kind of ideology to cover the activities of greedy men and scoundrels. One may ask: is this a true picture of America? Nobody can answer such a question definitively, or at least for anyone else, but certainly enough evidence has become available since Vietnam – of assassinations, secret wars, Watergate, Irangate, the Contras, the allegations concerning CIA involvement in crack cocaine, charges of collusion between oil interests and foreign governments – to say this portrait is at the very least a historically plausible interpretation.

To what extent does Stone himself believe this broad notion? There does seem to be a kind of running contradiction in his historical work. In interviews and in the films, he sometimes insists on the chaotic, multiple, relativist nature of history – in essence, on the untellibility of the truth of the past. But this does not prevent him from going ahead and directing films with stories that carry the force of truth. Indeed, more than simply storytelling, Stone uses the past for the purpose of delivering certain kinds of truths about our national life. They usually come through the words of most of his major characters – Chris Taylor, Richard Boyle, Ron Kovic, Ly Le Haslip, and Jim Garrison – all of whom are seekers after and tellers of the truth. In his insistence on the moral lessons of history, Stone seems to be exceedingly traditional.

His dilemma would seem to spring from a simple human problem: Stone wants to have it both ways at once without having to reconcile the differences. He wants to get the history right and yet he knows that such a task is essentially impossible. Perhaps this is why, in a film such as *JFK*, form seems to be at war with the contents – the razzle-dazzle multiple realities of the montage at odds with the tepid realism of Jim Garrison's home life and the limp domestic drama about why he doesn't spend more time with his family. Stone's sense that history is not a single story also can run against his notion that it is important to tell the truth of the past. This dilemma may be why he appears angry in so many interviews about whether his works should be labelled history or fiction. It is as if he dimly recognizes the dilemma and stymied by the contradiction, occasionally bursts into verbal violence, saying things like, 'Who knows what history is? It's just a bunch of stories people tell each other around the campfire'.

My suggestion is that history also resides in the kinds of works Stone has created for the screen. Given a society in which reading, particularly serious reading about the past, is increasingly an élitist endeavour, it is possible that such history on the screen is the history of the future. Perhaps in a visual culture, the truth of the individual fact is less important than the overall truth of the metaphors we create to help us to understand the past. Fact, we must remember, has not always been the primary tool for telling the past. The 'truth' contained in facts was never highly important to griots in Africa, or to history-makers in other oral cultures. Maybe Oliver Stone is a kind of griot for a new visual age. A person who, in a sense, makes history by making myths, and makes myths in order to tell truths. Wanting the myths he recounts to have a truth value. And in so far as they do, these are not the literal truths that our scientific age expects in print, but truths for a coming age (or one already here?) in which a visual culture expresses its own kinds of truth.

Let's face it: the problem that Stone and other film makers face is very real – how do you make the past serious to a large audience? How do you communicate lessons from the past to a public in a post-literate age. Surely public history in the future is less likely to be propagated by scholarly monographs than by stories presented on the large and small screen. Is this a shocking idea? To accept Stone or other directors as historians, one must understand that the theory and practice of history today are not what they were when I received my PhD almost four decades ago. For at least the last half century (and more in some quarters) the practice and truth claims of history have been under major attack from philosophers, literary and cultural theorists, post-modern critics, and historians themselves. The literature on this is far too huge to deal with here, so all I wish to do is to suggest that the cumulative weight of the arguments add up to the following: That written history, academic history, is not something solid and unproblematic, and certainly not a 'reflection' of a past reality, but the construction of a moral story about the past out of traces that remain. That history (as we practise it) is an ideological and cultural product of the Western world at a particular time in its development, one when the notion of 'scientific' truth, based on replicable experiments, has been carried into the social sciences, including history (where no such experimentation is possible). That history is actually no more than a series of conventions for thinking about the past. That these conventions have shifted over time – from the stories of Herodotus to the scientism of a Von Ranke – and that they will obviously shift in the future. That the 'truth' of history does not reside in the verifiability of individual pieces of data, but in the overall narrative of the past. If he does nothing else in his films, Oliver Stone – like Theodore Angelopoulos, the Taviani brothers, and many other directors – makes films that enter into, engage, comment upon, and contest the existing body of data and arguments on recent America that we professionals call the discourse of history.

Chapter 8

Engaging the discourse

W hat kind of a historical world does the dramatic film propose? One can admit the argument of my earlier chapters – that individual films, in depicting the past, can contribute to our understanding as well as to the larger discourse of history – and yet still wonder to what extent can a group of films, like several works of written history, be able to give a broader insight into a historical topic? Put another way: what might we learn from viewing a number of films devoted to a single incident or a major subject? To what extent will those films, taken together, relate to, comment upon, and add to the larger discourse? It is just such questions that I wish to approach in this chapter. To do so I have selected the Holocaust as the topic. It was not my first choice – in part because the subject is so vast and extreme, in part because so much has been written not only on the Holocaust but on also on its films. But those reasons have in the end become the precise ones for choosing it. The Holocaust is central to modern history, at least in the West, where this book is being written and, presumably, will be mostly read. My notion that it is difficult to evaluate an historical film unless you understand the larger discourse out of which it arises becomes another reason for taking up the Holocaust. Not only do I regularly devote part of a course in the Modern Age to the subject (and hence I am immersed in the discourse), but probably almost anyone reading these words has some, if not quite a bit, of knowledge of, or exposure to, the Holocaust. This makes it more likely that the reader has encountered at least some of the issues and films to be discussed.

Another good reason for using this topic is the long-running debate over whether the Holocaust can be told in any medium at all. Ever since the revelations about Auschwitz (as a shorthand phrase for all the death camps), some have argued that the events there surpass the possibilities and limits of representation.

Theodore Adorno said it first, with the much-quoted line, 'After Auschwitz to write a poem is barbaric' (Friedlander 1992: 242). In a practical sense, he was wrong, for people have never stopped representing the Holocaust in a variety of forms of expression, not just poetry, but novels, memoirs, essays, museum installations, architecture, paintings, plays, and oratorios ever since knowledge of the events that comprise it emerged. Still, in some quarters the idea persists that no medium or genre is up to the horrors of something so vast, deadly, and incomprehensible, that seems so far outside the boundaries of historical writing, at least as a rational discourse capable of describing and shedding light on our normal realm of human behaviour and morality.

Suspicions about the possibility of representing the Holocaust fall with particular force on the motion picture, particularly the drama, and more particularly the popular Hollywood drama. If Eli Wiesel, himself a survivor of the campus, finds the Holocaust 'unsayable' in normal language, he is even warier of having it put on film: 'One does not imagine the unimaginable. And in particular, one does not show it on screen' (Baron 2005: 1, 3). Some scholars and critics find that dramatized images of Auschwitz are so banal, overused, and normalizing of an experience that could never be called normal, that only by avoiding images of the camps can one depict the Holocaust. Claude Lanzmann, who does just this in his epic, nine-and-a-half-hour documentary, *Shoah*, bluntly attacked the whole notion of dramatizing the Holocaust in his angry response to Stephen Spielberg's enormously popular *Schindler's List*: 'Fiction is a transgression. I deeply believe that there are some things that cannot and should not be represented' (Baron 2005: 1, 3). A debate over just this issue roils the pages of a volume entitled *Spielberg's Holocaust*, in which scholars feel compelled to come down on one side or the other – as partisans of the documentary or the drama, of Lanzmann or Spielberg (Loshitzky 1977).

The problem of representing the Holocaust can also be seen as the core problem of history. Can we really represent the past, factually or fictionally, as it was, or do we always present only some version of the way it possibly was or may have been? And in our representations, don't we inevitably alter the past, lose some of its meaning to itself, that is, to its historical actors, and at the same time impose other meanings (our meanings) upon events and moments that those who lived through them might have great difficulty in recognizing? My own viewpoint (as you who have read this far in the book will know) is that we always violate the past, even as we attempt to preserve its memory in whatever medium we use – in words on the page, images on screen, paint on canvas, artifacts in a museum exhibition. Yet this violation is inevitable, part of the price of our attempts at understanding the vanished word of our forebears. In this the Holocaust is like any other historical problem, a series of events (admittedly more horrifying than almost any other, although the twentieth century did produce a few other enormities that are almost as vast and equally baffling) created by humans and inflicted upon humans, which continue to haunt our culture, and which we continue to deal with in various discourses, scholarly and popular, including film. Scholars may debate issues surrounding the possibility and wisdom of 'representation', but in fact the Holocaust is continually being represented on film. The question for this book is: what do those representations say? How do they reflect, relate to, intersect with, comment upon, contest or elaborate the data, questions, issues, and debates of the enormous literature on the topic? Or more simply: what do we learn from encountering them?

Approaching the Holocaust on film (for this chapter) is a daunting task. How and what films does one choose to analyze? The filmography is enormous. Between 1945 and 1999, 782 dramatic features (including theatre releases, TV and Cable TV productions, and works that went direct to video) were produced that deal with the topic in one way or another, and in the new century the list keeps growing. The largest number of such films were made in the United States, with Germany in second place. But virtually all the nations of Western and Eastern Europe have contributed to this total, as have Israel and a number of countries where films on the topic might seem unexpected – Australia, Pakistan, Japan, and China. In his excellent study, *Projecting the Holocaust into the Present* (2005), Laurence Baron characterizes these works in two helpful ways: by themes (e.g. resistance, survivors, rescuers, ghetto, neo-Nazis, war criminals, etc.), and by genres (spy, road, character, action, biopic, courtroom, comedy, love, pornography). Given such categories, one strategy might be to follow a particular theme or genre, but the catalogue still would be very large, not to mention skewed towards certain sub-topics. Happily, Baron in his first chapter has another helpful list, this one on the major films of the 1990s. Specifically, he names ten works, one made each year in that decade. With two deletions, those are the films I shall consider in this chapter. I understand that this way of choosing may seem arbitrary, even odd. But my hunch is that even such a random selection will end by providing insight to the experience of the Holocaust. If so, this will make the argument all the more powerful.

The list, notable for its breadth and scope, includes films made by directors from eight different countries – Germany (2), Poland (2), the United States, Israel, France, Australia, Italy, and Hungary. It contains works which are popular and those that are little known; Academy Award winners and films that have achieved no honours, as well as stories told in many genres: the biofilm, the family saga, the comedy, and the investigation. (That five of the films are biographical represents, according to Baron, a trend in Holocaust films in recent years.) The majority of the eight films are, literally, based on true stories which take up a variety of themes and sub-topics: the death camps, resistance, racial laws, rescuers, survivors, and the shadow of the Holocaust that falls over the next generation, both the children of those who died and those who survived.

In using these films as a way of exploring the Holocaust, I propose to deal with them in the order in which Baron lists them – that is, the order in which they were made. After each viewing, I will write about the image of the Holocaust provided by the film, then follow with a conclusion to the chapter that attempts to sum up and explain what I have found. Other than to make it read more smoothly than it does as I write these words on 17 August, 2004 at 7:33 a.m., I will not alter this introduction to the chapter but let it stand as is. Were we to give this method a lable (and there is no need to do so), you might call this chapter a piece of process history, one that incorporates its own time-frame or stages of composition into its argument. I understand that this may seem like a kind of academic stunt, and in a way I suppose it is. But if so, it serves two larger purposes. The first, to see how historical films chosen some-what arbitrarily create a historical world. And second, to keep you, the readers, interested in what is going on. One of my fears is that a chapter composed this way will end up being eight long summaries of films, and to me there is some-thing dull about reading such summaries – especially of films one has not seen. Certainly such summaries can drain my own enthusiasm from books on film, and I wish to avoid draining yours. So come with me on these viewings and my response. I'll do my best to make this interesting.

The Nasty Girl (1990), directed by Michael Verhoeven, unmasks the ambiva-lence German villagers feel towards a teenager who reveals the secret that their hometown was a site of a Nazi labour camp. It is an unusual work in that it is a film about the Holocaust in which not a single Jew appears. Even the word Jew, is used only a few times, and never before the story is more than half over. In a way it's a film about Holocaust denial, or at least the refusal of (some) Germans to remember what occurred during the Third Reich – and the need for them and their country to do so. The main character, Sonya, is a pre-cocious student with a strong religious background who lives in the comfort-able (and fictional) Bavarian town of Pfilzing. After winning a national essay contest in the mid-1960s on the theme of European Freedom, she enters another contest on the topic, 'My Home Town During the Third Reich'. Sonya is proud of Pfilzing and its citizens. Her aim in the new essay is to show 'How we resisted the Nazis', and how the church, especially, kept its integrity during that period. So confident is Sonya of this notion that she barely hears her mother's soft warning: 'Just write about positive things.'

Her plan to write a work based on interviews with older people comes to naught, for everyone, including the town's leaders – professors, priests, businessmen, politicians – seems to remember little about the period. After she graduates high school, gets married to her former teacher, and begins to have a family, Pfilzing's past still pulls at her. Sonya enters college to study history, determined to write about her town during the Third Reich. When she begins to do research, the local newspaper archive provides a few, oblique clues. Unexpectedly, Sonya discovers an editorial in favour of racial purity that was written by one of her highly respected professors, and she learns from news articles that some Jews were convicted for shady business practices and sent to a concentration camp which, much to her astonishment, existed just outside the town. In search of more data, Sonya goes to the town archives, only to be kept from seeing files for a shifting variety of reasons: first she is told they are out on loan; then that they are too old and brittle to be used; then that the material deals with people still living and their privacy cannot be violated. Coming to understand that she is being stiffed, Sonya (over the objections of friends and family) sues the town and wins a judgement against the Pfilzing archivist – only to be informed that now the documents have been lost. But through a series of smart actions, a bit of luck, and help from the national press, she finally obtains a few files that show what she has begun to suspect – that Jews who owned businesses were denounced by some of the Pfilzing's business and church leaders; and that they were put into the local camp, where some were killed, others deported east, and others made the subject of medical experiments.

Sonya's efforts are, to put it mildly, not appreciated. Snubs from old friends; nasty phone messages saying she is not a real German but a communist; threats that she had better get out of town or else; a dead cat nailed to her doorway; bricks tossed through her windows; a bomb hurled into her living room – such actions both precede and continue after her book, *My Home Town During the Third Reich,* is brought out by a Munich publisher. Honorary doctorates bestowed by the University of Vienna and the Sorbonne lead to an invitation to speak at the local university, where she generalizes local experience to all Germany, saying (with or without irony – it's not clear): 'Pfilzing was a town like any other.' But shouts, jeers, and waving fists greet the announcement that her next research project will be specifically devoted to the fate of the town's Jews. The single man willing to testify about local Nazi activity has his home torched while Sonya is recording his words on tape. Yet eventually (it's not exactly clear why, but perhaps due to her growing national fame) the tide of anger subsides and she becomes the town's 'dear Sonya' once again. Now considered a local hero, she is called to a public ceremony for the unveiling of a bronze bust in honour of her accomplishments. But at the event, Sonya grows angry and refuses the honour, shouting 'you want to shut me up', and flees to her lifelong refuge, a huge sacred tree on a hill outside of town.

To tell *The Nasty Girl* as a simple story is to miss many of the elements which resonate with historical overtones. The sacred tree, where Sonya and her friends go as girls to leave offerings and to pray for love and success (and where she prays, successfully, that the teacher will marry her), is a connection to a deep and good German past, as is Sonya's relationship with her grandmother, a woman once arrested by the Nazis for giving food to Jews in the camp, the only elder in the film who supports her granddaughter's quest and who repeatedly says to everyone from the first essay to the end, 'Try to follow Sonya's example.' The beer hall, always shot in dark tones, where crowds of young males (presumably the ones who throw bricks and bombs through windows) clink beer glasses and sing militant songs, certainly is meant to recall Nazi male bonding and violence, if not directly Hitler's famed beer hall putsch. The soft tones of the Bach's Goldberg variations, played while Sonya and her family view the wreckage of their rooms caused by the bomb, serve as an ironic reminder of a cultured Germany. Even the anti-realist aesthetic of much of the film – overt and often ironic narration by Sonya in the present, commenting on past actions; the occasional use of overt back projection rather than sets; sequences in which her living room seems to float through the town while the family listens to threats on their answering machine; the documentary style interviews with some of the characters – all these point to Brecht and his alienation effects, strategies which are meant to make you think about, rather than simply feel, the character's situations.

For its original German audience, the film would have gained more historical weight because it is based on the story of Anja Rosmus, who underwent similar experiences when she wrote a book about her home town, Passau, during the Third Reich. Clearly it is a cautionary tale about the need to stay in touch with the past, good or bad. Sonya, herself, voices the historian's credo when she says: 'You have to know where things come from to know where they are going.' The past includes the town's Jews who, while offstage, are still the absent presence which drives the film and gives it force. For an entire town to not only repress its history, but conspire to keep a neighbour from finding out the truth of the past, would seem to indicate that crimes of an enormous and shameful nature were committed. *The Nasty Girl* may in part be a kind of salvage effort to show that there has been a good Germany alongside the bad one (and who could doubt it?), but it is also quite clear that the major crimes of the Third Reich were committed against a single folk – and the fact that we never see a Jew in the film suggests something about the thoroughness with which the Nazis pursued their aims.

In *Europa, Europa* (1991) a Jew is centre stage – and more particularly, a Jewish penis with its absent foreskin. Directed by Agnieska Holland, this odyssey of a boy who is able to survive as a member of the Hitler Youth because of his Aryan face, begins with a traditional family (rabbi and bearded elders in a prayer shawl, father and other males with their heads covered, mother and other women looking on) chanting prayers at a briss (circumcision ceremony) and it ends with the main character and his long lost brother, standing side by side outdoors and urinating, while behind them wander dazed victims who have just been liberated from a concentration camp. That main character is young Salomon Perel (a real person who as an old man appears briefly on screen in a kind of coda to the film) whose facial features and perfect command of German, along with the ironic tides of history, allow him to get through much of the war as a member of the Hitler Youth. On the very day of his Bar Mitzvah in 1935, the family dry goods store is wrecked and looted, and his sister killed in a Nazi pogrom. In response, the family flees Germany for his father's hometown of Lodz, Poland. Four years later, the Germans invade and Solly's parents send him and an older brother east. During the flight, the two boys become separated, and Solly ends up in a Russian orphanage, where for two years he learns enough Russian and imbibes enough communist doctrine to join the Young Pioneers (the communist youth organization). Or is this only a survival tactic? For when the Germans overrun the area, and communists and Jews are being pulled out of prisoner lineups to be shot, Solly identifies himself as an orphan of pure German blood, and claims he wants to serve the fatherland. For a while he works as a translator for a front-line company, proving to be so popular and successful that the captain sends him off to a Hitler Youth school in Germany, where he more or less flourishes until captured by the Russians just as the Third Reich collapses.

The penis is central to the story because Solly's main problem all these years is to keep it from ever being seen. Many of the incidents at the front and in school (some of them quite humorous) have to do with concealing his penis – finding places to be alone to urinate, and to take showers or baths, or making up excuses to avoid doctor's examinations, or refusing to make love to a passionately Nazi girlfriend who wishes him to father her pure Aryan child – anything to avoid discovery and execution. In a sequence that has to be painful for every male in the audience, Solly pulls down the skin of his penis and sews it over the head in an effort to simulate a foreskin. But the tactic doesn't work; his organ gets infected and he has to abandon the experiment. By doing well in the school for Hitler youth, winning competitive foot races, clicking his heels and shouting Heil Hitler, shedding tears and joining his voice in *Deutschland Uber Alles* when Stalingrad falls, he manages to maintain his cover.

Solly, himself – and thus we in the audience – sees only bits of the larger tragedy of Europe's Jews. We do witness his indoctrination into the Hitler school, see the courtyards full of Nazi banners and flags, and strutting military leaders, and hear the bloodthirsty martial songs – 'We shall sink our knives into Jewish flesh.' In a vain attempt to locate his parents, Solly journeys to Lodz where, from a streetcar with frosted windows that carries Aryans through the walled-off ghetto, he glimpses the awful conditions of Jewish life – poverty, filth, malnutrition, and dead bodies littering the streets. Having heard early on from an officer at the front that the Jews were being shipped off to Madagascar, he doesn't have to confront the death camps until the very end of the film, when his Russian captors show him photos. But if Solly doesn't know about the final solution, he certainly understands the vicious racism of the theories that underlie it. At the Hitler Youth School, the professor in his class on racial science passionately contrasts the vermin-like characteristics of the Jew (stooped, hand wringing, hook nose, high forehead, inability to look you in the eye, desire to stab you in the back) with the noble characteristics of the Aryan (tall, blonde, blue-eyed, forthright, etc.), then calls Solly to the front of the room, measures his cranial features and pronounces him of Aryan stock. In Solly's mind (and ours) it always comes back to the question: why all this death and destruction over such a tiny bit of flesh as a foreskin?

Korczak (1992), shot in black and white and directed by Andrjez Wajda, takes us into the heart of a ghetto like the one glimpsed in *Europa, Europa* – but in this case it is the largest of all ghettos, Warsaw. Based on the life of Dr Janusz Korczak (real name Henryk Goldszmit), a beloved physician, host of well-known weekly radio show in the Polish capital, *The Old Doctor*, and head of a progressive orphanage, the film highlights the plight of those most innocent victims of Nazism, children, in a story that focuses on its hero's attempts to protect his charges from the growing horrors of the régime. An idealist to the point of saintliness, Korczak is a man who will do anything, undergo any humiliation, to protect his two hundred wards. Yet there is steel in him too. When the Germans enter Warsaw, he remains in his Polish army uniform. When it is decreed that Jews wear the Star of David armband, he refuses to do so, and is beaten and jailed. When he sees a German soldier kicking a child, he intervenes with the shout, 'Have you no shame?' When, more than once, gentile friends offer to smuggle him out of the ghetto, he angrily refuses, saying 'What would you think of a mother who abandoned her children?'

The creation of the ghetto in Warsaw means that the orphanage must move from a palatial suburban estate on the river to cramped quarters in old buildings in the city. Here the task of comforting the frightened children, keeping them from the evils that flourish in the streets (the doctor has the windows walled up and orders that all activities take place indoors), trying to keep up morale ('I don't want to be a Jew' one youngster cries), and feeding them becomes the doctor's chief concern. As all begin to lose weight from their meagre rations, Korczak marches through the ghetto carrying not his physicians bag but a burlap sack as part of a relentless search for food. He is not above stooping into the gutter to pick up a few stalks of wheat, or nagging and harassing anyone and everyone for money and foodstuffs – store owners, the middle class and wealthy in their smart apartments, members of the Judenrat (the Jewish governing council), and criminals in night clubs. When a young militant confronts him and asks how he can deal with gangsters who suck the blood of their own people, he answers, 'I will see the devil to protect my children'.

Korczak's peregrinations provide a window onto the growing horrors inside the ghetto. This is no small neighbourhood, but more like a large densely packed city, an idea underscored when the doctor mentions that it contains 100,000 children. Here the random violence of German soldiers – the arbitrary beatings, arrests, and killings – are the background to a general deterioration of Jewish life. People hurry through the streets, hungry, furtive, fearful. Young kids risk forays through and beyond the ghetto wall in a perpetual search of food. Holed up in their apartments, the rich eat well, while the bodies of those who have died of starvation lie unattended in the gutters. In the nightclub where criminals gather to eat, drink, gamble, make deals, and listen to a torch singer, a gangster boasts to the doctor that at this very time, great business is being done in the ghetto, that many are getting rich from various shady activities, including the sale of stuff to the Germans. A major moral dilemma for the community centres in the Judenrat, those men who have taken power in answer to a German demand that the community govern itself. Their burden is not a happy one; their rationale: that people would be worse off without them. But having to create a Jewish police force to keep order, allocating the limited food supplies in full knowledge that at best they can perhaps save the lives of a small percentage of the population, its members know, as the head man says, 'God and history will judge if we make bad decisions'. One decision is his refusal to sign an order for the deportation of the Jews, and for that the SS beats him almost to death. When the deportations begin anyway, we see him dead, presumably by his own hand.

Despite all he sees, Korczak remains something of an optimist, one who can say at the end of an afternoon when he has managed to collect a lot of food, 'I've had a good day'. Or who can tell a young couple who wish to marry that despite the world closing in on them, he can foresee a better future. But he can be a realist too. He has the children enact a play by Rabindrath Tagore which ends with the hero passing away because he wants to 'familiarize the kids with death'. When the inevitable arrives in the form of German soldiers, breaking into the orphanage shouting 'Raus', Korczak uses his influence with a gangster (who is at that moment trying to give the doctor an American passport so he can escape) to get the Germans to back off and not molest his children. Beneath a flag with the Star of David, they march out of the building and through the streets as if on a school outing, joining masses of Jews who climb into railway wagons waiting at the station. As the train steams through the countryside, the car with Korczak becomes detached and rolls to a stop. He and the children descend and walk off into the peaceful fields of the country-side, disappearing slowly into a growing white light while on the screen appear the words: 'Korczak died with his children in the gas chambers of Treblinka in August, 1942.'

This last scene in *Korczak* was criticized in some quarters as a kind of cop-out. By not taking the doctor and his children all the way to the death camps, the argument ran, it visually suggested some sort of redemption in a case where no redemption is possible. But this is surely an overly literal interpretation of what, after all, is meant as a symbolic scene, suggestive of the brilliance that shines from the doctor's actions, or perhaps of a religious faith that points towards the shining rewards of an afterlife. For something more literal, at least with regard to the arrival at Auschwitz and the entry into the gas chambers, we have *Schindler's List* (1993) – although in an equally controversial sequence, this film draws back from showing the actual gassing, and instead has the women who are crowded into the shower room doused with water from the spigots that usually expel the deadly Zyclon B.

As a most popular and no doubt the best-known film ever to be made on the Holocaust (it won seven Academy Awards, including Best Director and Best Picture), Spielberg's 3-hour-and-16-minute-work, shot in black and white – perhaps in an effort to deglamorize the topic, perhaps as a way of making it seem more like a film from the era it depicts – seems to bear a special burden. The story, which traces the transformation of a shady war profiteer, Oskar Schindler (played by Liam Neeson), into a rescuer seems (or so believe some critics) to reinforce old stereotypes. Schindler dominates the story and appears in almost every sequence. The camera delights in looking up at the tall, handsome, and distinctly Aryan looking Schindler, a commanding pres-ence, and down on the Jews who work for him, short, dark, passive and help-less folk, with two exceptions: the Jewish profiteer, who supplies him with rare delicacies such as caviar, champagne, and chocolates, and the quiet, stub-born, and yet somehow strong Itzhak Stern (Ben Kingsley), his accountant and business manager. Schindler who dresses elegantly, meets high Nazi offi-cials in swank night clubs, bribes and charms his way into a profitable business position, ownership of a metal factory which obtains large contracts to produce mess kits for the German Army. For a long time he views the workers, who he calls 'My Jews', as no more than a source of wealth. Protecting them from deportation to the death camps is largely a matter of good business, for only with their continued efforts can he become and remain rich.

The transformation of Schindler from profiteer to rescuer, a man who uses all his wealth to set up a special factory in Czechoslovakia and buy from corrupt Nazis 1100 of his workers to bring with him, thus saving them from Auschwitz, takes place over time. Clearly it happens as the result of his exposure to an environment in which atrocities are increasingly common and the norms of traditional social life have been replaced by acts of violence and murder, both random and organized. From the first sequences that show German clerks registering and processing Jews, typing their names on lists, confiscating their property (clothing, jewels, articles of furniture – all are carefully sorted and stored, ready to be sent back to Germany) and conscripting them as labourers, to later ones, where they are herded into bleak and wintry concentration camps, we are witness to major steps in the process of bureaucratic dehumanization by which a people becomes stripped of its humanity, and thus are converted into anonymous objects ready for transportation to the death camps. If Auschwitz is shown in only one brief sequence, and if Schindler's women who have been taken there by mistake actually are among the rare ones who visit a genuine shower room, they also pass by a line of people who are descending into the gas chamber next to the crematorium, with its huge smoke stack belching flames and cinders into a dark sky.

The glamorous sequences that focus on Schindler doing business in night clubs and at parties, drinking champagne and dancing with beautiful women, are counterpointed by repeated incidents of mayhem, atrocity, and destruction. No less than 21 sequences of the film are devoted to atrocities inflicted on Jews by Germans. Some are random incidents in which an angry officer shoots someone in the street. Many involve the commander of the concentration camp, Amon Goeth (Ralph Fiennes), sitting in his home above the camp, using a high-powered rifle to pick off prisoners for recreation, for reprisals, or simply as a means of terrorizing them. Central to the film is the harrowing 20-minute section (and in a film, a sequence of this length can seem like an eternity) devoted to the official clearing of the Cracow Ghetto. Before the action, Goeth makes a proud speech saying 'this is a historic day', for after 600 years of residence, at last the Jews will be out of Cracow. What follows is a horrendous depiction of brutal soldiers shouting and shoving, dogs barking, people being brutally pushed and herded out of their houses and crammed into trucks. Some are casually clubbed, shot, or tossed off balconies. Patients in hospitals are shot in their beds, children and the elderly gunned down in the streets. Heightening the effect is Spielberg's handheld camera, which jerkily shows us horrors so close up that it's as if we become participants in the action, ducking, fleeing, hiding to save our own lives from the homicidal torrent inundating us (Baron 2005: 212).

Set in an Israeli orphanage in 1954, *Under the Domim Tree* (1994), directed by Eli Cohen, deals with the devastating effects of the Holocaust on the mentalities of those who somehow survived and now live on with its horrors and losses never absent from their conscious minds. The survivors here are all children, living together in a kibbutz, a collective farm. On the surface, this is a peaceful land, attuned to the rhythms of the farm animals and the growing season. But what happened 'there', the euphemism everyone uses for Europe and the death camps, marks virtually every day of their lives. It fills the heated meal-time debates over the question of reparations from Germany – can money do anything to bring loved ones back? Is this a way of punishing the Germans or letting them off the hook? It underlies the inexplicable suicide which opens the film, the death of one of three brothers who survived the war by hiding in a Polish forest, living off the land like what the other kids call 'wild animals'. It marks the bizarre behaviour of the remaining brothers, aged eight and fourteen, who on misty nights race through the kibbutz, the young one riding on the shoulders of the older one, howling like a wolf. It enters the relationships of the European orphans to Aviva, the single Sabra among them, whose father is long dead and whose mother is confined to a mental ward (she keeps talking as if she had witnessed horrible deeds 'there', when in fact she was in Palestine all through the war), for the others treat her as if, raised in the safety of Palestine, she can't possibly understand what it is to sustain a deep personal loss.

Befitting the shattered, disconnected nature of these children's lives, there is not so much a plot to the film as a series of moments and incidents that reveal the shifting hopes, dreams, nightmares, and fears of these young survivors. Some struggle with issues of language and names. They turn to the Sabra to learn the correct pronunciation of Hebrew words or worry about decisions as to whether to change their European names those which sound more Israeli. When a girl learns that her father has turned up in Poland alive, her comrades can both be happy and depressed (if it happened to her, it could happen to me, but why did it have to happen to her not me?). Eagerly they join together to help prepare her for the trip to Warsaw, sewing her new clothes and teaching her forgotten Polish words. But then news comes, in the middle of a joyous farewell party, that her father has suddenly died, and everyone slips into mourning with a sadness that is as much for themselves as for her – once again they have learned that hope is a luxury in which it is a mistake for them to indulge.

A major story concerns a tough, rather combative newly-arrived girl with scars on her back, who expresses contempt for the pains and dreams of the others. She, herself, cannot remember anything that happened 'there', but when a couple show up claiming they are her parents, she flees, and when they arrive again to take her 'home', she insists they are not her parents, but only people who first claimed her on the boat that brought them from a camp in Italy to Israel. Worse, her scars are, she says, due to violent beatings administered by the old man. When directors of the orphanage protect her, the case ends up in court. Friends of the couple testify that this is indeed their child, though some admit that even if she's not the right child, she is a girl of the same age who could take the place of their daughter who was killed 'there'. The judge seems sympathetic to such arguments, and only a last minute recollection of her mother's blue eyes, and her brother's name, and finally the family name, saves her from being given to parents who are not really her own. If the outcome is happy, the metaphor is a devastating measure of the horrors 'there' which the film never shows us – a young generation, an entire people, severed from their roots to the point that personal identities become shaky, unknown, a kind of mystery to each individual who must repeatedly ask, who am I? And even more important: why was I chosen to survive?

The connection between *Shine* (1996) and the Holocaust may seem tenuous, yet the Final Solution haunts the work, however distantly, as if to suggest that the crimes of the Nazi régime will live on in unexpected ways in generations that did not experience the death camps. This biofilm, directed by Scott Hicks, is based upon the life of Australian-born David Helfgott (Geoffrey Rush), a child prodigy on the piano, his choice of instrument and career in music encouraged by his father. Yet after his first great success as a young adult (a brilliant performance at the Royal College of Music in London of the extremely difficult third concerto by Sergei Rachmaninoff, a work his father always urged him to play), David collapses into a mental disorder which remains with him for the rest of his life – or at least the rest of the film. The syndrome is one that has him, after a period of hospitalization and electric shock treatment, talking in a repetitive poetic gibberish that only makes sense if you take the time to listen closely (which most people don't), and living like a child, unable to support or care for himself or make relationships with others. He dwells in squalor, remains unkempt, on occasion leaves his room undressed, to get lost wandering the streets at night. Sometimes he is brought back from such rambles to his boarding house by friendly strangers. Through one of them, a restaurant owner with a piano bar, he begins to play nightly to the great enthusiasm of her customers, and there he eventually meets a mature, understanding woman who agrees to marry him and then helps to launch him on the road to a career as a concert performer.

Where, you might ask, is the Holocaust in all this? Suffusing the family relationships that provide the cause of his breakdown, Helfgott's parents are survivors for whom the events in Europe are very much part of daily life. Never is it made clear what were their own experiences – did they hide out? were they in the camps? What we do learn is that the father's family was obliterated; his parents and siblings vanished into the gas chambers and ovens. From this, the old world style patriarch has drawn an iron-clad lesson: a family must never be separated. More than a lesson, this is a law which he drums into his children. A law that makes him refuse to allow the teenage David, already a rising star in the small world of 1950s Australia, to accept full scholarship to study piano at a top school in the United States, and has him repeating the action when a similar offer arrives from the Royal College of Music. When the normally cowed and obedient David stands up for his rights to go off even without permission, his father beats him, and when he refuses to capitulate, throws him out of the house, tells him never to return, and later refuses to answer any of his son's letters from London. These actions, the film suggests, are the underlying cause of the breakdown. In the UK, instances of peculiar behaviour surface even before his collapse after his success with Rachmaninoff. After David returns to Australia as an invalid, his father still will not visit, although other family members do so. Only shortly before his father's death, after David's first big concert, does the old man show up for an awkward and brief reconciliation. It doesn't remove the son's disabilities, but it does seem to allow him to go on to a new career.

The Harmonists (1997), directed by Joseph Vilsmaier, is a familiar kind of genre film about the formation, problems, eventual success, and ultimate dissolution of a glitzy, pop music group in the years between the world wars, in this case a sextet of male jazz singers. At first it seems far too light to have anything to do with a serious topic like the Holocaust because for some time the problems of the characters are no more than those of the genre. The organizer of the ensemble, Harry Frommerman, has a vision of a new kind of German music group which will perform a kind of a capella American jazz. His struggles are to bring together the personnel, create arrangements that are unique, oversee the endless rehearsals it takes in the search for the best combination of sounds, find a booking agent willing to take on such an unusual act and get it an audition. Finally he has to keep the men together through the normal tensions one expects (from having seen similar films) among active young vocal artists –

including the requisite struggle between two of them, Harry and Robert Biberti, the bass, over the same girl, Erna Eggstein, who works in a music store owned by Jews. Even though the Harmonists seem to rise fairly quickly to the top of the club and recording circuit, they do so in a Germany of the late twenties, that period when the frantic nightlife of Berlin (the clubs filled with American jazz musicians, overt sexual behaviour both hetero and homo, and the open use of drugs like cocaine are well rendered on screen) is counterpointed by the rise of the puritanical, racist street thugs in uniform, the Brown Shirts.

Paralleling the Harmonists movement towards becoming not only the most popular singing group in the country, but also an international success, is the Nazi movement towards power. Individual belligerence (at a resort, a young tough and former classmate of Erna's, first calls into question the manliness of the singers, then upbraids her for dating the Jewish Harry) and acts of social violence (the windows of the music store owned by a Jewish couple are painted over with Stars of David), begin to foreshadow the coming world of the Third Reich (at least for those in the audience). But the musicians on screen are for a long time little concerned with the growing upheaval around them, even though three were born as Jews (one has converted to Christianity), and one of the Christians in the group is married to a Jewish woman. Their apparent indifference to anything but music and success, which continues after the Nazis take power in 1933, appears to be a product of two beliefs: the notion that Germany is ultimately a civilized and orderly country of laws (a sentiment expressed by the store owner), and the feeling that they are so successful both in Germany and abroad that they will be immune from any interference with their careers or lives. Only when Storm Troopers (led by the same young tough) smash the Jewish-owned music store, and drag off Erna, while a Brown Shirt holds Ulrich at knife-point and another beats up Robert, does the threat begin to seem serious.

Even so, the only time the question of race surfaces among them is during a subsequent tour of the United States when Harry suggests that they do not return to Germany and they all join in a vigorous debate. Voted down by the others, Frommerman at first claims he will stay in America, then reluctantly joins his comrades for the return journey. Soon he and Robert are facing a Nazi official in the Reich Music Association, a fan who has them autograph a record for his nephew. The problem, he tells them, is not simply that there are Jews in the group. It's also the fact that they sing so many songs written by Jewish composers (Harry and other Harmonists). If they would just perform more works composed by Germans, they would be free to continue their engagements – as they do until the Nazi leader and theoretician Julius Schleicher attends a concert and invites them to his house. There Schleicher requests that they perform not one of their usual light, satirical tunes, but a folk song much favoured by the Nazis. Harry, literally choking on the words, cannot do so, and Schleicher dismisses them. It is the end. After a final concert, when they receive a standing ovation from their fans, the group breaks up, for the three Jewish members have decided to go into exile. Erna, who has long been wavering between Robert and Harry, joins the latter on the platform of the station as they board a train for Vienna. A postscript tells us that both the group in exile and the ones who stayed in Germany formed singing groups, but that both of them broke up in 1941.

Sunshine (1999) is a saga made by Istvan Szabo that both covers four generations of the Sonnenschein family and sketches a history of Hungary from the reign of Hapsburg Emperor Franz Josef in mid-nineteenth century through the First World War, the break-up of the Austro-Hungarian Empire, the rise of the right wing, the harsh interlude of the German occupation, the coming of the Red Army, and the early years of a repressive communist régime. The story charts the trajectory of a Jewish family in this modern era, recounting the movement from a small town to the big city, from poverty to riches, from business to professions like medicine and law, from traditional, synagogue-centred values to competition in Olympic Sports, from Orthodox Judaism to conversion to Catholicism. It is at the same time an extended metaphor on the fate of Jews during the processes of modernization, and a kind of warning against the futility of attempting to assimilate – at least in middle Europe of the twentieth century.

It begins when young and penniless Emmanuel Sonnenschein ('Sunshine' in English) migrates from a small town to Budapest with a single item of value: a secret formula for a medicinal tonic developed by his late father. This drink, marketed throughout the land, becomes the basis of the family fortune. By the time he is in late middle age, the now bearded Emmanuel presides over a huge, luxuriously furnished mansion that houses his wife, three children, and several servants. As befitting a patriarch, he is a conservative who advises his offspring to remain true to their Jewish faith and to avoid trouble. The children have their own ideas. Seeing themselves less as Jewish than Hungarian, they change their name to Soros and pursue professional careers (applauded by the father). One son, Gustav, becomes a medical doctor, and the other, Ignatz, a judge. The new century brings the political conflicts of the country into the household. Arguments flare between Gustav, a socialist who identifies with the workers exploited by the burgeoning capitalist system, and Ignatz, a conservative who thinks the dual monarchy embodies the most admirable of political and social systems. One of the high points of his life is a personal interview with the Emperor Franz Josef, who applauds him for his work as a punitive judge in military courts during the First World War.

The road to assimilation continues into the third generation. Adam, son of Ignatz, not only hides his Jewish background, but converts to Catholicism to further his career. A brilliant fencer, he becomes part of a team that consists of upper-class military men. When a competing group with a Jewish manager offers him a huge sum of money to join them, he flies into an anti-Semitic tirade: 'Those people think they can buy anything!' Conversion, connections, and the gold medal he won at the 1936 Olympics in a Berlin stadium hung with swastika banners do nothing to protect Adam when Hungarian Nazis take control of the country under the aegis of their German overlords. In a work camp, he is tortured to death in front of a mass of prisoners which includes his young son, Ivan, for refusing to admit aloud that he is Jewish. As an adult, Ivan, for a long time follows in his father footsteps, denying not only his religious heritage, but the humanism that went along with reform Judaism, as he rises within the communist government – until the time when he begins to encounter an ill concealed anti-Semitism within the party itself. Only then does he begin to recover some of the values of his tradition, symbolized his acts of leaving the Party and officially changing his name back to Sonnenschein.

Criticizing the Hollywood historical film can be a kind of reflex reaction among academics. If the usual grounds are its 'fictions', (dealt with in earlier chapters), another source concerns its aesthetics – the seamless camera work, the match-on-move editing, the broad palate of colours, the smooth integration of standard shots and sound effects meant to convince the viewer (or so the theory runs) that she or he is looking through a window at a real world rather than at a careful construction of one. Worse yet (the argument goes) are the stories of the past on film, with their fascinating characters, exotic locales, emotional highs, and (often) happy endings serve only to entertain viewers rather than helping to inform them, move them towards a critical consciousness or political action, or allowing them to face and work through the traumas of the past. If this is true for standard historicals, how much more deplorable it can seem if such entertainment values suffuse films about the Holocaust. What is desperately needed, says one specialist in German culture, are 'films that deal with Nazism and the Holocaust in ways that challenge the narrowly circumscribed Hollywood conventions of storytelling and not only reflect self-critically on the limit and impasses of film but also utilize its specific potential in the representation of the past' (Kaes 1992: 208).

Filling such a role are, presumably, such complex and difficult works as Claude Lanzmann's *Shoah*, with its nine-and-a-half-hours of interviews of survivors and no images from the 1940s, or Hans-Jurgen Syberberg's, *Hitler – a Film From Germany* (1977), which uses puppets, sets, historical objects, actors, and back-projection to create the Third Reich on what is clearly shown to be a sound stage. But sympathetic as I am to the often dazzling contributions of innovative or post-modern works of history on film (see Chapters 1 and 9), I don't understand the necessity for thinking in terms of an either/or. Written history uses different genres to present the past, so why not film? That the dramatic feature aims to entertain an audience does not rule out its ability to inform and move us, or to provide a sense of the past. One of the mistakes in the critique of Hollywood is to assume that the audience only learns from the central story and the fate of individual characters. But a historical film is much more than its story – it is an experience, the presentation of a world whose moments, characters, and images – particularly if they are strong – are capable of staying with the viewer long after the specific plots and resolutions have disappeared.

Aside from *The Nasty Girl*, with its quasi-Brechtian moments, the other seven works discussed here are more or less standard dramas. Though some are more Hollywood in their stories than others, and several have distinctly downbeat endings, all are full of the emotional highs and resolutions we expect from that genre. Greatly do they vary in artistry, style, tone, and production design – from the gorgeous black and white of *Schindler's List* to the harsher greys of *Korczak*; from the sumptuous mansions, offices, and concert halls where Sonnenscheins move, to the cramped and crowded spaces of the kibbutz of *Under the Domim Tree*; from the fluid camera movements of *Europa, Europa* to the more jagged shots of *Shine* in the days of Helfgott's madness. But however much the aesthetics are an inseparable part of the meaning conveyed by each work, I want to focus on the historical world they create, the images and moments these eight films collectively provide for seeing, experiencing, and understanding something of the Nazi years.

To simply consider locales, characters, and situations of the works present is to find an enormous breadth. The geographical spread falls across several countries – Germany, Poland, Russia, and Austria-Hungary – with shadows of the events darkening Israel and far off Australia. The timeframe runs from the late nineteenth century (*Sunshine*) to the latter half of the twentieth (*Shine, Nasty Girl*). Settings include crowded ghettos, apartments both modest and swanky (*Korczak, Harmonists*), elegant mansions, night clubs, concentration camps, concert halls, bars, synagogues, the royal palace in Vienna (*Sunshine*), and Auschwitz. Among the gentile characters are Protestants (*Nasty Girl*) and Catholics (*Schindler, Sunshine*); people friendly to Jews (*Harmonists*) and those who are indifferent to or annoyed by them; casual anti-Semites, doctrinaire Nazis, rescuers, and stubborn seekers after truth (*Nasty Girl*). Among Jews, the range of backgrounds and character are very broad. Included are the orthodox, the mildly religious (*Europa, Korczak*), the indifferent (*Harmonists*), and those who convert to Christianity (*Sunshine*); the poor, the middle class, and the rich; artisans who work with their hands, professionals who get ahead using their education and brains, and racketeers who hustle money in the shadow of destruction. Here one finds optimists and the pessimists, the brave and the fearful, collaborators and Kapos (Jews who work as police for the Nazis), the members of the Judenrat, and a few who dare to fight back against the system (*Korczak*).

The diversity of characters and places is matched by the wide range of worlds, experiences, and situations. The films portray the smart urban life of Berlin and Budapest in the 1920s and 1930s, when assimilated and inter-married Jews seem no different from their neighbours; the beginnings of Nazi thuggery as Jews are insulted on the street and their synagogues and stores trashed in the thirties (*Europa, Harmonists*); the results of the racial laws as people are first forced to wear the Star of David, then made to hastily pack their belongings, give up their apartments and possessions, and join the crowds moving towards cramped quarters in the squalid ghetto; the violence of speeches denouncing them as vermin, of lectures on the racial superiority of the Aryan, and the murderous words of anti-Semitic songs (*Europa*); the humiliations of being forced to stand in endless lines for processing, to strip for physical examinations, to be prodded and poked, to have their appearance (their dress, sideburns, beards) derided, and to be compelled to perform actions such as shovelling snow or dancing for common German soldiers in the streets (*Korczak*); the pains and rigour of life in the concentration camps, where one can be shot for the tiniest infraction of rules or for no reason at all; the terror of being packed like cattle into a railway wagon and carried cross-country and through the gates of Auschwitz. In these films, we enter a world in which violence and terror are ever present, from the perpetual shouts, kicks, and shoves of soldiers, to the casual and then well-organized murders; we are confronted with images of men, women, and children pushed off roofs, clubbed to death, or shot at randomly in the streets or in the camps, or lined against walls and gunned down in masses, or led into the gas chambers. We also gain some sense of the lingering effects of the régime – the Germans who refuse to face their past, the traumas borne by the next generation, in Europe, in Israel, and in Australia.

I could continue – but to this kind of description there is no real end. So much happens within the motion picture frame that the details contained in these eight films deny any real possibility of a neat or adequate summary. All I mean to do is to point towards the wealth of information – locales, characters, and situations – about the Holocaust and its aftermath that are delivered to us in their more than 16 hours of screen time. It is true that many aspects of the topic are left untouched in these dramatic features. They don't attempt to explain anything about the cultural, social, psychological, economic, or political causes of anti-Semitism or Nazism; show almost nothing of the men at the top who prepared for and planned the Final Solution; virtually ignore issues of collaboration by conquered peoples such as the Poles with the Germans; mention nothing about the reactions (or lack of them) of the Allied leadership to know-ledge of the depredations being worked on Europe's Jewish population. Which is only to say that, like all historical films, this group is not capable of explain-ing long-running national, European, or world geopolitical developments.

Yet I would argue that to the larger discourse of the Holocaust, a field in which debates over its causes, complicities, and course are still bitterly con-tested (witness the flap over Daniel Goldhagen's book, *Hitler's Willing Executioners*, in the late 1990s, or the rumpus among German historians, the so-called *Historikerstreit* or Historian's Debate a few years earlier), these eight movies add an important experiential quality. They do this by exploiting the great potentialities of the medium – by giving us the illusion that, for a little while, we witness, or even live, the problems, angers, fears, joys, and pains of other lives set in other times. Doing so, they provide us with what surely is a kind of historical insight and understanding. To see these eight films, to live through them, is to be exposed to some of the worst and best of human behaviour as played out in an appalling régime during one of humanity's dark-est ages. To consider the knowledge gained from that anything other than historical is to ignore the evidence of three major conduits of learning – one's eyes, body and heart.

Chapter 9

Film on history

In the fall of 2000 I made a lecture tour of several universities and cultural centres in Japan. My topic for the tour was a short version, illustrated with film clips, of what is now Chapter 7 of this book – its title: 'Oliver Stone as Historian.' After my lecture at the American Center in Tokyo, I went out for food and beer with some former students from the year I was a Fulbright professor at Kyushu University. One of them, a mathematician who is now a major figure in the Genome Project in Japan, and who is also a serious student of Buddhism, told me the following: my explanation about the history film reminded him of the beginnings of Buddhist paintings in Japan. The priests (and here we are, no doubt, in the sixth or seventh century) realized that an illiterate population could not read the sacred Sanskrit texts, so they decided to create visual works, paintings (the mandala is one of the forms we know best) to instill in the population the ideas of Buddhism. Smart and educated men, these priests realized that these paintings could not contain all the information and all the complex ideas that were part of the sacred texts, that they were in fact a kind of simplification of those written texts. Yet they strongly felt that the more public and more accessible medium of painting would convey the spirit, the feeling, and the meaning of Buddhism to the general public who did not have the skills to read. Over the centuries, these visual representations of Buddhist ideas began to take on an integrity of their own, as more and more people came, and still come, to know the ideas of the religion through these images rather than through the sacred texts that were their inspiration. Today they have for most people, including priests, taken the place of those texts; indeed, some find them more characteristic and revealing of Buddhism than the original texts.

More than any comment made on my efforts to understand and explicate the role of the history film, more than anything said by any critic, fellow historian, narratologist, or cinema studies expert, this idea struck home. For it seemed to point directly to some of the major questions with which I have been struggling ever since beginning to write on film. The question of how to think about or understand the relationship between history on the screen and history on the page. The question of whether this is a lesser or simply a different realm of history. The question of how and what and if the work of history on the screen adds to historical understanding. At least this brief story suggests that surely if there is more than one way of understanding the doctrines of a lengthy and complex religious tradition such as Buddhism, with a history in Japan that goes back almost 15 centuries, then there can be more than one way of understanding the past and more than one medium in which to convey that understanding.

Even if one accepts this insight, it leads to more questions: what exactly is *historical understanding*? What do we mean when we use that term. And is such understanding, whatever it is, always and everywhere the same, or is historical understanding (as it must be) itself historically determined? To say we understand the past surely means we know more than simply the traces of the past we call data or facts, otherwise chronicles would be a perfectly adequate way of knowing. Clearly understanding has to do with how we put those traces together to mean something to us today. The most common device for doing so is narrative. We come to understand the past in the stories we tell about it, stories based on the sort of data we call fact, but stories which include other elements that are not directly in the data but arise from the process of story telling. Through the work of recent theorists, we have come to know that this narrative of the past is itself a device – our narratives select some of those traces, and in doing so, 'constitutes' them, that is makes them into the 'facts' that we then link together to show and explain and interpret what happened – to, in short, produce meaning. By now we also know enough about narrative history to suggest that a great deal of this 'meaning' often precedes the 'facts' and is part of the process that helps to constitute them.

As mentioned in the Introduction to this book, I came to think and write about historical film well into my career as an historian. Before turning to film, I produced, along with a number of essays and articles, three works of narrative history, though to be precise, the second was a biography and the third a series of three interlaced biographies. When I was writing these books, I certainly did not think about the relationship between facts and narrative, or even about the truth claims of what I wrote. I simply worked within a discipline that had standards of procedure which did not very much reflect upon themselves or their origins. You followed those standards and produced historical truth – which somehow included historical understanding.

Personally I grew restless with the traditional narrative form. My second book, *Romantic Revolutionary: A Biography of John Reed* (1975) took several small steps away from the linear, and my third was a full blown experiment in a different way of writing history. Perhaps influenced by my own experience and its unusual theme, how living and working in Japan changed three nineteenth-century American sojourners, my book, *Mirror in the Shrine* (1988), was a self-reflexive work that told its story in multiple voices, was written in the present tense and sometimes the second person, and utilized occasional direct address to the audience or to my characters. As a one-time sojourner myself, I wished to share something about the immediacy of the experience of an alien culture, the shock of its sights, smells, personal encounters. In a sense, I wanted to create on the page the kind of encounter with the world of the past (in this case nineteenth-century Japan) that film so effortlessly seems to provide. The book was generally well received, but some reviewers chided me for lapsing into the first or second person, worried that I was not writing proper 'history', or was indulging in 'fiction' because I had stepped outside the normal narrative boundaries.

Even before undertaking this narrative experiment, I had begun to teach and write about historical film. Like many historians who introduce film in the classroom, I at first did so in a somewhat unconscious and wholly untheoretical way. When talking about the twentieth century, it seemed useful to share some of the common images, which meant showing a film like *The Jazz Singer* (1927) to demonstrate something about immigrant groups and the changing culture of the 1920s, or *Grapes of Wrath* (1940) for a flavour of the Dust Bowl, or *Triumph of the Will* (1935) to give a sense of the Nazi self-image, or *Battleship Potemkin* (1925) for the founding ideology of the Soviet State. My use of film expanded from an occasional one to an entire course in historical film in 1977 after attendance at my once over-subscribed class on radical and revolutionary movements, shrank from 35 students to 2. Changing the topic to Radicalism and Revolution on Film served to boost my enrolments back to their previous numbers. It also provided another level of history, another discourse to talk about in class, although I would not have put it that way at the time. What was soon clear was that the written works of history and those on film pointed to the same topics but dealt with them in different ways, raising different sorts of questions and providing different sorts of answers about the past.

The issues raised by this double discourse became more important when I began to write about film in the early 1980s. This happened largely because two of my written works were used, more or less, as the basis for films. One of them, *The Good Fight* (1982) was a feature-length documentary about the

Americans who fought in the Spanish Civil War. Since this was precisely the topic of my first book, *Crusade of the Left: The Lincoln Battalion and the Spanish Civil War* (1969), I became the chief historical consultant on a project funded by the National Endowment for the Humanities and undertaken by three young filmmakers. More than simply adviser, I ended up writing the narration for the film. The whole experience, beyond the insight it provided into the process of making a documentary, let me see how much such a work was shaped by the beliefs and agendas of the film-maker historians, and how much its narrative strategies and structure shared with the dramatic feature – such things as the need for interesting characters, a plot with a sense of development, and a conclusion suffused with a strong moral position.

The other film was the big budget Hollywood feature, *Reds*. While I was still in the process of writing *Romantic Revolutionary* (1975), I was contacted by Warren Beatty, who had learned at the Houghton Library at Harvard University, which houses Reed's papers, that I was at work on the topic. The year was 1972, and if you wanted to talk to someone in detail about Jack Reed, his friends, milieu, and times, I was the one. Beatty and I talked on and off for the next seven years, until the film went into production and I joined the production company as historical consultant. This was a loosely-defined job. Basically both I and my files were available to help the film makers (writers, director, producers, production designer, cinematographers, wardrobe, etc.) with any questions they had about anything to do with Reed and the worlds in which he moved. I also read and made critiques of various versions of the script, suggested some changes of actions or language (I have a couple of lines of dialogue in the film), and went on location with the company for a few weeks in Spain, where I was gratified to see copies of my book being read by people all over the set and was treated to the great pleasure of having director of photography Vittorio Storaro (who won one of his four Oscars for *Reds*) tell me that my book was his Bible, that he never lit a scene and set up a camera until he had re-read the relevant part of *Romantic Revolutionary*.

The experiences of working on these films, created in part from my own research, made me start to wonder exactly what happened on the way from the page to the screen. But only after a request from the journal, *Reviews in American History*, did I write my first essay on film, '*Reds* as history'. In retrospect, it seems like a naïve essay. While it praised some aspects of the film and yet took it to task for some of its historical errors – in part for getting certain details wrong; in part for missing what I thought to be the overall important theme of John Reed's life – the essay never stopped to consider that film was such a different medium from the written word that it had to be judged by different criteria (Rosenstone 1982). But to say that is to get ahead of myself.

It took some years for me to realize how easy it is to criticize historical films for errors. And how much more difficult to figure out how the products of this visual medium sit with relation to written history. Or to try to understand just how, and what do they convey, about the past?

This excursion into autobiography seems necessary because working on film provides more than a little insight into what sorts of things can and cannot be done on screen – either through normal dramatic practice or the limitations (and demands) of the medium. These experiences helped me to understand, if only unconsciously, how film of necessity did and had to do something different from the written word. Figuring out what that is, and how to think about it, has been my task, on and off, ever since. What seems clear is that too many academics critique film naïvely, unthinkingly – as I did in my first essay. Why? Because movies run against our notion of proper history. It still runs against that notion in me, but I have come to see – as you will know if you have read the earlier chapters – that film is not history in our traditional sense, but it is a kind of history nonetheless. An important kind which may well have already changed the way we see and describe the past. Film has given us tools to see reality in a new way – including the realities of a past which has long since vanished from our sight.

A second reason for indulging in autobiography is to explain to the reader the choice of movies which I have used to illustrate my theme. I am well aware that they have been largely devoted to war, social upheaval, and catastrophe. As the books on Spain and John Reed indicate, the early part of my career was devoted to the study of radical social and political movements of both modern Europe and the United States. For years as a researcher, I delved deeply into the discourse of radicalism, while as a teacher of a course called The Modern Age, I of necessity focus to a great extent on movements dealing with social upheaval – the two world wars, the Russian Revolution, Nazism, and the Holocaust. One result is that, in line with my belief that it is necessary to know the discourse of the particular field to be able to write in depth on the history film, my choice has been limited to works depicting such events. (Another area of my research, the relation between the United States and Japan in the nineteenth century, has produced too few films to warrant explication.) If I am right in my arguments about the history film, then they apply to other fields in the past as well, to questions, say, of industrial development, the growth of the middle class, to family and gender history, cultural change, international relations, colonialism, to any topic which involves people in the past about whom a story can be told. I am aware, too, that a large number of the films analyzed in this book deal with specific, documentable people and events, but one could easily do a book like this analyzing films that, like a couple of those in the chapter on the Holocaust (e.g. *Under the Domim Tree, Sunshine*) deal with fictional characters placed into specific historical settings.

As I pursued my studies on the history film over several years (usually in response to requests that I present a paper or take part in a panel on the increasingly popular, to both historians and people in cinema studies, topic of history and film), I for a long time kept trying to look at films with an historian's eye, trying to make film fit into the rules and conventions we academic historians use to construct a past. Early on it became obvious to me that some film makers were obsessed by the past in the same way that historians are. Oliver Stone, Ousmane Sembene, Carlos Diegues, Rainer Werner Fassbinder, Margarethe von Trotta, Andrejz Wajda, Istvan Szabo, the Taviani brothers – all kept returning to the past for their subjects, and dealing with serious moments, events, and people in their respective nation's histories. So why, I asked myself, weren't they considered historians? Just because they worked in a popular medium? My 'Aha!' experience came after viewing Alex Cox's *Walker* and going back to read everything about that nineteenth-century adventurer – and seeing that this black comedy about the American invasion of Nicaragua engaged precisely the same questions that engaged historians about American involvement in Central America. This was the moment I could set aside my training and ask: Why not just accept that a Cox or the others are already historians and take a look at how such film makers create their histories – *why not investigate their rules of engagement with the traces of the past, rules of engagement that come out of the possibilities and practices of the medium in which they work.* Rather than criticizing historical films for doing or not doing this or that, why not try to figure out what we would want the ideal historical film to be? From that point on, my attention focused on films and film makers who obviously (from an historian's point of view) were attempting to create a meaningful historical world – which to me means a world on the screen that engages the kind of historical issues about which historians also write – ethnicity, war, revolution, social change, gender relations, colonialism, race.

To accept film makers as historians, as I have been proposing throughout this book, is to accept a new sort of history. The medium and its practices for constructing a past – all ensure that the historical world on film will be different from that on the page. In terms of informational content, intellectual density, or theoretical insight, film will always be less complex than written history. Yet its moving images and sound scapes will create experiential and emotional complexities of a sort unknown upon the printed page. Like the Buddhist paintings, the historical film can convey much about the past to us and thereby provide some sort of knowledge and understanding – even if we cannot specify exactly what the contours of such understanding are.

Lest I seem terribly naïve, let me say that I understand there is another, perhaps more likely possibility: that the visual media will simply wipe out history or any sense of the past as we have known it for the last couple of hundred or couple of thousand years. That the mixing of past and present, the kind of pastiche used in advertising and literary fiction and film, the flattening of reality, the jumble of images from different ages and cultures, about which so many post-modern theorists such as Frederick Jameson have worried, will destroy history as we have known it. Since we historians don't predict the future, I have no answer to that critique except the gut feeling that one of the constants of human history is that people always want to have some knowledge, however imperfect, about where they and their ancestors came from, literally and figuratively. And that as long as screens, large and small, are a major medium for showing and telling us about our world, then film will be one way of rendering the past.

However we think of it, we must admit that film gives us a new sort of history, what we might call history as vision. It's earliest predecessor, oral history, tends to create a poetic relationship to world. Then over a two-thousand-year period, written history has created an increasingly linear, scientific relationship. Film changes rules of the game and creates its own sort of truth, creates a multi-level past that has so little to do with language that it is difficult to describe adequately in words. Certainly the historical world created by film is potentially much more complex than written text. On the screen, several things occur simultaneously – image, sound, language, even text – elements that support and work against each other to create a realm of meaning as different from written history as written was from oral history. So different that it allows us to speculate that the visual media may represent a major shift in consciousness about how we think about our past. If this is true, then it may well be our film maker historians are probing the possibilities for the future of our past.

What kept and continues to keep historians from fully coming to grips with film as history is our traditional reflex: empiricism. However much we might enjoy a dramatic feature set in the past, the specialist of the period represented is bound at many points to cry 'foul' – and to argue that a particular scene, a character, a moment, a bit of dialogue or a whole sequence of events is not an accurate reflection of the sources, but only an invention. Such judgements are not mistaken. Settings, actors, costumes, gestures, dialogue, music and other elements on the screen – all of necessity, as Pierre Sorlin pointed out 20 years ago, partake of a good deal of the imaginary. Certainly the screen provides no clear window onto a vanished past; the best it can do is to provide a construction of proximate realities to what once was. Here we face the larger point, the more fundamental issue raised but never fully explored by Sorlin: if the bulk of what historical films show on the screen is fiction, how can we consider them to be history?

Maybe one should not insist upon the word – at least not in its capitalized form. The best and more serious kind of historical film does 'history' only in so far as it attempts to make meaning out of something that has occurred in the past. Like written history, it utilizes traces of that past, but its rules of engagement with them are structured by the demands of the medium and the practices it has evolved – which means that its claims will be far different from those of history on the page. To give but a few examples. The basic element of the medium, the camera, is a greedy mechanism which, in order to create a world, must show more precise details – arrangements of furniture, the way tools are handled, stances or gestures, the exact locations of warriors in a landscape or strikers before a factory – than historical research could ever fully provide. The dramatic structure, which means the need for plausible characters and psychic tension, and the limitations on screen time, ensures that dialogue will have to be created, events and characters condensed, compressed, altered – even invented. However counter intuitive it may seem, what we see on the screen is – and in this sense precisely like written history – not a window onto the past but a construction of a simulated past, not a literal reality but a metaphoric one.

The notion that written history works as metaphor has been powerfully argued by more than one theorist in recent years. Even those who do not accept the position that metaphor is central to historical understanding have come to realize that works of history cannot literally recreate the past but can only enfold its trace elements into a verbal construction, a text that attempts to explain vanished people, events, moments, and movements to us in the present. Doing so involves much more than the literal. Even the most scholarly histories are, in the words of Robert Berkhofer, 'more structures of interpretation than the structures of factuality they purport to be' (Berkhofer 1995: 57). Indeed, the literary job of historical realism, the only mode of writing historians recognize as legitimate – and one to which most film makers slavishly adhere – is to 'make the structure of interpretation appear to be (the same as) the structure of factuality'. What this suggests is that both written history and films invoke the authenticity (or reality) that comes from using those traces, that documentary evidence we call 'facts', and then go on to employ a literary or filmic vocabulary to create 'history'.

Whatever they share in terms of interpretive structure, the relationship of data to discourse, historical books and films divide on one crucial issue: invention. The most radical theorists may talk of the fictive qualities of all narrative, but however metaphoric, historical narrative is always built on blocks of verifiable data. The dramatic film, by contrast (and here is where it parts company most sharply with the documentary and gets closest to the historical novel), indulges in the invention of characters, dialogue, incidents, and events; indeed, some historical films are made up of wholly invented characters placed into a documented setting or situation. This practice of invention may be enough to remove from the dramatic film the word 'history', but certainly not the ideas of historical 'thinking' or 'understanding'. Not if by that phrase we mean coming to grips with the issues from the past that trouble and challenge us in the present – questions of social change, gender relations, individual and group identity, class, ethnicity, war, colonialism, revolution, ideology, and nationalism,

It is just these kinds of major social and cultural issues that are explored in what one might call 'the new historical', a film with roots in the past – Eisenstein's *October* or Carl Dreyer's *Joan of Arc* (1928) are among the forebears – which have become increasingly common in the last 30 years. The break-up of the Hollywood studio system, the creation of film capabilities in newly-independent Third World countries, the activism of the 1960s, the collapse of the Soviet Bloc, the creation of lightweight, less expensive film and video equipment, the vast expansion of television channels and cable systems – such factors no doubt underlie, but don't exactly explain, the flourishing of this genre of dramatic motion pictures (which has a counterpart in the proliferation of documentaries, sponsored by television channels) that downplay or eschew traditional romance and attempt to deal seriously with the meaning of the past.

The term, 'new historical', may seem to imply a movement, but it would be more accurately described as a tendency, and a diffuse one at that. Individual examples of such films have been produced just about everywhere movies are made, but they also tend to appear in two sorts of clusters: as either several works by a single director (Andrzej Wajda, Poland; Oliver Stone, US; Theo Angelopolous, Greece; Ousmane Sembene, Senegal) or several films in a single country in a brief period of time (the New German Cinema or the Cinema Nuovo of Brazil, both in the 1970s; Cuban film in the 1960s). Attempts to pinpoint the cause of such clusters can be no more than speculation. Financial and business considerations must certainly be involved, yet such movies tend to appear at moments when nations are undergoing some kind of cultural or political stress, change or upheaval – the attempt to come to grips with the trauma of Vietnam (Oliver Stone); the corruption and internal conflicts that presaged the end of communism (Wajda); terrorism, repression, and the legacy of the Third Reich (New German Cinema); the breakup of a nation (the cinema of the former Yugoslavia in the 1990s); the desire to find (or create) a heritage for a post-colonial country (Sembene, Cinema Nuovo, Australia in the 1980s); or to justify a revolutionary change of régimes (Cuba).

For the traditional historian, my argument for the film as a form of history may be indigestible. But to those historians with faces set towards the future, it may seem more like common sense. Even if the film could deliver data as well as the written word (which it cannot, as a practical matter, do very well), what would be the point? We already have books. To attend the cinema, or to watch a television screen, is to undergo an experience far different from that of reading words on a page. That difference lies at the heart of the history film. However we define, measure, and analyze that difference – and none of this has yet been undertaken very convincingly, perhaps because of the great slippage involved in translating a multi-media experience into linear words – we can at least understand that the experience is different enough to let us think that ultimately the historical film takes us back to the most basic questions: what do we want from the past? Why do we want to know it? What else might we want to know that we don't already know? To learn by example? To feel (or think we feel) what others (may have) felt in given situations? To experience, if only distantly, what others experienced in war, revolution, political crisis, times of trouble and times of plenty? Or perhaps, as in the history once practised by the Greeks, to be inspired into ethical or aesthetic contemplation of the human condition?

It may seem counter intuitive, even downright insulting to suggest the film as a new form of historical thinking. Yet living in an increasingly visual age, we must be prepared to at least entertain such a notion. For visual thinking of the past, metaphor and symbol may become far more important than amassing data or creating a logical argument. Theorist Frank Ankersmit has already argued that even with regard to written history, 'the metaphorical dimension . . . is more powerful than the literal or factual dimensions', and has broached the notion that in the future we need to focus less on the past itself than on the language we use for speaking about the past (Ankersmit 1994a: 180). This at least suggests that we might judge historians less by their data and more by the aptness of their metaphors. In a world of film, these would be visual metaphors – or perhaps something we can simply call vision. Here is a major point shared by both films and books – each is more than the sum of its parts. A written work is based upon data, but the totality of its words transcend the data and launch into a realm of moral argument and metaphor. Film also utilizes data, if in a rather more casual way, before it too launches into the same realm. Vision, metaphor, overall argument or moral is precisely the point at which film and written history come the closest to each other. The details of the past are necessary, interesting, even fascinating but what we really want to know is how to think about them, what they mean. The printed page and film are both ready to tell us.

If the dramatic film can successfully meditate upon, interrogate and analyze the past, or explore that which has been repressed by official histories, as I have tried to show in earlier chapters, then surely it plays part of the role we assign to traditional History. More than a quarter of a century ago, Marc Ferro, in the essay which suggested that some directors had already created a filmic writing of history, went on to claim that in a more general way, motion pictures provide what he called a 'counter discourse' on contemporary society. Let me take his idea one step further and claim that the history film creates a counter discourse on the past. An unusual discourse, to be sure, for it bridges Aristotle's distinction between history and poetry – such films include both what happened and what might have happened.

To change the medium of history from the page to the screen, to add images, sound, colour, movement, and drama, is to alter the way we read, see, perceive, and think about the past. All these elements are part of a practice of history for which we do not yet have a decent label. Nor do we have a good sense of its coordinates, how and where it sits in time, space, and in relation to our other discourses. Yet this kind of history is a challenge, a provocation, and a paradox. If its world can never be taken literally, the history film creates rich images, sequences, and visual metaphors that help us to see and think about what has been. Its truths are metaphoric and symbolic, not literal. The history film not only challenges traditional History, but helps return us to a kind of ground zero, a sense that we can never really know the past, but can only continually play with, reconfigure, and try to make meaning out of the traces it has left behind.

Guide to key reading

While there has been an increasing amount of writing on the topic of history and film in the last quarter of a century, it's difficult to point to many texts as 'key' to what still must be seen as a field (or sub-field or sub-sub-field) in search of a methodology. The Ur texts in the field are four collections of essays and one single authored work, all of them published between 1976 and 1981. Three of these volumes more or less emerged out of conferences on film and history held at such places as University College, London, the Imperial War Museum, and the Universities of Utrecht, Gottingen, and Bielefeld. The essays in Paul Smith (ed.), *The Historian and Film* (Cambridge: Cambridge University Press, 1976), deal mostly with questions of how historians can evaluate newsreel as historical evidence and how to use films in the classroom, while K.R.M. Short (ed.), *Feature Films as History* (Knoxville: University of Tennessee Press, 1981), considers dramatic features and the issue of how clusters of them made in certain periods can serve as windows into exploration of particular ideologies or climates of opinion. The largest and broadest of the collections, Karsten Fledelius *et al.* (eds), *History and the Audio-Visual Media* (Copenhagen: University of Copenhagen, 1979) divides its essays into three revealing categories: didactic problems, film and TV materials as source materials for historians, and content analysis and mass communications.

The kind of analysis pursued in *History on Film/Film on History*, which sees the visual media as a legitimate way of representing the past, begins with two books – the suggestive essays of Marc Ferro that are collected in *Cinema et histoire* (Paris: Editions Denoel, 1977), especially the last essay, 'Does a Filmic Writing of History Exist?', and the work by Pierre Sorlin entitled *The Film in History: Restaging the Past* (Totowa, NJ. Barnes and Noble, 1980), which examines feature films that deal with the American Civil War, the Russian

Revolution, and the Italian *Risorgimento* and broaches the issue of the truth of such fictional works. An important marker is the short essay by D.J. Wenden, 'Battleship Potemkin – Film and Reality', in Short (ed.), *Feature Films as History*, 37–61 (1981), which suggests that film may create a different kind of work about the past, history as 'symbol' rather than as 'reality'.

The range of topics in these initial five works show that the study of film and history has developed simultaneously in several different directions. The one followed in these pages, the one that considers the question of to what extent historical films can actually 'do' history, got a boost from a 55-page *AHR* Forum in the December, 1988 issue of *The American Historical Review* (Vol. 93: 1173–1227). Here my own lead essay, 'History in Images/History in Words: Reflections on the Possibility of Really Putting History on Film', argued the case for film, and was responded to with varying degrees of enthusiasm and criticism by four historians, including Hayden White, David Herlihy, John E. O'Connor, and Robert Brent Toplin. As part of his commentary, White coined an invaluable new term 'historiophoty', which he defined as 'the representation of history and our thought about it in visual images and filmic discourse'.

In the 15 years since 1988, three historians based in the United States (Natalie Davis, Robert Brent Toplin, and I) have produced books which, in a sense, build upon that forum. None of these volumes are a comprehensive study. Each consists of a group of essays or a series of chapters focused around individual films, or types of films, particular themes that suggest larger issues. My own book, *Visions of the Past: The Challenge of Film to the Idea of History* (Cambridge, MA: Harvard University Press, 1995a) groups its essays (originally published in journals) under three headings: History in Images, the Historical Film, and The Future of the Past. The latter section features a piece entitled 'Film and the Beginnings of Post-modern History', which argues that it is experimental film makers rather than historians who are creating a realm of post-modern history, which has previously only been theorized rather than practiced. Because of this essay, I have not felt the need to deal with the post-modern history film in this book, other than to point to some examples of it in Chapters 1 and 4. Equally diverse is a collection that I edited, entitled *Revisioning History: Filmmakers and the Construction of a New Past* (Princeton, NJ: Princeton University Press, 1995b). Here each of 11 specialists from different historical fields in American, European, and Japanese history analyzes a single film in terms of how it relates to the larger discourse surrounding its topic.

The most sustained attempt to understand 'what kind of historical inquiry' films can undertake has been made by the well-known historian of early modern France, Natalie Davis, in *Slaves on Screen: Film and Historical Vision* (Cambridge, MA.: Harvard University Press, 2000). Since a number of pages in chapter one are devoted to analyzing that book's strategies and contribution, here let me only say that Davis goes farther than anyone previously has in her attempt to set five films (on the topic of slavery) within a broader framework of historical discourse. This is more than Robert Brent Toplin does in either of his two well-meaning but conceptually limited books, *History by Hollywood: The Use and Abuse of the American Past* (Urbana, IL: University of Illinois Press, 1996) and *Reel History: In Defense of Hollywood* (Lawrence, KS: University Press of Kansas, 2002). By explicating a variety of major productions, he does provide certain insights into the Hollywood historical, but Toplin's attempt in the latter volume to explain the historical film as a genre fails to come to grips with the all-important referential aspect of historical representation. More subtle and interesting in its argument is an essay by J.E. Smythe, 'Young Mr Lincoln: Between Myth and History in 1939', *Rethinking History: The Journal of Theory and Practice*, 7 (Summer 2003), 193–214, which argues that this particular classic feature, and by extension other works made during the studio hero, create a new form of history on screen, works that hover between fact and fiction and are meant to undo the false mythologizing of the past.

Other volumes of essays (sometimes the outgrowth of conferences) account for a good deal of the writing by historians on film – at least apart from the reviews that have begun to appear in the pages of most historical journals. These works tend to mix together diverse approaches to the topic; they include pieces that deal with films as cultural artefacts which can be explicated as a way of understanding the age in which they were created; criticisms of the factual or conceptual shortcomings of individual works or groups of films; and (very occasionally) appreciations of particular films as having something worthwhile to say about the past. Among such volumes are John E. O'Connor and Martin Jackson (eds), *American History/American Film: Interpreting the Hollywood Image* (New York: Frederick Ungar, 1979); Peter C. Rollins (ed.), *Hollywood as Historian: American Film in a Cultural Context* (Lexington, KY: The University Press of Kentucky, 1983); John W. Chambers II and David Culbert (eds), *World War II, Film, and History* (New York: Oxford University Press, 1996); Vivian Sobchack (ed.), *The Persistence of History: Cinema, Television, and the Modern Event* (New York: Routledge, 1996); Donald F. Stevens (ed.), *Based on a True Story: Latin American History at the Movies* (Wilmington, DL: Scholarly Resources, 1997); Peter C. Rollins and John O'Connor (eds), *Hollywood's World War I: Motion Picture Images* (Bowling Green, OH: Bowling Green State University Popular Press, 1997);

Tony Barta (ed.), *Screening the Past: Film and the Representation of History* (Westport, CN: Praeger, 1998); Jeff Doyle *et al.* (eds), *Our Selection on Writings on Cinemas' Histories* (Canberra: NFSA/ADFA, 1998); David W. Ellwood (ed.), *The Movies as History: Visions of the Twentieth Century* (Phoenix Mill, UK: Sutton Publishing, 2000); Marcia Landy (ed.), *The Historical Film: History and Memory in Media* (New Brunswick, N.J: Rutgers University Press, 2001); Gary Edgerton and Peter C. Rollins (eds), *Television Histories: Shaping Collective Memory in the Media Age* (Lexington, KY: University of Kentucky Press, 2001); Claire Monk and Amy Sargeant (eds), *British Historical Cinema* (London: Routledge, 2002); Peter C. Rollins and John O'Connor (eds), *Hollywood's White House: The American Presidency in Film and History* (Lexington, KY: The University Press of Kentucky, 2003); Martha W. Driver and Sid Ray (eds), *The Medieval Hero on Screen: Representations from Beowulf to Buffy* (Jefferson, NC: McFarland, 2004).

Among single-author volumes are several which take up specialized historical topics, including Maria Wyke, *Projecting the Past: Ancient Rome, Cinema, and History* (New York: Routledge, 1997), and John Abert, *A Knight at the Movies: Medieval History on Film* (New York: Routledge, 2003). The Holocaust has drawn the efforts of several authors – these include Ilan Avisar, *Screening the Holocaust: Cinema's Images of the Unimaginable* (Bloomington: Indiana University Press, 1988); Annette Insdorf, *Indelible Shadows: Film and the Holocaust* (Cambridge: Cambridge University Press, 2nd edn, 1989); Judith E. Doneson, *The Holocaust in American Film* (Syracuse: Syracuse University Press, 2nd edn, 2002); as well as Yosefa Loshitzky (ed.), *Spielberg's Holocaust: Critical Perspectives on Schindler's List* (Bloomington: Indiana University Press, 1997). Most suggestive about film as a way of telling the Holocaust, most widespread in its geographic reach, and most up-to-date in its analysis of films of the last 15 years is Lawrence Baron, *Projecting the Holocaust into the Present: The Changing Focus of Holocaust Feature Films Since 1990* (Oxford: Rowan & Littlefield, 2005).

Mixtures of different approaches to the history film mark special issues of journals devoted to history and film, as well as a number of publications in languages other than English. Among the former are the following: 'One Film – Many Histories: An Inquiry into *Before the Rain*', *Rethinking History: The Journal of Theory and Practice*, 4 (No. 2, Summer 2000), 127–92; 'Film and History in Africa', *South African Historical Journal*, 48 (2003), 1–137; 'History, Historians, and Visual Entertainment Media', *The Public Historian*, 25 (No. 3, Summer 2003), 9–102. Foreign works include Joaquim Romaguera and Esteve Riambau (eds), *La Historia y el cine* (Barcelona: Editorial Fontamara, 1983); Sylvie Dallet (ed.), *Guerres revolutionnaires: Histoire et*

Cinema (Paris: Editions L'Harmattan, 1984); Rainer Rother (ed.), *Bilder schreiben Geschichte: Der Historiker im Kino* (Berlin: Klaus Wagenbach, 1991); and Judith Keilbach (ed.), *Die Gegenwart der Vergangenheit* (Berlin: Vorwerk, 2003). Journals with relevant sections include 'Cinema, Le temps de l'Histoire', *Vingtieme Siècle* (46, Avril–Juin 1995), 2–175; 'Le cinema face a l'Histoire', *Vertigo*, 16 (1997), 13–182; and 'Cinema-Historia', *O Olho da historia*, 1 (No. 5, Set. 1998), 105–72. A recent unique and provocative volume by a historian that places a variety of films, including historicals, into a deep context of the past century is Shlomo Sand, *Le vingtieme siècle a l'ecran* (Paris: Edition de Seuil, 2004).

Unlike almost any other tendency in historical theory, when one deals with the visual media you have to refer largely to texts that are not produced by historians themselves, and are well outside the realm of academia. Worse yet in the eyes of some academics, most of these texts (movies) are nakedly commercial cultural products. All this means that the reaction of many historians (professional, journalistic, and popular) when considering historical presentations in the media is to excoriate films for their factual and conceptual errors. Examples of this approach abound in many of the reviews of films that appear in scholarly journals such as *The American Historical Review* or *The Journal of American History*. You can also find it alive and well in several books which may be seen as key to not much more than the blind traditionalism of historians and historically-minded journalists – works such as Kenneth M. Cameron, *America on Film: Hollywood and American History* (New York: Continuum, 1997); Marc C. Carnes (ed.), *Past Imperfect: History According to the Movies* (New York: Henry Holt, 1995); Joseph Roquemore, *History Goes to the Movies* (New York: Random House, 1999); and, to a lesser extent (since it does find some films worthwhile), George MacDonald Fraser, *The Hollywood History of the World* (New York: William Morrow, 1998).

Historians hardly have a monopoly on writing about historical film. In recent years, academics in fields like literature, cinema studies, and communications have turned their attention to how the past is represented on screen. Since the scholarly stakes in those fields are rather different from those in history, such works can often seem (at least to this historian) a species of self-contained analysis that cares little about the world of historical discourse, the past itself, or anything which lies outside the frame of the screen. Yet some of these works are both provocative and interesting. Among the best ones are Robert Burgoyne, *Film Nation: Hollywood Looks at U.S. History* (Minneapolis: University of Minnesota Press, 1997); *Leger Grindon, Shadows on the Past: Studies in the Historical Fiction Film* (Philadelphia: Temple University Press, 1996); Marcia Landy, *British Genres* (Princeton: Princeton

University Press, 1991); Marcia Landy, *Cinematic Uses of the Past*
(Minneapolis: University of Minnesota Press, 1996); George F. Custen,
Bio/Pics: How Hollywood Constructed Public History (New Brunswick, N.J:
Rutgers University Press, 1992); and the special issue of *Biography: An
Interdisciplinary Quarterly*, 23 (Winter 2000) edited by Glen Man and
devoted entirely to 'the biopic'. Other contributions from those in ancillary
fields are contained in books devoted either to particular directors or national
cinemas. This literature is large, but among studies I have found particularly
useful with regard to historical film are the following on individuals: Francoise
Pfaff, *The Cinema of Ousmane Sembene: A Pioneer of African Film* (Westport,
CN: Greenwood, 1984); Peter Brunette, *Roberto Rossellini* (New York: Oxford
University Press, 1987); James Goodwin, *Eisenstein, Cinema, and History*
(Ubana and Chicago: University of Illinois, 1993); Thomas Elsaesser,
Fassbinder's Germany: History, Identity, Subject (Amsterdam: Amsterdam
University Press, 1996); Andrew Horton, *The Films of Theo Angelopoulos: A
Cinema of Contemplation* (Princeton, N.J.: Princeton University Press, 1997);
Robert Brent Toplin (ed.), *Oliver Stone's USA* (Lawrence: University Press of
Kansas, 2000); John Orr and Elzbieta Ostrowska, *The Cinema of Andrzej
Wajda: The Art of Irony and Defiance* (London: Wallflower Press, 2003).

     With regard to national cinemas, the most suggestive are: Michael Chahan,
The Cuban Image: Cinema and Cultural Politics (Bloomington: Indiana
University Press, 1985); Anton Kaes, *From Hitler to Heimat: The Return
of History as Film* (Cambridge, MA: Harvard University Press, 1989);
Marcia Landy, *Italian Film* (Cambridge: Cambridge University Press, 2000);
Dina Iordonova, *Cinema of Flames: Balkan Film Culture and the Media*
(London: British Film Institute, 2001); Dina Iordanova, *Cinema of the
Other Europe: The Industry and Artistry of East Central European Film*
(London: Wallflower Press, 2003).

     While literature on the documentary film is substantial, only a single work
has been devoted entirely to those which deal with history. David Ludvigsson,
*The Historian-Filmmaker's Dilemmma: Historical Documentaries in Sweden
in the Era of Hager and Villius* (Uppsala: University of Uppsala PhD dissertation, 2003), is a much broader study than the title might indicate; indeed, it
is the only work to attempt to define the nature and scope of the history
documentary. Works which examine the form and rhetorical strategies of
the documentaries and thus give insights that can be applied to the historical include Bill Nichols *Representing Reality* (Bloomington: University of
Indiana Press, 1991) and *Introduction to Documentary* (Bloomington: University of Indiana Press, 2001); Carl L. Plantinga, *Rhetoric and Representation in Nonfiction Film* (Cambridge: Cambridge University Press, 1997);

William Guynn, *A Cinema of Nonfiction* (London and Toronto: Associated University Presses, 1990), and Michael Renov (ed.), *Theorizing Documentary* (New York: Routledge, 1993). More general histories of the form will mention the origins of the compilation film and provide some examples, but none delves into its relation to historical discourse. Among the better ones are Eric Barnouw, *Documentary: A History of the Non-Fiction Film* (New York: Oxford University Press, 1983); Richard M. Barsam, *Nonfiction Film: A Critical History* (Bloomington: Indiana University Press, 1973, revised 1992); and Maria Antonia Paz and Julio Montero, *Creando la realidad: El cine informativo* (Barcelona: Editorial Ariel, 1999). Two useful works that deal with the films of perhaps the best known of current American directors of historical documentary are Robert Brent Toplin (ed.), *Ken Burns's The Civil War: Historians Respond* (New York: Oxford University, 1996), and Gary R. Edgerton, *Ken Burns's America* (New York: Palgrave, 2001).

Finally, for the ideas that underlie my approach to understanding the history film, I would have to point to a huge body of writing about the theory and practice of history, particularly in its post-structuralist and deconstructive modes. Rather than undertaking the nearly impossible task of listing all the works that have influenced me, let me point you to the Guide to key to reading in the brilliant inaugural volume in this series, Alun Munslow, *The New History* (London: Pearson-Longman, 2003). Its wonderful suggestions will keep anyone interested in the topic busy for years to come.

Bibliography

Ambrose, Steven E. (2000) '*Nixon*: Is it History?' in Robert Toplin (ed.) *Oliver Stone's USA*.

Ankersmit, F.R. (1994a) *History and Tropology: The Rise and Fall of Metaphor*, Berkeley and Los Angeles: University of California Press.

Ankersmit, F.R. (1994b) 'Historiography and post-modernism' in Ankersmit, *History and Tropology*, 162–81.

Avisar, Ilan (1988) *Screening the Holocaust: Cinema's Images of the Unimaginable*, Bloomington, IN: University of Indiana Press.

Backscheider, Paula R. (2000) *Reflections on Biography*, New York: Oxford University Press.

Barnouw, Eric (1983) *Documentary: A History of the Non-Fiction Film*, New York: Oxford University Press.

Baron, Lawrence (2005) *Projecting the Holocaust into the Present: The Changing Focus of Contemporary Holocaust Cinema*, Larham: Rowan & Littlefield.

Barta, Tony (ed.) (1998) *Screening the Past: Film and the Representation of History*, Westport, CN: Praeger.

Bercuson, David J. and Wise, S.F. Wise (eds) (1994) *The Valour and the Horror Revisited*, Montreal: McGill-Queen's University Press.

Bergan, Ronald (1983) 'What Ever Happened to the Biopic?' *Films and Filming*, 346 (July): 22.

Bergan, Ronald (1997) *Sergei Eisenstein: A Life in Conflict*, Woodstock, New York: The Overlook Press.

Berkhofer, Robert F. Jr. (1995) *Beyond the Great Story: History as Text and Discourse*, Cambridge, MA: Harvard University Press.

Bordwell, David (1993) *The Cinema of Eisenstein*, Cambridge, MA: Harvard University Press.

Brik, Osip (1988) 'The Lef Ring: Comrades! A Clash of Views!', Richard Taylor and Ian Christie (eds) *The Film Factory: Russian and Soviet Cinema in Documents*: Cambridge, MA: Harvard University Press.

Broue, Pierre and Temime, Emil (1961) *La revolution et la guerre d'espagne*, Paris: Les editions de minuit.

Brunette, Peter (1987) *Roberto Rossellini*, New York: Oxford University Press.

Burchard, Peter (1965) *One Gallant Rush: Robert Gould Shaw and His Brave Black Regiment*, New York: St Martin's Press.

Burgoyne, Robert (1997) *Film Nation: Hollywood Looks at U.S. History*, Minneapolis: University of Minnesota Press.

Cameron, Kenneth M. (1997) *America on Film: Hollywood and American History*, New York: Continuum.

Carnes, Mark C. (ed.) (1995) *Past Imperfect: History According to the Movies*, New York: Henry Holt.

Chamberlin, William Henry (1935) *The Russian Revolution, 1917–1921*, 2 Vols, New York: Henry Holt.

Chapsal, Madeleine (1963) *Mourir à Madrid*, Paris: Edition Seghers.

Corney, Frederick Charles (1997) *Writing October: Memory, Identity, and the Construction of the Bolshevik Revolution*, Ann Arbor, MI: UMI Dissertation Services.

Crusells, Magi (2003) *Las Brigadas Internacionales en la pantalla*, Ciudad Real: Universidad de Castilla-La Mancha.

Custen, George F. (1992) *Bio/Pics: How Hollywood Constructed Public History*, New Brunswick, N.J.: Rutgers University Press.

Custen, George F. (2000) 'The Mechanical Life in the Age of Human Reproduction: American Biopics, 1961–1980' *Biography* 23 (1), 127–59.

Davis, Jack E. (2000) 'New Left, Revisionist, In-Your-Face History: Oliver Stone's *Born on the Fourth of July* Experience' in Robert Toplin (ed.) *Oliver Stone's USA*.

Davis, Natalie Zemon (2000) *Slaves on Screen: Film and Historical Vision*, Cambridge MA.: Harvard University Press.

Doneson, Judith E. (2002) *The Holocaust in American Film*, 2nd edn, Syracuse, NY: Syracuse University Press.

Duncan, Russell (ed.) (1994) *Blue-Eyed Child of Fortune: The Civil War Letters of Robert Gould Shaw*, New York: Avon Books.

Edgerton, Gary G. (2001) *Ken Burns's America*, New York: Palgrave.

Eisenstein, Sergei (1949) Jay Leyda (ed. and translator) *Film Form: Essays in Film Theory*, New York: Harcourt, Brace & World.

Eisenstein, Sergei (1976) *Three Films*, London: Lorrimor Publishers.

Eisenstein, Sergei (1995) *Beyond the Stars: The Memoires of Sergei Eisenstein*, London: British Film Institute.

Elsaesser, Thomas (1989) *New German Cinema: A History*, New Brunswick, N.J.: Rutgers University Press.

Emilio, Luis F. (1995) *A Brave Black Regiment: History of the Fifty-Fourth Regiment of the Massachusetts Volunteer Infantry, 1863–1865*, New York: Da Capo.

Evans, Richard J. (1989) *In Hitler's Shadow: West German Historians and the Attempt to Escape from the Nazi Past*, New York: Pantheon Books.

Farr, James R. (2000) 'The Lizard King or Fake Hero?: Oliver Stone, Jim Morrison, and History' in Toplin (ed.) *Oliver Stone's USA*.

Ferro, Marc (1977) *Cinema et histoire*, Paris: Editions Denoel. Translated by Naomi Green (1988), *Cinema and History*, Detroit: Wayne State University Press.

Figes, Orlando (1998) *A People's Tragedy: The Russian Revolution, 1891–1924*, New York: Penguin.

Fledelius, Karsten *et al.* (eds) (1979) *History and the Audio-Visual Media*, Copenhagen: University of Copenhagen.

Fledelius, Karsten (2004) private email to author.

Fraser, Ronald (ed.) (1979) *Blood of Spain: An Oral History of the Spanish Civil War*, New York: Pantheon.

Friedlander, Saul (ed.) (1992) *Probing the Limits of Representation: Nazism and the 'Final Solution'*, Cambridge, MA: Harvard University Press.

Goodwin, James (1993) *Eisenstein, Cinema, and History*, Urbana and Chicago: University of Illinois.

Grindon, Leger (1996) *Shadows on the Past: Studies in the Historical Fiction Film*, Philadelphia: Temple University Press.

Gubern, Roman (1986) *La guerra de Espana en la pantalla*, Madrid: Filmoteca Espanola.

Guynn, Richard (1990) *A Cinema of Nonfiction*, London and Toronto: Associated University Presses.

Haslip, Le Ly (1999) *When Heaven and Earth Changes Places*, New York: Plume.

Haslip, Le Ly (2000) 'Heaven and Earth' in Toplin (ed.) *Oliver Stone's USA*, 178–87.

Heilbrun, Carol G. (1993) 'Is Biography Fiction' in *Soundings: An Interdisciplinary Journal 86* (Summer/Fall), 295–304.

Hicks, Granville (1936) *John Reed: The Making of a Revolutionary*, New York: Macmillan.

Homberger, Eric (1990) *John Reed*, Manchester: Manchester University Press.

Horton, Andrew (1997) *The Films of Theo Angelopoulos: A Cinema of Contemplation*, Princeton, N.J.: Princeton University Press.

Insdorf, Annette (1989) *Indelible Shadows: Film and the Holocaust*, 2nd edn, Cambridge: Cambridge University Press.

Jackson, Gabriel (1965) *The Spanish Republic and the Civil War, 1931–1939*, Princeton, N.J.: Princeton University Press.

Jenkins, Keith, and and Munslow, Alun (2004) (eds) *The Nature of History Reader*, London: Routledge.

Kaes, Anton (1989) *From Hitler to Heimat: The Return of History as Film*, Cambridge, MA: Harvard University Press.

Kaes, Anton (1992) 'Holocaust and the End of History' in Saul Friedlander (ed.) *Probing the Limits of Representation*.

Kagan, Norman (2000) *The Cinema of Oliver Stone*, New York: Continuum.

Kellner, Hans (1980) *Language and Historical Representation: Getting the Story Crooked*, Madison: University of Wisconsin Press.

Kurtz, Michael L. (2000) 'Oliver Stone, *JFK*, and History' in Toplin (ed.) *Oliver Stone's USA*.

LaFeber, Walter (2000) '*Salvador*' in Robert Toplin (ed.) *Oliver Stone's USA*.

Lagny, Michele *et al.* (1976) *October: Ecriture et ideologie*, Paris: Editions Albatros.

Lagny, Michele *et al.* (1979) *La revolution figuree: film, histoire, politique*, Paris Editions Albatros.

Landy, Marcia (1996) *Cinematic Uses of the Past*, Minneapolis: University of Minnesota Press.

Landy, Marcia (2000) *Italian Film*, Cambridge: Cambridge University Press.

Lehman, Daniel W. (2002) *John Reed and the Writing of Revolution*, Athens, OH: Ohio University Press.

Lerner, Gerda (1995) 'Joan of Arc: Three Films' in Mark C. Carnes (ed.) *Past Imperfect: History According to the Movies*, New York: Henry Holt, 54–59.

Leyda, Jay (1960) *Kino: A History of Russian and Soviet Film*, Princeton, N.J.: Princeton University Press.

Leyda, Jay (ed.) (1976) *Three Films by Sergei Eisenstein*, London: Lorrimer.

Loshitzky, Yoshefa (1977) (ed.) *Spielberg's Holocaust: Critical Perspectives on Schindler's List*, Bloomington: Indiana University Press.

Lukacs, George (1983) *The Historical Novel*, Lincoln, NB: University of Nebraska Press.

Ludvigsson, David (2003) *The Historian-Filmmaker's Dilemma: Historical Documentaries in Sweden in the Era of Hager and Villius*, Uppsala: University of Uppsala PhD dissertation.

Mackey-Kallis, Susan (1996) *Oliver Stone's America*, Boulder, CO: Westview Press.

McPherson, James M. (1995) 'Glory' in Mark C. Carnes (ed.) *Past Imperfect: History According to the Movies*, New York: Henry Holt, 128–31.

Maier, Charles S. (1988) *The Unmasterable Past: History, Holocaust, and German National Identity*, Cambridge, MA: Harvard University Press.

Man, Glen (ed.) (2000) 'The Biopic' a special issue of *Biography: An Interdisciplinary Quarterly*, 23 (Winter).

Medieval History at the Movies, http://www.fordham.edu/halsall/medfilms.html

Medvedev, Roy (1979) *The October Revolution*, London: Constable.

Monk, Claire and Sargeant, Amy (eds) (2002) *British Historical Cinema*, London: Routledge.

Munslow, Alun (1997) *Deconstucting History*, London: Routledge.

Munslow, Alun (2003) *The New History*, London: Pearson–Longman.

Nadel, Ira (1984) *Biography: Fiction, Fact, and Form*, New York: St. Martin's Press.

Nichols, Bill (1991) *Representing Reality*, Bloomington: University of Indiana Press.

Nichols, Bill (2001) *Introduction to Documentary*, Bloomington: University of Indiana Press.

Novick, Peter (1988) *That Noble Dream: The Objectivity Question and the American Historical Profession*, Cambridge: Cambridge University Press.

Orr, John and Ostrowska, Elzbieta (2003) *The Cinema of Andrzej Wajda: The Art of Irony and Defiance*, London: Wallflower Press.

Orwell, George (1980) *Homage to Catalonia*, New York: Harcourt, Brace, Jovanovich.

Piotovsky, Adrian (1988) 'October Must be Re-Edited' in Richard Taylor and Ian Christie (eds) *The Film Factory: Russian and Soviet Cinema in Documents*: Cambridge, MA: Harvard University Press.

Pipes, Richard (1991) *The Russian Revolution*, New York: Alfred A. Knopf.

Pipes, Richard (1993) *Russia Under the Bolshevik Regime*, New York: Vintage.

Pipes, Richard (1995) *A Concise History of the Russian Revolution*, New York: Vintage.

Plantinga, Carl R. (1997) *Rhetoric and Representation in Nonfiction Film*, Cambridge: Cambridge University Press.

Rabinowitch, Alex (1968) *Prelude to Revolution: The Petrograd Bolsheviks and the July 1917 Uprising*, Indiana: Indiana University Press.

Rabinowitch, Alex (1976) *The Bolsheviks Come to Power: The Revolution of 1917 in Petrograd*, New York: Norton.

Reed, John (1934) *Ten Days That Shook the World*, New York: Boni & Liveright.

Reed, John (1959) *Insurgent Mexico*, New York: International.

Renov, Michael (1993) (ed.) *Theorizing Documentary*, New York and London: Routledge.

Rentschler, Eric (1988) (ed.) *West German Filmmakers on Film: Visions and Voices*, New York: Holmes & Meier.

Roberts, Graham (1999) *Forward Soviet!: History and Non-fiction Film in the USSR*, London: I.B. Tauris.

Roberts, Randy and Welky, David (2000) 'A Sacred Mission: Oliver Stone and Vietnam' in Toplin (ed.) *Oliver Stone's USA*.

Roquemore, Joseph (1999) *History Goes to the Movies*, New York: Random House.

Rosenstone, Robert A. (1969) *Crusade of the Left: The Lincoln Battalion in the Spanish Civil War*, New York: Pegasus.

Rosenstone, Robert A. (1975) *Romantic Revolutionary: A Biography of John Reed*, New York: Alfred A. Knopf.

Rosenstone, Robert A. (1982) '*Reds* as History' in *Reviews in American History* 10: 299–310.

Rosenstone, Robert A. (1988) *Mirror in the Shrine: American Encounters with Meiji Japan*, Cambridge, MA.: Harvard University Press.

Rosenstone, Robert A. (1989) '*The Good Fight*: History, Memory, Documentary' in *Cineaste* 17 (1), 12–15.

Rosenstone, Robert A. (1992) 'Walker: The Dramatic Film as Historical Truth' in *Film Historia*, 2 (1), 3–12. Reprinted in *(1995) Visions of the Past: The Challenge of Film to Our Idea of History*.

Rosenstone, Robert A. (1994) 'The Historical Film: Looking at the Past in a Postliterate Age' in Lloyd Kramer *et al.* (eds) *Learning History in America*:

Schools, Cultures, and Politics, Minneapolis: University of Minnesota Press, 141–60.

Rosenstone, Robert A. (1995a) *Visions of the Past*, Cambridge, MA: Harvard University Press.

Rosenstone, Robert A. (ed.) (1995b) *Revisioning History: Filmmakers and the Construction of a New Past*, Princeton, N.J.: Princeton University Press.

Rosenstone, Robert A. (2001a) 'Introduction to Experiments in Narrative' in *Rethinking History: The Journal of Theory and Practice*, 5: 411–16.

Rosenstone, Robert A. (2001b) '*October* as History' in *Rethinking History: The Journal of Theory and Practice*, 5: 255–74.

Rosenstone, Robert A. (2004) 'Inventing Historical Truth on the Silver Screen' in *Cineaste*, 29 (2) (Spring), 29–33.

Rosenthal, Alan (2005) The Problems and Challenges of the History Documentary. Keynote address at the Annual Film and Literature Conference, Florida State University, 28 January, devoted to the topic, 'Transnational Film and Literature: Cultural Production and the Claims of History'.

Rokotov, T. (1988) 'Why is *October* Difficult?,' in Richard Taylor and Ian Christie (eds) *The Film Factory: Russian and Soviet Cinema in Documents*: Cambridge, MA: Harvard University Press.

Schickel, Richard (1984) *D.W. Griffith: An American Life*, New York: Simon and Schuster.

Scott, Walter (1984) *Ivanhoe: a Romance* (1900), Boston: Dana Ester & Co.

Short, K.R.M. (ed.) (1981) *Feature Films as History*, Knoxville: University of Tennessee Press.

Shub, Esfir (1988) 'This Work Cries Out' in Richard Taylor and Ian Christie (eds) *The Film Factory: Russian and Soviet Cinema in Documents*: Cambridge, MA: Harvard University Press.

Silva, Fred (ed.) (1971) *Focus on The Birth of a Nation*, Englewood Cliffs, N.J.: Prentice-Hall.

Smith, Paul (ed.) (1976) *The Historian and Film*, Cambridge: Cambridge University Press.

Smythe, J.E. (2003) 'Young Mr Lincoln: Between Myth and History in 1939' in *Rethinking History: The Journal of Theory and Practice*, 7 (Summer) 193–214.

Sorlin, Pierre (1980) *The Film in History: Restaging the Past*, Totowa, NJ: Barnes and Noble.

Sorlin, Pierre (1995) '*The Night of the Shooting Stars*: Fascism, Resistance, and the Liberation of Italy' in Robert A. Rosenstone (ed.) *Revisioning History: Film and the Construction of a New Past*.

Stevens, Donald F. (1997) *Based on a True Story: Latin American History at the Movies*, Wilmington, DE.: Scholarly Resources.

Stone, Oliver (2000) 'Stone on Stone's Image' in Robert Brent Toplin (ed.) *Oliver Stone's USA: Film, History, Controversy*, Lawrence: University Press of Kansas.

Taylor, Richard and Christie, Ian (eds) *The Film Factory: Russian and Soviet Cinema in Documents*: Cambridge, MA: Harvard University Press.

Thomas, Hugh (1961) *The Spanish Civil War*, New York: Harper and Brothers.

Toplin, Robert Brent (2000) *Oliver Stone's USA*, Lawrence: University Press of Kansas.

Toplin, Robert Brent (2002) *Reel History: In Defense of Hollywood*, Lawrence: University Press of Kansas.

Toplin, Robert Brent (2004) 'Cinematic History: An Anatomy of the Genre' in *Cineaste* 39 (2) (Spring), 34–39.

Tredell, Nicolas (ed.) (2002) *Cinemas of the Mind*, Cambridge: Icon Books.

Wenden, D. J. (1981) 'Battleship Potemkin – Film and Reality' in Short (ed.) *Feature Films as History*.

White, Hayden (1978) *Tropics of Discourse: Essays in Cultural Criticism*, Baltimore: Johns Hopkins University Press.

White, Hayden (1988) 'Historiography and Historiophoty' in *The American Historical Review*, 93: 1193.

Windschuttle, Keith (1996) *The Killing of History: How Literary Critics and Social Theorists are Murdering Our Past*, New York: The Free Press.

Wyke, Maria (1997) *Projecting the Past: Ancient Rome, Cinema, and History*, London: Routledge.

Index